Early Childhood Grows Up

International Perspectives on Early Childhood Education and Development

Volume 6

Early childhood education in many countries has been built upon a strong tradition of a materially rich and active play-based pedagogy and environment. Yet what has become visible within the profession, is, essentially a Western view of childhood, preschool education and school education.

It is timely that a series of books be published which present a broader view of early childhood education. This series seeks to provide an international perspective on early childhood education. In particular, the books published in this series:

- Examine how learning is organized across a range of cultures, particularly indigenous communities
- Make visible a range of ways in which early childhood pedagogy is framed and enacted across countries, including the majority poor countries
- Critique how particular forms of knowledge are constructed in curriculum within and across countries
- Explore policy imperatives which shape and have shaped how early childhood education is enacted across countries
- Examine how early childhood education is researched locally and globally
- Examine the theoretical informants driving pedagogy and practice, and seek to find alternative perspectives from those that dominate many Western heritage countries
- Critique assessment practices and consider a broader set of ways of measuring children's learning
- Examine concept formation from within the context of country-specific pedagogy and learning outcomes

The series covers theoretical works, evidence-based pedagogical research, and international research studies. The series also covers a broad range of countries, including majority poor countries. Classical areas of interest, such as play, the images of childhood, and family studies, will also be examined. However, the focus is critical and international (not Western-centric).

Linda Miller · Carmen Dalli · Mathias Urban
Editors

Early Childhood Grows Up

Towards a Critical Ecology of the Profession

Foreword by Peter Moss

 Springer

Editors
Prof. Linda Miller
North End 120
SG8 5NZ Royston, Herts
Bassingbourn
United Kingdom
l.k.miller@open.ac.uk

Prof. Carmen Dalli
Institute for Early Childhood Studies
Victoria University of Wellington
PO Box 600
Wellington 6140
New Zealand
carmen.dalli@vuw.ac.nz

Dr. Mathias Urban
Cass School of Education and Communities
University of East London
Water Lane
E15 4LZ London
United Kingdom
m.urban@uel.ac.uk

ISBN 978-94-007-2717-5   e-ISBN 978-94-007-2718-2
DOI 10.1007/978-94-007-2718-2
Springer Dordrecht Heidelberg London New York

Library of Congress Control Number: 2011942268

Springer is part of Springer Science+Business Media (www.springer.com)

Foreword

Early childhood education and care may be on the up at present, attracting the favourable attention of national and international policy makers and politicians, identified as a 'good' sector of the welfare state deserving of expansion and investment. Yet it seems to me that its apparent healthy exterior hides many of the prevailing ills of our time, which, if ignored, may make the current attention something of a mixed blessing. What ills do I mean?

First is the technoscience, which as Edgar Morin puts it,

> has invaded every tissue of the developed societies, implanting at an organisational level the logic of the artificial machine. This logic has penetrated the sphere of daily life and repressed the democratic power of citizens in favour of the experts and specialists (Morin & Kern, 1999, p. 68).

This logic of the artificial machine is fragmented, compartmentalised, reductionist; it is taken up with efficiency, predictability, calculability and specialisation; it avoids or seeks to control context and complexity; and it cedes our responsibility.

The second ill is the primacy given to an extreme instrumental rationality, 'preoccupied with calculation and quantification, with the relationship between inputs and outputs, with finding the most economical application of means to a given end' (Taylor, 1995). It is a prime example of what Lyotard (1984) terms 'performativity', which Stephen Ball defines as 'a disciplinary system of judgements, classifications and targets towards which schools and teachers must strive and through which they are evaluated' (1998, p. 190). This instrumental rationality is focused intently on defining and implementing an unwavering relationship between prescribed practices and procedures (often given the shorthand of 'quality') and prescribed outcomes (for example, learning or developmental goals). Process, everyday life, the unexpected, which account for so much of life and make life so often worth living, have no place here.

The third ill, expressed in the words of historian Carlo Ginzburg (1998), is 'constantly being offered solutions before we have asked the critical questions'. Putting technical practice first, obsessed by the technical question 'what works?', and assuming we can contract questions and answers to experts and specialists, education is drained of its essential political and ethical dimensions, dimensions that are needed to first generate then begin to find answers to key critical questions.

Questions such as: What is our image of the child? Of the educator and preschool? How do we understand concepts such as education, care, learning and knowledge? What is the purpose of education? What are fundamental values of education? What do we want for our children, here and now and in the future?

Fourth, there is the ascendency of economistic thinking in an age of resurgent neo-liberalism. This resurgence has brought about a one-dimensional way of thinking, with the collapse of the social into an overwhelming economic sphere, a process vividly described by Nikolas Rose:

> Social government must be restructured in the name of an economic logic... (and) the relation of the social and economic is rethought. All aspects of social behaviour are now reconceptualised along economic lines – as calculative actions undertaken through the universal human faculty of choice. Choice is to be seen as dependent upon a relative assessment of costs and benefits of 'investments' in the light of environmental contingencies (Rose, 1999, pp. 141–142).

Economistic thinking in early childhood education takes two main forms. First, the reduction of early childhood education to a simple matter of economic investment, justified in terms of delivering a certain level of economic return, typified by the oft quoted (and in my view dubious) claims that a dollar invested in early childhood education giving returns of $6 upwards. Second, the commodification, privatisation and marketisation of early childhood education: In this way of thinking, early childhood education becomes a tradable commodity to be provided by businesses competing in the market place. The parent is a customer, engaged in an act of private consumption, an autonomous subject ('autonomous' understood as meaning independent of others, a separate entity with complete control over personal decisions) responsible for managing her own risks, in this case purchasing care and education to meet the needs of herself and her child, but at the same time relieved of responsibility for others beyond her immediate family. The child is the object of the service, to be cared for, perhaps to be educated, the passive recipient of the service purchased by his or her parents.

Of course, this is a selection of current ills, there are many to choose from, and there is much inter-connectedness and overlap. But I think they give a flavour of my thinking; as things are going we are in danger of governing children more, relying on early childhood to fix the deep structural problems in our societies, and imposing standardisation at the expense of plurality and critical self-awareness. If, as Morin suggests, the challenge facing our endangered species and ravaged planet is to think in context and think complexity, the way much early childhood education and care is going today will not pass muster.

Equally disturbing, important relationships are badly out of kilter and early childhood education is caught up in this wider process too: the relationship between mankind and the environment; between prosperity and well-being; between coherence and diversity; and between poetry and prose. Another cue from Edgar Morin: Human life, he argues, is a mixture of prose and poetry, both necessary, both woven together, the prose side encompassing work, survival and aiming at targets, the main site for the practical, utilitarian and technical; while poetry is a way of life involving participation, love, eagerness and joy. But today the relationship between the two is quite unbalanced. Having separated prose and poetry, modern western civilisation has relegated poetry to private life. We need a powerful counter-offensive of poetry, and not least in education, at a time when human beings spend most of their lives surviving and where the future on offer seems to be ever more prose as we look forward to more years of paid work in an ever more competitive economy where the constant cry of the manager is more productivity and the constant cry of government and business is to compete better and consume more (see also Vea Vecchi, 2010, for a discussion of the place of 'poetic languages' in early childhood education).

It is in this somewhat dismal context that I welcome this book, as another sign of a growing movement of resistance and diversity. With its cross-national perspective, it makes us think of context and diversity, that perhaps not everywhere and everyone has the same values, goals, traditions and concepts – though some of that rich diversity may be lost by having to work in the modern *lingua franca* of English, not the first language of seven contributors. We are led to think too about different images and understandings of the child, the centre and the pedagogical work that takes place in it.

The book's focus on the everyday – relating as it does to some of the work done by an international team of researchers collaborating on a project titled *A Day in the Life of an Early Years Practitioner* – leads us to think about process and the meaning of living part of one's life, whether child or adult, in early childhood centres. It raises the critical question behind my colleague Alison Clark's Mosaic approach (Clark & Moss, 2001) to listening to young children, 'what does it mean to be in this place?' It acknowledges, too, the irreducible element of uncertainty when working with children and adults (and not just in nurseries one might add), reminding us that the concept of outcomes may have some use only if it allows for the surprising and unexpected, not just the predefined and normative.

The book delves into critical questions about pedagogy, relationships and professionalism. And the inclusion in one chapter of the term 'new public education' encourages us to contest the dominance of privatisation and marketisation, the 'new private education', and to open up for thinking what a new public education might mean and what it might offer our strained, fractured and unjust societies. One element of that 'new public education', for me, would be the valuing of collective over individual choice in many key areas, thus bringing democracy into the nursery as a foundational value and practice.

I have been critical of the technical, the managerial, the economic. Each though has its place, but it is a sign of a democratic, flourishing and just society that that place is debated and that the technical, the managerial and the economic are put at the service of richer and more important purposes – in the back seat, not the driving seat, tools at the disposal of the workforce not the other way round. Which brings me to a final observation: The growing attention given to early childhood education and care is bringing a welcome attention also to the workforce in these services, and not before time given the low levels of education and often disgracefully low pay deemed sufficient for many members of this workforce, in particular for those working with children under 3 years and in so-called childcare services. But – despite this attention and the higher levels of initial and continuing education it is giving some rise to – unless the technical, the managerial and the economic are reined in, and unless more space is made for the discussion of professionalisation, we may end up having achieved only a transition from the worker as substitute mother to the worker as lower or higher grade technician. I hope this book contributes both to the space needed for that discussion and to the discussions that take place in that space.

London, UK   Peter Moss[*]

References

Ball, S. J. (1998). Performativity and fragmentation in 'postmodern schooling'. In J. Carter (Ed.), *Postmodernity and the fragmentation of welfare* (pp. 187–203). London: Routledge.

Clark, A., & Moss, P. (2001). *Listening to young children: The Mosaic approach.* London: National Children's Bureau.

Ginzburg, C. (1998). *Ledtrådar: Essäer om konst, förbjuden kunskap och dold historia (Threads. Essays on art, forbidden knowledge and hidden history).* Stockholm: Häften for Kritiska Studier.

Lyotard, J.-F. (1984). *The postmodern condition: A report on knowledge.* Minneapolis, MN: University of Minnesota Press.

Morin, E., & Kern, A. B. (1999). *Homeland earth: A manifesto for the new millennium.* Cresskill, NJ: Hampton Press.

Rose, N. (1999). *Powers of freedom: Reframing political thought.* Cambridge, UK: Cambridge University Press.

Taylor, C. (1995). *Philosophical arguments.* Cambridge, MA: Harvard University Press.

Vecchi, V. (2010). *Art and creativity in Reggio Emilia: Exploring the role and potential of ateliers in early childhood education.* London: Routledge.

---

[*] **Peter Moss** is Professor of Early Childhood Provision at the Institute of Education, University of London. His academic interests include services for children and their workforces, the relationship between care, employment and gender, democracy in education, and social pedagogy. He coordinates an international network on parental leave policy and research.

Acknowledgements

This book has been an exciting and stimulating project that has pulled together the work of colleagues spread across the globe. We thank each contributor for their enthusiasm, hard work and collegiality.

In particular, we would like to acknowledge the contribution of the six early childhood practitioners who shared their perspectives and experiences with us, put up with our cameras and questions, and provided the basis for what has become a fascinating example of 'practice-based evidence' for the day-to-day ecology of the early childhood profession. Without Anna (Sweden), Bette (New Zealand), Josie (Australia), Julie (England), Maija (Finland) and Frau Müller (Germany) this book would not have been possible.

Our thanks go to the *European Early Childhood Education Research Association* (EECERA) at whose annual conferences this book was conceived.

Finally, we thank Susan Kaiser at the Jessie Hetherington Centre for Educational Research at Victoria University of Wellington, New Zealand, for her invaluable assistance in putting the manuscript together. Without her impeccable eye for detail, and her unfailing good humour, our role as editors would have been much harder.

Linda Miller
Carmen Dalli
Mathias Urban

Contents

About the Editors

Carmen Dalli is Professor of Early Childhood Education and Director of the Institute for Early Childhood Studies at Victoria University of Wellington in New Zealand. Her research combines an interest in professionalism in the early years with a focus on policy and pedagogical issues and the intersection of these with child development knowledge. She has a particular interest in group-based early childhood education and care provisions for children aged under 3 years.

Linda Miller is Emeritus Professor, Early Years at the Open University, United Kingdom. Her research interests centre on workforce policy issues and the professionalisation of the early years workforce in England, where she has been involved in national consultations and government working parties. Linda has published widely in this field, most recently, a Critical Issues in the Early Years Series for SAGE publishers.

Mathias Urban is Reader in Education at the Cass School of Education and Communities, University of East London, United Kingdom. His research interests unfold around questions of quality and professionalism in working with young children, families and communities in diverse socio-cultural contexts, diversity and equality, and participatory evaluation. He has a particular interest in international policy and professional epistemology.

About the Authors

Irene Balaguer Felip is President of Associació de Mestres Rosa Sensat, the Barcelona-based Teachers' Association founded in 1965 in response to 40 years of fascist dictatorship in Spain. Her main interests focus on teacher education and the quality of education for all ages, especially for children from 0 to 6. She is committed to defending public education as a right for all children with no discrimination of any kind.

Carrie Cable was a Senior Lecturer in Education at the Open University until 2011 and is now an Educational Consultant. Her research interests include English as an additional language and bilingualism, and for 3 years she was director of a major research project examining the learning and teaching of languages in primary schools.

Gill Goodliff is a Senior Lecturer and Head of Qualifications for Early Years in the Department of Education at The Open University, United Kingdom. Her research interests include the professional identities of early years practitioners and expressions of spirituality by children aged under 3 years.

Kirsti Karila is Professor of Early Childhood Education at the University of Tampere, Finland. She has conducted research projects concerning professionalism, professional identities, professional interaction and parent–practitioner collaboration in early childhood education. Recently, she has examined the new curricular practices in Finnish early childhood education and care.

Jarmo Kinos's first profession was as a kindergarten teacher. He subsequently worked as a lecturer and researcher at the University of Turku and is currently acting professor at the University of Tampere, Finland. His main research interests lie in history, professionalism and pedagogical practices of early childhood education. His latest research topic deals with the academisation and scientification of early childhood education in Finnish universities.

Marja Kuisma worked for many years as a Senior Lecturer in curriculum studies and special education at Uppsala University in Sweden before she retired in February 2011. Her research interest in the links between theory and practical studies in teacher education focused on teacher thinking and professionalism.

Pamela Oberhuemer was based for many years at the State Institute of Early Childhood Research in Munich, Germany, and currently works as a freelance researcher and journal editor. Her research foregrounds cross-national perspectives relating to early childhood education and care systems, curricular frameworks, and initial and continuing professional development. Her most recent book (with Inge Schreyer and Michelle Neuman) on the 27 European Union countries is *Professionals in Early Childhood Education and Care Systems – European Profiles and Perspectives*.

Jan Peeters is the co-ordinator of the Research and Resource Centre for Early Childhood Education and Care of the Department of Social Welfare Studies at Ghent University (Belgium). Together with colleagues from different countries, he founded 'DECET', the European Network on working around diversity in the early years and 'Children in Europe', a network of 17 magazines in ECE. He is on the board of ISSA, an Eastern European and Middle Asian network of 27 countries. His main topics of interest are the under threes, gender, diversity, and professionalism in the early years.

Anette Sandberg is Professor of Early Childhood Education at Mälardalen University, Sweden. Her current research concerns preschool teachers' competence, and preschool as the context for language development in children. She is also involved in two international research projects *Preschool teachers' views on children's learning* and *Support for preschool teachers' professional development.*

Christine Woodrow is Associate Professor at the Centre for Education Research in the School of Education at the University of Western Sydney in Australia. Her particular research interests include early childhood policy, leadership and constructions of professional identity. She is passionately interested in the role early childhood can play in community building and social change.

List of Acronyms

BA/BTeach	Bachelor of Arts/Bachelor of Teaching
BUPL	Danish Federation of Early Childhood Teachers and Youth Educators
CAF	Common Assessment Framework
CETL	Centre for Excellence in Teaching and Learning
CWDC	Children's Workforce Development Council
DCSF	Department for Children, Schools and Families
DfEE	Department of Education and Employment
DfES	Department for Education and Skills
ECE	Early childhood education
ECEC	Early childhood education and care
ECEGO	Expertisecentrum Ervaringsgericht Onderwijs
ECTS	European Credit Transfer System
EJE	Éducateur jeunes enfants
ELGs	Early Learning Goals
EPPE	Effective Provision of Pre-school Education
ERO	Education Review Office
EU	European Union
EYFS	Early Years Foundation Stage
EYP	Early Years Professional
EYPS	Early Years Professional Status
GBP	Great Britain Pounds
GDP	Gross domestic product
GDR	German Democratic Republic
HMT	Her Majesty's Treasury
IQF	Integrated Qualifications Framework
ISCED	International standard classification of education
ITERS	Infant Toddler Environment Rating Scale
Lpfö98/06	Swedish Ministry of Education 1998/2006
OECD	Organisation for Economic Co-operation and Development
Ofsted	Office for Standards in Education, Children's Services and Skills
QCA	Qualifications Framework

SEEPRO	Systems of early education/care and professionalisation
SEN	Special educational needs
STAKES	National Research and Development Centre for Welfare and Health
UNICEF	United Nations Children's Fund

Part I
Professionalism in Local and Cross-National Contexts: Towards a Critical Ecology of the Profession

Chapter 1
Early Childhood Grows Up: Towards a Critical Ecology of the Profession

Setting the Scene

Carmen Dalli, Linda Miller, and Mathias Urban

1.1 Introduction

This book makes two key arguments. The first is that early childhood education has grown up; the second is that we need to contemplate a new future for early childhood education – one in which the profession is marked by a critical ecology.

1.2 Our First Argument: Early Childhood Education Has Grown Up

By growing up we mean that from a sector that historically has been the Cinderella of the education system (Dalli, 1993; Opper, 1993) – undervalued and under-funded – in recent years early childhood education has slowly but surely travelled up the priority list of national policy agendas across the globe (Miller & Cable, 2011; Moss, 2008, 2010; OECD, 2006). As a result, there has been an unprecedented interest in the professionalisation of the early years workforce, often linked to the argument that the quality of early childhood services, and the improvement of opportunities for children and families, are associated with more highly trained staff (OECD, 2006). National pedagogical and regulatory practices have been introduced in many countries in an attempt to develop and enhance professional practice and there has been an expansion of opportunities to obtain higher level qualifications.

C. Dalli (✉)
Institute for Early Childhood Studies, Victoria University of Wellington, Wellington 6140, New Zealand
e-mail: carmen.dalli@vuw.ac.nz

L. Miller (✉)
Faculty of Education and Language Studies, The Open University, Milton Keynes MK76AA, UK
e-mail: l.k.miller@open.ac.uk

M. Urban (✉)
Cass School of Education and Communities, University of East London, London E15 4LZ, UK
e-mail: m.urban@uel.ac.uk

L. Miller et al. (eds.), *Early Childhood Grows Up*, International Perspectives on Early
Childhood Education and Development 6, DOI 10.1007/978-94-007-2718-2_1,
© Springer Science+Business Media B.V. 2012

An increasing number of university degrees are contributing to the notion that there is a profession in early childhood and an associated need for professional development (Miller & Cable, 2008).

This book bears witness to the fact that this global trend, perhaps an outward sign of 'growing up', has opened up a space for those engaged in early childhood education – the insiders of this historically undervalued sector – to engage in debate about the nature of their practice. Is early childhood education a profession? Should it be considered as one? What would it take for this to be so? What does professionalism mean in early childhood education? Is there a difference between profession and professionalism?

In large part, this book is the outcome of activity in one *insider space* opened up as a special interest group (SIG) on early childhood professionalism formed in 2004 by researchers from across the globe within the European Early Childhood Research Association (EECERA). Most of the authors in this book were present at the first meeting of that SIG and have since met regularly at the EECERA annual conference. What brought us together with our diverse individual, disciplinary and institutional backgrounds was a shared interest in understanding the complex realities of practitioners working with young children, families and communities in various occupational, institutional and socio-cultural settings.

To explore what turned out to be an increasingly complex, contested and often contradictory issue, the SIG developed a number of activities including international seminars and joint publications (Dalli & Urban, 2008, 2010). The backbone of Part I of this book (Chapters 2, 3, 4, 5, 6 and 7) is a project entitled A *Day in the Life of an Early Years Practitioner* (from now on referred to as the *Day in the Life* project) which was first discussed at the second meeting of the SIG in Dublin in 2005. We should note that in this book we use the terms 'early years' and 'early childhood education and care' (ECEC) interchangeably reflecting common practice across the countries represented in the book. For example, in England (Chapter 3) the term 'early years' is used to denote a concerted attempt to move towards holistic services which do not separate out care and education. On the other hand, ECEC is more commonly used in the other countries involved in the *Day in the Life* project: Australia, England, Finland, Germany, New Zealand and Sweden. We outline the broad framework of the *Day in the Life* project later in this chapter where we also explain how, through exploring early years practice in six different geographic localities, the project researchers came together as a *community of practice* (Wenger, 2006) or a learning community (Kilkpatrick, Barrett, & Jones, 2003) engaged in a collective learning endeavour about a shared interest. The fact that the geographic contexts of the project crossed both national and continental boundaries – from Finland, Germany and Sweden in continental Europe to England, and Australia and New Zealand in Australasia – made the community of practice not only a long-distance one but also a diverse one linguistically, historically and socio-politically. By coming together in the project we shared local knowledge and, from our diverse socio-cultural realities, constructed new understandings, knowledge and questions about our shared interest in professional early childhood practice, its commonalities and differences.

It became clear, for example, that the day-to-day realities in diverse local contexts shared some similarities: all the practitioners worked in complex situations with individuals and groups; they juggled multiple demands; they balanced a planned day with flexibility to respond to the unexpected; and each exhibited a practice that was essentially relational and based on intimate knowledge of children and their context. Across each case study, there is a story of practice whose undertones are familiar: behind the appearance of trivial and routine activities, acting professionally in the different contexts means bringing together multiple layers of understanding and thinking in interacting with children, families and colleagues, in situations that are sometimes ethically challenging, within a curriculum that might look outwardly fragmented but is intricately connected.

At the same time there are also differences in the way the practitioners in the *Day in the Life* project articulated their work role, and these reflect the diverse socio-historical and political contexts in which the practitioners lived their lives. For example, the Australian case study (Chapter 2) shows that, in a context where corporate provision of early childhood services is fast becoming the norm, Josie's view of professionalism is articulated as a rejection of what she calls the outward 'trappings' of 'professionalism' – such as branded centre clothing. Instead, along-side the affective and relational dimension of her role, Josie identified leadership within her early childhood centre and broader early childhood community, and a strong sense of moral purpose as the centre of her lived 'professionalism'. In New Zealand, within a policy context that promoted a fully qualified workforce and included a holistic and open-ended curriculum (*Te Whāriki*) that encourages autonomous programme planning, Bette's reflective, articulate and agentic style of practice appears to conform to the structural and societal expectations for her role. For the Finnish and English practitioners, Maija and Julie, each working in contexts where multi-professionalism has been offered as a solution to the multi-faceted nature of early childhood work, the practitioners' views of their practice reveal the complex and often challenging relational dynamics between staff with different roles and qualifications working within the same space. Similarly, in the Swedish case study Anna's focus on working from an ethical base of respect appears in line with the democratic values embedded in the Swedish preschool curriculum (*Lpfö 98/06*). There is a challenge in the German case study where Frau Müller emerges as an 'uncertain expert' whose expertise resides precisely in her ability to deal with ambiguity and uncertainty when societal expectations from her role are about technical expertise and certainty. Thus, in each case, the practitioners offer us not only a snapshot of practice but also an entry point into their own con-structions of their lived professional practice: sometimes these constructions are consistent with policy formulations; sometimes they reveal tensions and contradic-tions. Inevitably, however, there is a link between individual action and broader policy frameworks. When doing what they do, the practitioners enact a reality that constructs its own knowledge, revealing that acting and knowing are two sides of the same coin.

By sharing this knowledge across contexts through this book, we hope to open up a new space where that knowledge construction, within and across localities, can speak for itself. We return to the argument that early childhood education has grown up, and that the profession can speak for itself, in the concluding chapter.

Part II of the book takes us a step away from the intimate playing out of the day-to-day reality of lived practice portrayed in the chapters in the first part of the book. Drawing on the work of members of the SIG outside of the *Day in the Life* project, the chapters in Part II view professionalism from a more structural perspective and reveal aspects of the bigger socio-political context that impact on day-to-day practice. Highlighting the limited systematic information about the early childhood workforce in Europe, Pamela Oberhuemer argues that early childhood work contexts across Europe are sites of change with diverse country-specific traditions. She argues that each tradition needs to be investigated individually if a common thread of understandings about professionalism is to be identified. Jan Peeters' chapter draws attention to the policy context of Flanders and provides an account of how a comparative study by childcare advocates helped bring about change: it created a consensus in the Flemish childcare community about the need to focus on qualifications and regulations to increase professionalism in the childcare workforce. Writing about the *Associacío de Mestres Rosa Sensat* based in Barcelona, Irene Belaguer Felip likewise highlights the ability of practitioners to create change. Indeed, she emphasises the importance of criticality, ethical and political action, and activism for transformation, as essential elements of professionalism. These three chapters act to contextualise the micro-level analyses presented in the case study chapters; they open up another way of looking at the topic of professionalism. They also add weight to the argument that early childhood education has grown up and is developing its own scholarly field, including through policy and critical analysis.

1.3 Our Second Argument: Towards a Critical Ecology of the Early Childhood Profession

Our second argument is that professionalism in early childhood practice cannot be defined in simple universalistic and immutable terms, or through finite lists of qualities and attributes. Rather, the chapters in this book collectively illustrate that early childhood professionalism is something whose meaning appears to be embedded in local contexts, visible in relational interactions, ethical and political in nature, and involving multiple layers of knowledge, judgement, and influences from the broader societal context. In researching lived realities in six diverse localities, the *Day in the Life* project created space for practitioners 'to name the[ir] world' (Freire, 2010, p. 88) and thus to own it, to transform and re-create it 'in action-reflection' (p. 88). What became apparent in this process is that there were several layers of interactions that crucially influenced the practitioners' constructions of professionalism.

Using terminology from Bronfenbrenner's (1979) ecological systems theory and adopted by many other authors (e.g., Garbarino, 1992), we can relate these layers to the *micro-*, *meso-*, *exo-* and *macrosystem* of an ecology of the early childhood profession. Bronfenbrenner suggested these distinct but interrelated ecological levels to systematise the complexity of individuals' experiences in society. He described these levels as 'a set of nested structures, each inside the next, like a set of Russian dolls' (Bronfenbrenner, 1979, p. 22). He later suggested an additional *chronosystem* to describe changes in the ecological system over time (Bronfenbrenner, 1986).

In early childhood contexts – such as in teacher preparation programmes – the ecological model is probably best known as a perspective on children's development, which is how Bronfenbrenner (1979) first used it. Since its introduction, however, ecological perspectives have been employed by a wide range of disciplines that deal with the complexities of human behaviour, ranging from cross-cultural psychology (e.g., Worthman, 2010) to 'lifestyle, leisure and travel research' (e.g. Woodside, Caldwell, & Spurr, 2006). In this book we suggest that a new conceptualisation of professionalism is required that is able to reflect the complex realities in which early childhood practitioners live their lives and their profession, and how practitioners' realities are inextricably linked to their wider context. We also suggest that Bronfenbrenner's ecological model can be helpful in explaining this new conceptualisation. However, we suggest that a slightly different angle, or extended perspective, is necessary in our field: *a critical ecology of the early childhood profession*.

It is not within the scope of this book to present a detailed discussion of Bronfenbrenner's theoretical model. However, a brief definition of key terms and how they are relevant to our argument is appropriate. The following definitions in Table 1.1 focus on the early childhood practitioner and her interactions.

The phrase *a critical ecology of the early childhood profession* was coined within discussions of the SIG in whose space the *Day in the Life* project was conceived.

Elsewhere we have already argued that in a critical ecology of the early childhood profession, the early childhood community would be characterised by critical thinking about 'practices at every layer of the early childhood professional system'

Table 1.1 Definitions of ecological system terms as used in this book (adapted from Garbarino, 1992)

Ecological level	Definition	Examples
Microsystem	Situations in which the practitioner is physically present and has face-to-face contact with influential others	Practitioners interacting with: Children Co-workers Parents
Mesosystem	Relationships between the *microsystems*; connections between situations	Team connections Multi-/inter-professional work
Exosystem	Settings in which practitioners do not participate but in which significant decisions affecting them are made	Local/regional body authority Parents' workplace
Macrosystem	'Blueprints' for a particular society; assumptions about 'how things should be done'	Values, shared assumptions, broad ideological patterns of a particular culture; socio-economic and political context
Chronosystem	Developments of the ecological system over time	Socio-historical context

(Urban, 2008, p. 145), a stance of enquiry that is 'informed by the political and social realities' (p. 146), an alertness to challenges in the settings one acts in, as well as to 'the strengths that might be brought to bear on the present to make the present better' (Dalli, 2007, p. 3, 2010). Within a critical ecology of the early childhood profession, practitioners would be 'reflective, self-critical and perpetually open to responsive growth in their local context' (Dalli, 2007, p. 3). In this way, practitioners within a profession that has a critical ecology would be able to effect the kind of changes described by Irene Belaguer Felip (Chapter 10): transforming practices from within. We give more substance to this argument in the concluding chapter where we discuss the issues, themes and points of tension raised in this book through the use of terminology borrowed from Bronfenbrenner's (1979, 1986) ecological systems theory.

1.4 The Framework of the *Day in the Life* Project

We turn now to a fuller description of the *Day in the Life* project. At its simplest the project can be described as a set of six case studies which investigated how early childhood practitioners 'acted as a professional' in six different local contexts.

The idea of observing 'a day in the life' has been used before, perhaps most notably in Tobin, Wu, and Davidson's (1989) seminal work *Preschool in Three Cultures* featuring daily life in Japanese, American and Chinese pre-schools. The particular seeds for our *Day in the Life* project were sown during conversations between one of the editors (Linda Miller) and colleagues at the Open University (Julia Gillen and Roger Hancock). Gillen and Hancock had worked on a project which explored constructions of early childhood by analysing film footage of a day in the life of a 2.5-year-old girl in each of five countries (Gillen et al., 2007). Bringing the seeds of those conversations to a SIG pre-conference meeting in 2005 on a sunny August day in Dublin proved the beginning of a 5-year collaboration across six countries that has culminated in this book.

1.4.1 Who Is the Early Years Professional?

One of our questions for the project was the following: who is the early years professional? Work involving caring for young children has traditionally been a female-dominated occupation. In the 20 countries surveyed in the OECD report *Starting Strong 11*, men were found to represent less than 1% of the workforce in ECEC (OECD, 2006). Early childhood work has historically been positioned as 'women's work', and as not being of sufficient importance to be properly remunerated and valued, or considered to be a 'real profession', despite significant cultural and economic shifts which have affected the construction of gender. These historical discourses concerning the 'naturalised' differences between men and women tend to exclude, or at least discourage, men from participating in the ECEC workforce

(Roberts-Holmes & Brownhill, 2010). Not surprisingly, therefore, the practitioners in each of the six case studies featured in this book are female.

Moss (2008) has argued that it is important to address our understanding of the early childhood professional – as we have tried to do in this book. He argued for an early years practitioner who is a 'democratic and reflective professional' and who would value the qualities of: dialogue; critical thinking; researching; listening and openness to otherness; uncertainty and provisionality; subjectivity; border crossing, multiple perspectives and curiosity (pp. 125–126). According to Moss, these qualities can be achieved through education and continuous professional development, and expressed in everyday practice. As Moss notes, this conceptualisation of the early childhood practitioner is encompassed within Oberhuemer's (2005) description of *democratic professionalism*. Oberhuemer listed the following aspects of the role of the democratic professional: interacting with children; centre management and leadership; partnership with parents; and acting from a professional knowledge base. Taking a different approach, one of us (Dalli, 2008), surveyed New Zealand practitioners' perceptions about their role and offered a 'ground-up' definition of the professional early childhood practitioner. This is structured around the three core components of pedagogical strategies, professional knowledge and practice, and collaborative relationships.

1.4.2 Getting Organised: What We Did and How We Did It

Our aim within the *Day in the Life* project was to explore the notion of professionalism with individual practitioners, each working in an early childhood setting in their country context.

From the outset we were mindful of the need to consider the policy agendas in each of the six countries represented in the study. This is because each country has different routes to 'becoming a professional' as well as different policy infrastructures to support early childhood services.

We were also mindful that although the *Day in the Life* research group came to know each other well as part of a learning community (Kilkpatrick et al., 2003; Wenger, 2006), we needed to know more about the general socio-cultural, historical, economic and political context in which we were each working. Thus, one of the first tasks for the project researchers was to compile a country profile, or contextualising description, to inform the rest of the project team about the context in which they were researching. At the 'macro level', each country profile outlined the policy background to ECEC including: recent developments, the purpose of the services, administration and delivery, regulation and funding. At a 'micro level' the reports described the local context in which the practitioner was working, including: the setting and its organisation, staffing and staff roles, the nature of the curriculum and programme, and details about the practitioner. The descriptions were later used to provide the context for the participating practitioners' working lives in each of the case study chapters. Table 1.2 summarises key contextual details for each case study as a way of sketching an overall picture of the practitioners in the project before they

Table 1.2 Contextual details of each case study

Name and country of case study practitioner	Experience as a practitioner	Qualification background	Type of setting; policy auspices: education/care/ social welfare	Numbers of children in a class/group; age-range; staff:child ratio	Urban/rural location; opening hours	Job title of practitioner and age range worked with	Name of curriculum document or government guidance and age range covered	School starting age
Josie: Australia	3 years as director; over 9 years as childcare practitioner	• Post-secondary Technical and Further Education (TAFE) childcare certificate; • Bachelor's degree in Early Childhood teaching; • Diploma in Children's Services; • Currently enrolled in Master degree by research	Long daycare centre providing accredited full time centre-based care and education for children aged 0–5 years for a minimum of 48 weeks of the year. Department of Education, Employment and Workplace Relations (DEEWR) (National Policy) Department of Education and Communities (NSW state policy)	61 licensed places for a full day, up to 5 days a week Age range: 0–5 years Staff:child ratio varies by child age as follows: 0–2 years = 1:4 2–3 years = 1:8 3–5 years = 1:10	Lower foothills on outskirts of a large capital city on South Eastern seaboard of Australia 07.30–18.00	Centre director 0–5 years age range	*The Practice of Relationships*: A curriculum framework developed in 2002 for state of New South Wales. *Being, Belonging and Becoming: A national learning framework for Australia (since* July 2009) (0–5 years age range)	6 years

Table 1.2 (continued)

Name and country of case study practitioner	Experience as a practitioner	Qualification background	Type of setting; policy auspices: education/care/social welfare	Numbers of children in a class/group; age-range; staff:child ratio	Urban/rural location; opening hours	Job title of practitioner and age range worked with	Name of curriculum document or government guidance and age range covered	School starting age
Julie: England	7 years in daycare	• National Vocational Qualification (Level 3 work-based, competency framework qualification); • Level 4 Certificate; • Intention to progress to a Foundation degree	Private daycare centre Department for Children Schools and Families (since 2010 Department for Education)	154 children enrolled with 66 attending at any one time Age range: 0–5 years Minimum staff: child ratio varies by child age as follows: <2 years: 1:3 2 years: 1:4 3–7 years: 1:8 or 1:13	Urban setting 07.30–18.30	Nursery manager (0–5 years age range)	Early Years Foundation Stage (0–5 years age range)	Term after child's 5th birthday
Maija: Finland	20 years as kindergarten teacher	• 3-year tertiary level training; • further studies (education, pre-school education) at university	Public daycare centre under the auspices of the Ministry of Social Affairs and Health	135 children in full daycare, 80 in part time play groups. Age range: 1–7 years Staff:child ratio = 1:7 in groups of 21 children	Suburban area 06.30–17.30	Kindergarten teacher (4–6 years age range)	National Curriculum Guidelines on Early Childhood Education and Care	7 years

Table 1.2 (continued)

Name and country of case study practitioner	Experience as a practitioner	Qualification background	Type of setting; policy auspices: education/care/social welfare	Numbers of children in a class/group; age-range; staff:child ratio	Urban/rural location; opening hours	Job title of practitioner and age range worked with	Name of curriculum document or government guidance and age range covered	School starting age
Frau Müller: Germany	20 years as 'Erzieherin' (educator)	• 3-year Higher Education degree 'Erzieherin', qualified under GDR regulations; • 're-qualified' according to new legislation introduced after German reunification 1990	'Kindertagesstätte' (full day early childhood education and care centre) run by non-profit welfare organisation (German Red Cross). Fully regulated under State and federal legislation.	112 children in full daycare, in 6 groups: 2 groups: 0–2 years; 4 groups: 3–6 years. Age range: 0–6 years Staff:child ratio 0–2 years = 1:6 3–6 years = 1:13 In Frau Müller's group there were approx 25 children	Small town in the State of Saxony-Anhalt, former eastern part of Germany. 06.00–18.00	Erzieherin[a] (4–6 years age range)	Bildung:elementar (mandatory early childhood curriculum framework for all publicly funded EC services in the State of Saxony-Anhalt. (0–6 years age range)	6 years
Bette: New Zealand	8.5 years as a kindergarten teacher	• Two-year diploma of teaching ECE; • intention to upgrade to a degree qualification	State kindergarten. Fully regulated by NZ Ministry of Education	Maximum of 45 children in each morning and afternoon session; Age range: 3–5 years Staff:child ratio = 1:8	Urban setting; Daily am sessions from 08.30–11.30; three pm sessions per week 12.45–15.15	Kindergarten teacher	Te Whāriki (1996) (0–6 age range)	Compulsory school age is 6 years; most children start on their 5th birthday.

Table 1.2 (continued)

Name and country of case study practitioner	Experience as a practitioner	Qualification background	Type of setting; policy auspices: education/care/ social welfare	Numbers of children in a class/group; age-range; staff:child ratio	Urban/rural location; opening hours	Job title of practitioner and age range worked with	Name of curriculum document or government guidance and age range covered	School starting age
Anna: Sweden	26 years as preschool teacher	• Two-year tertiary level training. • Followed by further studies (education, pre-school education) at university.	Public full-time daycare centre. Ministry of Education and Sciences.	Maximum 108 children in six units: 3 units: 3–5 years 2 units: 1–3 years 1 unit: 1–4 years Overall staff:child ratio = 1:8 In Anna's unit there were 19 children aged 3–5 years with 2 full-time teachers and one daycare attendant	Suburban area 06.30–18.30	Preschool teacher with (3–5 years age range)	National Curriculum Guidelines on Early Childhood Education and Care (0–6 years age range)	7 years

[a] Qualified for working with children from birth to adolescence according to German federal legislation. 'Erzieherinnen' may work in a wide range of settings including residential care but mainly work in early childhood education and care (birth to compulsory school age)

are introduced individually in Chapters 2, 3, 4, 5, 6 and 7. We urge readers to remember that each chapter presents the voice of an early childhood practitioner who, in Freireian tradition, is naming her world and thus claiming it.

1.4.3 Choosing Case Study Research

A key understanding among the project team was that the *Day in the Life* project could not be about a 'typical practitioner' or a 'typical' early childhood setting. We were clear that this would not have been possible even *within* countries as there are no such phenomena as typical practitioners or settings. We agreed instead to work with a practitioner with whom we already had a working relationship, thus creating what might be called a 'convenience sample' of cases across contexts (Cohen, Manion, & Morrison, 2000). We did, however, agree on a number of other criteria: the practitioner had to have at least 3 years' post-qualification early childhood experience; she had to have achieved the minimum level of qualification required within her local context; and she had to work with children aged 3 years or more. Additionally, we formulated three questions which provided the overall framework and some structural equivalence for the project across the different contexts. The questions focused on:

1. what it means to act professionally in a particular context
2. perceptions of what being a 'professional' in early childhood means – including practitioners' self-perceptions and external perspectives
3. common features of practice in each context.

Given our intention to explore meanings about professionalism from the practitioners' experience of their role, we adopted a qualitative case study approach. We were not seeking 'verification of predetermined hypotheses' (Merriam, 1988, p. 13) but rather an in-depth understanding of a phenomenon that we knew from our previous discussions shared some common features, but also differed in country-specific and other ways. As a group of cross-national researchers, qualitative case studies allowed us to adapt our investigation to the specific conditions within which the early childhood practitioners lived their professional lives. Within each country setting, the researchers gathered data using non-participant observation of a full 'day in the life' of the chosen practitioner using video recording and case notes. We also interviewed the practitioner about *her* perception of the day and about her views of professionalism. Our hope as researchers was that through entering the world of the practitioners, we would be able to see the world from their perspective and that this would lead to shared meaning making. We use the words of Robert Stake (1999) to explain our interest in the individual practitioners:

> We are interested in them [cases] for both their uniqueness and commonality. We seek to understand them. We would like to hear their stories. We may have reservations about some things the people (I will call them actors) tell us, just as they will question some of the

things we will tell about them. But we enter the scene with a sincere interest in learning how they function in their ordinary pursuits and milieus and with a willingness to put aside many presumptions while we learn. (p. 1)

Pragmatically, case studies were also an efficient way for the project group to make full use of limited resources. They afforded us a way to understand complexities in unique situations even when ultimately we were also 'interested in the general phenomenon or a population of cases more than in the individual case' (Bassey, 1999, p. 436).

1.4.4 Working as a Learning Community

The project presented some logistical challenges: we were a group of researchers located across six countries with limited possibilities for regular contact and a need to develop a way of working together. Nonetheless, with a clear shared interest, and a desire to work towards a common goal, the project team in effect soon became an example of what Wenger (2006) calls: 'communities of practice... formed by people who engage in a process of collective learning in a shared domain of human endeavour' (p. 1). Our shared *domain*, or area of interest, was the notion of professionalism from both a theoretical and practice perspective which we were seeking to understand as a locally constructed notion. We were a *community* because we 'engaged in joint activities and discussions, help[ed] each other, and share[ed] information' (p. 2) and we also built relationships that enabled us to learn from one another. In terms of our *practices*, we soon 'develop[ed] a shared repertoire of resources: experiences, stories, tools, ways of addressing recurring problems' (p. 2) through, for example, developing a research outline that was circulated and agreed within the wider group. We also developed other generic documentation including: a practitioner interview schedule; consent forms; letters to the early childhood centre inviting the practitioner's participation; information pamphlets about the project; parental consent form for parents of children included in the filming, and a consent form for the participating practitioner. The researchers in each country were responsible for ethics approval from their own institution and for raising funding for their local case study. The broad guidelines in the overall research proposal were followed by each of the project researchers with adaptations to local conditions as necessary. At the same time, we acknowledged that within the scope of the overall project, each participant needed to tell their own country story, to look both inside and outside the individual case study and then to reflect upon what had been learnt (Wenger, 2006).

The project proceeded in two phases. In Phase one, we met as and when we could in various locations across Europe and also communicated through e-mail as we gathered our data, wrote and circulated case reports, and started our thematic analyses guided by principles from grounded theory and focused on opening up understandings and meanings around our project aims (Richards, 2009; Strauss & Corbin, 1998). In Phase two, we undertook dissemination of our early analyses through meetings and joint conference presentations, and also the writing up of the case studies and country reports.

Throughout both phases we remained focused on the idea that the *Day in the Life* project was not about *comparing* the practices we observed. While we collated case reports which shared a common conceptual and methodological framework, like Gillen et al. (2007) and Penn (1998) we recognised the impossibility of direct comparisons or matching of experiences across cultures, because of the contextual parameters under which the research in each country was conducted. As Penn eloquently put it: 'all that is possible is to listen to the separate voices and try to hear their stories' (p. 14). What the project aimed to achieve was to give voice to the practitioners working in each of the six countries but also to look for some common themes and elements (see Chapter 11 for a discussion of these). As with Tobin et al.'s (1989) study, the focus has been on eliciting meanings within each context and then sharing what we found.

1.4.5 Capturing the Practitioner's Day

In order to capture the reality of the practitioner's day, we filmed each practitioner for one complete day following a process of familiarisation in each early childhood centre. In some countries the researchers did the filming themselves. In England and New Zealand we were fortunate to have a professional film crew. As researchers we were present throughout the filming but tried to remain unobtrusive. As soon as possible after the day of filming, we did a follow-up interview with the practitioner which we also filmed or audio taped. The focus of the interview was to explore the practitioner's view of the day captured on film, including examples of 'acting' professionally'. We also investigated the practitioner's perception of being an early childhood professional, and key features of her practice. All interviews were transcribed either by the researchers or a professional transcriber. When the data-gathering was complete, we viewed, edited and analysed the films with input from the practitioners along the way.

Research progressed at different rates in each country. Once the data were collated, and where time permitted, each country researcher/s produced a case report for circulation, discussion and dissemination. As we have already noted, ongoing discussion and dissemination also took place informally – at conference meal times, and on evenings out – and more formally at pre-conference project meetings and in shared conference presentations.

1.4.6 Presenting the Case Studies: Singularities Versus Generalisations

The outcome of the activity within the learning community of the *Day in the Life* project is presented in the next six chapters as country case studies in alphabetical order of the country, starting with Australia. We have chosen this order as an organisational device to avoid any impression of privileging the experiences of one practitioner in any country over that of others. To us this is also a way of honouring the diverse historical and policy contexts of the countries represented in the project; each has something to offer and none is more exemplary than the other. What they each illustrate is that the cultural context is important to the professionalism that is manifested. They demonstrate that there is no one 'model' of professionalism or early childhood professional, either within or across countries; each practitioner faced different dilemmas and challenges and 'framed' their professionalism in different ways.

We have aimed to bring the case studies to life by illustrating them with 'vignettes' – short descriptions of episodes or situations which occurred throughout the practitioners' day – selected by the researchers. These are useful in 'allowing voices to speak with immediacy' (Abbott & Gillen, 1999, p. 49) and can provide a partial 'picture' of what is happening. At the same time, we are mindful of the concern that case studies tend to 'embalm' (Bassey, 1999, p. 35) practices rather than depict them as fluid and changing: By naming this tendency we acknowledge that we do not claim to have 'caught' practices as they will always be. Rather, throughout the project, we had Bassey's notion of 'fuzzy generalisations' (p. 12) as part of our frame of reference. Fuzzy generalisations arise from studies of *singularities* and are statements which make no absolute claim to knowledge but hedge their claim with uncertainties. Typically claiming that 'it is possible, or likely, or unlikely that' what was found in the one situation will be found in similar situations elsewhere, a fuzzy generalisation rules out ideas of certainty and absoluteness. The use of the term 'fuzzy' allows for the human complexity operating within each individual case – as in this project. The notion of fuzzy generalisations thus allowed us to seek common elements across the project but also to acknowledge the complexity of each individual case, and its likely differences from other cases in its local context, and within the wider policy frameworks of the six countries.

1.5 Concluding Thoughts

The stories contained in Chapters 2, 3, 4, 5, 6 and 7 belong to the practitioners at the centre of each individual example within the *Day in the Life* project. As researchers we sought to illuminate common practices, issues and themes and to give public voice to the shared understandings that emerged of what professionalism means for the practitioners involved. At the same time, as we strove to illuminate the three questions posed at the outset of the study, we were aware that any interpretation is necessarily subjective and that in making choices certain data may be favoured or given a greater voice over others. A key realisation was that there is no such thing as *the universal* early childhood profession (see Chapter 11) but that 'there are always new and surprising ways of being and doing' (Duhn, 2011, p. 133) that require and deserve our attention and curiosity. This message is evident also in the second part of the book: the socio-political contexts in which practitioners live their lives are many and varied, making their impact an integral part of the way professionalism is enacted, and their result worthy of our curiosity and attention.

We have written this book with an audience in mind of early years professionals working mainly at the postgraduate level, and for practitioners engaged in continuing professional learning. We hope it will also be of interest to researchers and academics working in the field of early childhood education. The aim of this book is to bring a critical perspective to thinking about professional early years practice by offering a lens through which to view the socio-political and working contexts in which early years practitioners live their life.

References

Abbott, L., & Gillen, J. (1999). Revelations through research partnerships. *Early Years: An International Journal of Research and Development, 20*(1), 43–53.

Bassey, M. (1999). *Case study research in educational settings*. Buckingham: Open University Press.

Bronfenbrenner, U. (1979). *The ecology of human development: Experiments by nature and design*. Cambridge, MA: Harvard University Press.

Bronfenbrenner, U. (1986). Ecology of the family as a context for human development. *Developmental Psychology, 22*(6), 723–742.

Cohen, L., Manion, L., & Morrison, K. (2000). *Research methods in education* (5th ed.). London: Routledge Falmer.

Dalli, C. (1993). Is Cinderella back among the cinders? A review of early childhood education in the early 1990s. *New Zealand Annual Review of Education, 3*, 223–252. Available at http://www.victoria.ac.nz/nzaroe/1993/pdf/text-dalli.pdf

Dalli, C. (2007, August). *Towards a critical ecology of the profession*. Paper presentation at SIG discussion forum on Professionalism, EECERA Conference, Prague.

Dalli, C. (2008). Pedagogy, knowledge and collaboration: Towards a ground-up perspective on professionalism. *Special edition of the European Early Childhood Education Research Journal: Professionalism in Early Childhood Education and Care, 16*(2), 171–185.

Dalli, C. (2010). Towards the re-emergence of a critical ecology of the early childhood profession in New Zealand. *Contemporary Issues in Early Childhood, 11*(1), 61–74.

Dalli, C., & Urban, M. (2008). *Special edition of the European Early Childhood Education Research Journal: Professionalism in Early Childhood Education and Care, 16*(2), 131–280.

Dalli, C., & Urban, M. (Eds.). (2010). *Professionalism in early childhood education and care: International perspectives*. London: Routledge.

Duhn, I. (2011). Towards professionalism/s. In L. Miller & C. Cable (Eds.), *Professionalization, leadership and management in the early years* (pp. 133–146). London: Sage.

Freire, P. (2010). *Pedagogy of the oppressed*. New York: Continuum.

Garbarino, J. (1992). *Children and families in the social environment* (2nd ed.). New York: Aldine de Gruyter.

Gillen, J., Cameron, C. A., Tapanya, S., Pinto, G., Hancock, R., Young, S., et al. (2007). A day in the life: Advancing a methodology for the cultural study of development and learning in early childhood. *Early Child Development and Care, 177*(2), 207–218.

Kilkpatrick, S., Barrett, M., & Jones, M. (2003). *Defining learning communities*. Paper presented at the Australian Association for Research in Education. Retrieved from http://www.aare.edu.au/03pap/jon03441.pdf

Merriam, S. (1988). *Case study research in education: A qualitative approach*. San Francisco: Jossey-Bass.

Miller, L., & Cable, C. (Eds.). (2008). *Professionalism in the early years*. Oxon: Hodder Education.

Miller, L., & Cable, C. (Eds.). (2011). *Professionalization, leadership and management in the early years*. London: Sage.

Moss, P. (2008). The democratic and reflective professional: Reforming and rethinking the early years workforce. In L. Miller & C. Cable (Eds.), *Professionalism in the early years* (pp. 121–130). Oxon: Hodder Education.

Moss, P. (2010) We cannot go on as we are; The educator in an education for survival. *Contemporary Issues in Early Childhood, 11*(1), 8–19.

Oberhuemer, P. (2005). Conceptualising the early childhood pedagogue: Policy approaches and issues of professionalism. *European Early Childhood Research Journal, 13*(1), 5–15.

OECD. (2006). *Starting Strong 11: Early childhood education and care*. Paris: OECD.

Opper, S. (1993). Kindergarten education: Cinderella of the Hong Kong Education system. In A. B. M. Tsui & I. Johnson (Eds.), *Teacher education and development* (Education Papers No 18, pp. 80–89). Hong Kong: Faculty of Education, The University of Hong Kong.

Penn, H. (1998). Comparative research: A way forward? In T. David (Ed.), *Researching early childhood education: European perspectives* (pp. 7–24). London: Paul Chapman.

Richards, L. (2009). *Handling qualitative data: A practical guide*. London: Sage.

Roberts-Holmes, G., & Brownhill, S. (2010). Where are the men? A critical discussion of male absence in the early years. In L. Miller & C. Cable (Eds.), *Professionalization, leadership and management in the early years* (pp. 119–133). London: Sage.

Stake, R. (1999). *The art of case study research*. London: Sage.

Strauss, A., & Corbin, J. (1998). *Basics of qualitative research: Techniques or procedures and developing grounded theory*. London: Sage.

Tobin, J. J., Wu, D. Y. H., & Davidson, D. H. (1989). *Preschool in three cultures: Japan, China, and the United States*. New Haven, CT: Yale University Press.

Urban, M. (2008). Dealing with uncertainty: Challenges and possibilities for the early childhood profession. *European Early Childhood Education Research Journal, 16*(2), 135–152.

Wenger, E. (2006). *Communities of practice: A brief introduction*. Retrieved August 6, 2010, from http://www.ewenger.com/theory/index.htm

Woodside, A. G., Caldwell, M., & Spurr, R. (2006). Advancing ecological systems theory in lifestyle, leisure and travel research. *Journal of Travel Research, 44*(3), 259–272.

Worthman, C. M. (2010). The ecology of human development: Evolving models for cultural psychology. *Journal of Cross-Cultural Psychology, 41*(4), 546–562.

Chapter 2
Relationships, Reflexivity and Renewal: Professional Practice in Action in an Australian Children's Centre

Christine Woodrow

2.1 Introduction

This Australian case study was conducted on the cusp of significant change in the landscape of Australian early childhood policy and practice. Australia has had a very fragmented approach to early years provision (OECD, 2001; Press, 2006). This has given rise to a perceived ambiguity of purpose in early childhood provisions and established fertile ground for corporate provision of childcare to thrive and expand across Australia over the last decade (Press & Woodrow, 2005). This fragmentation has also undoubtedly been instrumental in entrenching an artificial dichotomy between care and education in early childhood policy and practice.

Now, a new era characterised by the rhetoric of 'national partnerships' (DEEWR, 2009a) has seemingly arrived, coinciding with re-invigorated political attention to the early childhood years. The emerging prominence of words such as 'new agenda', 'reform', 'workforce development', 'leadership' and 'investment', evident in the new *National Early Childhood Development Strategy* (DEEWR, 2009a), holds promise for: a higher profile for early childhood on the agendas of government; better working conditions; stronger articulation of shared visions; and more streamlined provision through the development of unified systems, standards and regulations across the nation. One significant element of the recent National Strategy is the requirement for all early childhood settings to include 4-year university-trained personnel in their staffing profile. Recent Australian studies (Fenech, Sumsion, & Goodfellow, 2006, 2008; Sumsion, 2002) have identified significant challenges to achieving these growth targets for qualified staff, including the complex problems of recruitment and staff retention associated with pay and conditions. Clearly, the context of early childhood in Australia is very dynamic, and many

C. Woodrow (✉)
Centre for Education Research, School of Education, University of Western Sydney, Sydney,
NSW, Australia
e-mail: C.Woodrow@uws.edu.au

of the factors that influence the production of early childhood professional identities and individual and collective understandings of professionalism are in a state of change.

A number of key elements and emerging issues relating to policy and practice in the broad Australian context emerged in the case study. As a way of contextualising the case study, the chapter begins with a brief description of some of the salient features of early childhood provision in the Australian context. Following this is a presentation and discussion of data from the study. The chapter concludes with a discussion of some implications from the findings.

2.2 Understanding and Defining the Field of Early Childhood in Australia

Consistent with international definitions, Early Childhood Education and Care (ECEC) in Australia typically denotes a range of care and education programmes for children aged between birth and 8 years (Press, 2006). This locates early childhood provision in a diverse range of settings, regulatory contexts, policy discourses and political jurisdictions. The mainstream settings for early childhood provision in Australia are currently described and categorised as:

Preschools	Primarily, but not always, sessional early education programmes catering for 3–5-year-olds (sometimes called kindergartens) and almost always staffed by trained teachers.
Childcare or Long Daycare	Catering for children from shortly after birth through to school commencement and primarily understood as responding to the needs of working parents. It has a mixed staffing profile – including unqualified, those with vocational qualifications and teaching qualifications – with variation in regulatory requirements across jurisdictions.
School	For children aged 4.5–8 years and staffed by qualified teachers, with many jurisdictions providing a pre-compulsory year ahead of the first year of primary school variously called preparatory, transition or kindergarten.

Increasingly, programmes directed at supporting children (and their families) living in vulnerable communities are also considered to be early childhood programmes, reflecting the international trend towards integrated service provision (Siraj-Blatchford, Clarke, & Needham, 2007).

2.2.1 Purposes of Early Childhood Provision: Care and/or Education?

In Australian policy discourse, there appear to be three main understandings of the purposes of early childhood provision: substitute care for parents whilst they participate in the paid workforce; preparation for school; and early intervention and support for vulnerable families (Ailwood, 2004; Press, 2006).

The new national reform agenda for early childhood education in Australia places great significance on the establishment of early learning and care centres (DEEWR, 2009a). This new emphasis on learning *and* care is an advance on the historical positioning of care and education as different and distinctive sites of policy and practice (OECD, 2001; Press & Hayes, 2000) and signals a new policy intention of institutionally embedding the integration of childcare and early years education in the one site (Valentine, Katz, & Griffiths, 2007). This represents a significant institutional shift in Australia.

Much has already been written on the impact and implications of the artificial divide between these two conceptualisations of early childhood work (Ailwood, 2004; Fasoli, Woodrow, & Scrivens, 2007; Moss, 2006; Press, 2007; Woodrow, 2002). These implications include issues such as the low status of the profession, salaries and conditions (Sumsion, 2002) and how the dichotomy perpetuates distinctions between care and education, serving to maintain the status quo of much less favourable conditions for people working in childcare settings, despite the strong educational component to these programmes.

2.2.2 Regulating Quality

Currently in Australia, regulation of programme quality and standards for childcare settings occurs within a two-layered overlapping system, in which one layer is managed at a national governmental level, and the other by state departments. The state systems address structural dimensions of quality (e.g., qualifications, staff child ratios, adequacy of facilities) which are managed through a regime of compliance inspections and renewal of licences on an annual basis. The second layer of quality management is a nationally administered quality assurance process, designated as the Quality Improvement and Accreditation System (QIAS), but commonly referred to as 'Accreditation'. For parents to receive the federal government funding of a fee subsidy, the centre must have achieved a minimal level of accreditation which incorporates elements of programme quality (for example, dimensions of interactions with children, approaches to educational and developmental programme, and levels of parental involvement). There has been widespread dissatisfaction with the burden of compliance, and increased understanding of the complexity associated with a multi-layered system – recent research has shown that overlaps between accreditation and licensing processes can impede quality standards and practice

(Fenech et al., 2008). A new *National Quality Framework* (DEEWR, 2009a) released for consultation in 2009 and due to come into effect on 1 January 2012, will significantly change the regulatory environment and quality management in the sector.

2.2.3 Curriculum

Historically in Australia, the curriculum for early childhood settings outside the schooling system has typically been unregulated (Woodrow, 2004; Woodrow & Brennan, 1999). More recently, curriculum guidelines have been developed to support professional practice in the non-school settings. In the state of New South Wales – the site of this case study – a curriculum framework was developed by the state, *The Practice of Relationships* (DoCS, 2002), to guide professional decision-making in all early childhood settings, but in reality its use has been optional. In July 2009, the Federal Government launched a new learning framework based on three central ideas: *Being, Belonging and Becoming* (DEEWR, 2009b). Subtitled: *A National Early Years Learning Framework for Australia*, the document details four intended learning outcomes, a set of principles, and a statement about pedagogy and professional roles for educators. Learning through play is a central tenet of the document. This curriculum initiative could be read as marking a new era in unifying early years curricula nationally and an institutional acknowledgement of the growing importance of the early years. Ways in which such developments might be influential or constitutive of 're-making' professional identity in the field will be one important line of new research in the context of recent shifts in public policy support for early years education in Australia.

2.3 The Case Study Site

2.3.1 Overview

The Australian case study site is located in the lower foothills of a world heritage area on the outskirts of a large capital city on the south eastern seaboard of Australia. The region has regular rail and motorway access to Australia's largest city.

For this study, the centre has been renamed the Cherry Lane Children's Centre. It is designated a 'long daycare centre' signifying that it provides accredited full-time centre-based care for children aged 0–5 years for a minimum of 48 weeks of the year. Approximately 3000 such centres, varying enormously in size and context, exist across the country. This centre is managed by a 'not-for-profit' community-based volunteer committee.

Parents using this centre will typically be participating in paid employment or study, and will be eligible to receive a fee subsidy from the federal government according to their level of income.

2.3.2 Setting the Scene: Context and Staffing

The Children's Centre is licensed for 61 children who can attend an integrated care and education programme for a full day, up to 5 days a week. The centre is open from 7.30 am to 6 pm. It is purpose-built and comprises three separate play rooms, each with large separate outdoor play areas. Children are located in rooms according to age, and the staff are assigned to particular rooms to ensure continuity in relationships between adults and children. The staffing includes four qualified early childhood teachers (one as the director), nine staff members with post-secondary vocational education qualifications in early childhood (six at diploma level and three at certificate level), and two staff with extensive experience but no formal qualifications. The centre sees itself effectively integrating care and education through this staffing mix. Josie is the director of Cherry Lane and values the mix of qualifications and experience of her staff. In Josie's view, although formal qualifications are important, staff dispositions also have a big impact on the children's experience. Josie described these dispositions as including the 'ability to work well in the team and have good relationships with parents which are equally as important as the expert knowledge of a teacher, especially with the babies, and highlight the importance placed on relationality'.

2.3.3 Profiling the Practitioner

Josie had been at Cherry Lane Children's Centre for over 3 years as the director and was an experienced early years practitioner. She was studying for a master's degree specialising in early childhood and she hoped to continue on to doctoral study. Her career in early childhood could be characterised as a pathway of lifelong learning. She began as a voluntary worker in an early childhood setting and then completed an entry-level childcare certificate through the post-secondary Technical and Further Education system (TAFE). She subsequently and progressively completed a diploma in children's services and a degree in early childhood teaching. Josie communicated a strong sense of the role of early childhood education in addressing social justice concerns, and the indivisibility of care and education. She also clearly articulated her understanding of her leadership role in the centre as involving working constructively with staff to establish a respectful community, and supporting and raising pedagogical quality.

> I think my job here is to be a leader, to me that means being able to pass this knowledge onto others, empower them [the staff] to engage in critical reflection, inspire them to bring change and mentor them through this process. Professionalism is marked by the ability to first critically reflect on your own practice but secondly to make changes based on those reflections, and that's the hard bit . . . I have needed to support people in this process and it also means respect, values, and having a space to question without fear of retribution.

2.3.4 The Structure of Josie's Day

As the director, Josie's overall responsibility was for the daily operation of the centre: 'the children, the parents, the staff, the actual building, the policies'. According to Josie, staffing-related issues accounted for almost 90% of her working time, but she also acknowledged that many of these overlapped with curriculum issues as they related to staff involvement in the programme: 'We are going for best practice in accreditation; parents want a quality service for their children, so I need to make sure that what we are doing is the very best we can be doing'.

Josie had developed a structure to her day to enable her to meet these diverse responsibilities. Table 2.1 includes a précis of her activities in her day, accompanied by a relevant quote from the interview.

2.3.5 Curriculum and Pedagogical Approaches

Josie articulated a clear perspective on the role her centre plays in the lives of children and their families. She said relationships are at the heart of the early childhood experience.

> It's about trust, and it's about what parents want for their children... it's also about relationships: relationships between the staff and the children, between the staff and the parents, and of course between the children themselves – them learning how to relate, who they are... their identity and then their relationships with others.

She believed that when children leave the centre to start school, the biggest contribution the centre will have made will be to 'enhancing children's social competence, their social literacy' – by this she meant the children's capacity to get on with each other, to be 'respectful of difference', to be social and relate to other children and adults in caring and respectful ways...' to have friendships and to 'understand what's expected of you in different places'.

In talking about her philosophy of teaching, Josie reflected on where her current thinking was now about the experience of childcare, compared to previously:

> I've come to understand that this is a group programme, it's not home care, and it's not just substitute home care, we're not providing one-on-one care here like a home... it's a developmental programme... and it's still ok to talk about children's development... but it's a group programme – of course we care about the individual, and adapt to individual needs, but it's group education, the group programme – that is its strength, being part of a group, learning in a group, and we need to recognise this and we need to promote this.

During the interview, Josie said that it was acknowledging this reality that helped them with the changes they had made towards embracing the 'project approach' (Katz & Chard, 2001) to children's learning. Josie described the pedagogical approach at the centre as 'child-focussed and interest based', encompassing an emergent curriculum which she explained as involving:

> individual direct observations enabling staff to recognise and identify the strengths, abilities and possibilities of each child across all the developmental domains.

Table 2.1   Précis of Josie's day

Approximate time of day	Activities	Quote
7.00 am	Welcoming children, parents and staff Administration (emails, deliveries, phone messages, council re-building maintenance issues) Parent conversations, informal greetings and exchanges of information	*It's about trust, trust and respect – parent and staff being respectful, so much of our focus is on the children, but there are the parents . . . and the staff . . .*
8.30 am	Interaction with staff and children in the playrooms	*This is where I learn about the professional learning needs of the staff, and also see the relationships they have with the children, the kind of team work . . .*
9.30 am	Parent interview Tour of centre (Over 50s Club contact) Student appointment	
10.30 am	Planning staff-development activities Follow-up actions from staff meeting Planning for parent committee meeting Contact with health for special support for child with special needs	*This is my project work time, whatever are my priorities, usually to do with the staff, or the accreditation. For our inclusion of this child with autism, we get a funded person for 5 out of the 8 hours that the child attends*
12.00	Lunch with staff in centre staff room	*I try to sit down to have lunch with some of the staff, I sit and just talk and listen*
1.00 pm	Interactions with children and staff in playrooms, walking from room to room, helping out where needed.	*I make sure I catch up with the staff that I hadn't connected with in the morning, help where needed. Is everything going ok for the day, help give the babies their bottles*
2.00 pm	Project priorities work Planning staff-development activities Re-writing centre policies Follow-up actions from staff meeting	*Am I a visionary director? I put my vision out there, people embrace part of your vision and they have their own . . . you have to allow their vision as well . . . and mentor them, I give staff all the support they need*
3.00 pm finish		

Observations taken by the staff of children's interactions and activities were regularly given to parents, together with a feedback sheet, which the parents frequently returned. Josie noted that this was one of the ways that she and her staff learned about children's interests and got ideas about how to plan for their learning, as well as building relationships with parents.

Josie saw the Cherry Lane approach as based on developmental goals 'as a starting point', together with a more free-flowing adaptation of the project approach in which 'children can come in and out as their interest ebbs and flows'. The curriculum framework document *The Practice of Relationships* (DoCS, 2002) also provided a framework for curriculum planning and action in this setting. From Josie's perspective, the programme's commitment to providing the opportunity for children to 'reach their potential' is balanced with a concern for their comfort, security and safety 'in caring relationships'. The curriculum had a different focus and emphasis according to the children's age and developmental status. As Josie explained:

> ...for the infants [the curriculum] is ...care and attachment and building of trusting relationships, supporting developing skills and giving opportunity for experiencing success through these. For the 2 to 3s, it is self-help skills and self-knowledge e.g., eating, toileting, ...that relationships are friendships and helping [them] to get to know their own reactions and responses to frustrations. Social relationships become really important here, and identifying themselves, and who they are, and developing an empathy for others.

> For 3–4s [the curriculum] is building on developing skills, a sense of importance and agency in their world...a development of respect for the environment and for others... challenging beliefs, concepts and forming prejudices, and instilling a sense of power of themselves.

> For 4–5s, [the curriculum is] helping their sense of esteem...extending their skills and helping to support their problem-solving strategies and their creativity. ...establishing themselves as architects and artists of their own lives. ...helping the relationships they have formed and to break down stereotypes...expanding their world and honouring their accomplishments, skills and strengths. ...emotional literacy. ...skills for communicating...language, problem solving, asking for help....

This emphasis on communicating and relationships was reflected in the arrangement of the rooms and the way the curriculum was planned and enacted. Pedagogical strategies and techniques included the establishment of what Josie described as 'invitational-based learning centres', together with project work, individual activities, large group experiences with music and stories, as well as small group activities.

Josie explained that careful attention is paid to the setting up of the 'learning centres' in which objects and materials are laid out to invite children's participation. These were set up as distinct areas focussed around: books; dramatic play themes with some props to scaffold children's ideas; construction kits such as Lego; percussion instruments; drawing; painting; and recycled materials; and sometimes included a range of different hard and soft materials to 'encourage imagination'. Provision was made in the learning centres for small groups of children to participate together, reflecting Josie's valuing of the group experience and the social learning that she identified as an important strength of the centre's programme. She considered experiential learning through 'free' play to be at the heart of the children's daily experiences in the centre.

The children's day was structured around four main components in which the staff planned a balance of experiences between being indoors and outdoors: routines, semi-structured play, free play and circle group time.

2.3.6 Stepping Up to the Role of the Educator

Josie identified with a range of roles that early childhood educators undertake on a daily basis. In particular, she said that early years educators have roles that vary across 'those of guides, role models, facilitators, co-constructors and co-players' in their interactions with children. She stressed the importance of the relationships that early years educators form with children and with parents, but also recognised that putting children and parents at the forefront posed challenges for early childhood professional identity: 'often I see that staff won't assert themselves with parents, they do have expertise and they shouldn't be afraid of expressing this . . .'.

Josie expressed a view that it is time for early childhood educators to 'step up' and 'claim their expertise' in young children's learning. She said that whilst it is fundamentally important to have strong relationships with parents, teachers also need to 'own their responsibilities as educators' which are distinct from the roles parents play. She believed educators need to be more proactive in interacting with children, and '. . . more capable in leading learning'. To be able to do this, Josie explained that early years educators need to have more strongly developed practices of critical self-reflection. She believed that the new *Early Years Learning Framework for Australia* (DEEWR, 2009b) highlights the multifaceted role of the early childhood educator and the importance of reflective practice in effective educational decision-making which she expected would help support this shift across the field.

These perspectives are consistent with much of the contemporary literature on early childhood pedagogy (Anning, Cullen, & Fleer, 2008; MacNaughton & Williams, 2004), particularly that located within socio-cultural frameworks (Fleer et al., 2006) which establish an active role for the early years educator as a key informant and actor in children's learning.

2.3.7 Being Professional – Critical Self-Reflection and Ongoing Professional Learning

Since becoming the director at Cherry Lane, Josie had provided leadership in a significant curriculum renewal process aimed at enhancing the pedagogical work with children and more productive interpersonal relationships. Using the *Early Childhood Australia's Code of Ethics* (ECA, 2006) as a starting point, Josie had facilitated many opportunities to support the staff to discuss professionalism in the work place and issues of workplace culture, and encouraged them to 'be reflective . . . take ownership and responsibility for feelings, emotions and actions'. Using a critical pedagogy framework, Josie also had structured professional learning activities over the previous 2 years for staff to re-consider some of the taken-for-granted practices of the centre. This required staff to consider the value of these practices to themselves, the children and the families. As a consequence, individual child observational summaries prepared by staff and sent home to parents, and the long-standing practice of the daily journal, had been replaced by new practices which document children's learning in the context of the group. The playrooms now contained much visible evidence of children's project work, and children's comments, and co-constructed adult and child documentation of learning was publicly displayed.

According to Josie, the biggest challenge for her staff team has been the capacity for critical self-reflection, which she understood as essential for working with the children and families with 'real understanding:'

> You know the staff were doing all this work, writing the summaries of their observations, taking time away from the children, and sending them home to the families, and it's just about the individual. But really their children are learning in a group context so why do we keep doing the individual thing, and duplicate the work by sending the summaries, and with the journal just summarising the day without having time to think about what really was happening? It's better to do less but do it with real understanding – What are the children really learning? What can the parents learn about their child in the social context of other children? – these are what matter, but for some staff they need a lot of support and mentoring . . . for others, not much, just the time to think.

At the time of the interview Josie was about to start an action research project focussing on pedagogical quality which would involve all the staff. She anticipated that the staff skills and knowledge about reflecting critically on their work would be further developed.

Seeing herself still on a trajectory of learning, Josie had progressively added to her qualifications, working her way through various levels in the post-secondary vocational education system and subsequently using these credentials to gain university admission, first undergraduate and then postgraduate. In addition to her formal studies, Josie was a foundation member of the Critical Curriculum Group, a self-initiated activist group of early childhood teachers with a commitment to implementing a social justice agenda. She had also joined an early childhood professional mentoring programme, undertaken training in the role of mentor, and participated in a practitioner enquiry research circle.

Josie's commitment to ongoing professional learning was very evident. Much of her professional learning activities had been at her own expense and Josie reported that her management committee had needed to be convinced that they should support her. This highlighted some of the particular challenges and characteristics of the early childhood field at this time, including an ongoing widespread undervaluing in the wider community of the work and required expertise of early years educators.

In the teacher education research literature, there is an increasing conceptualisation of teacher education as occurring along a 'professional learning continuum that spans pre-service professional preparation, induction and continuing professional development' (Feiman-Nemser, 2001, p. 1039), accompanied by a growing acceptance of the responsibility of employing authorities for making provisions for ongoing professional development. In contrast, the reality for those professionals working in the 0–5 sector is that ongoing professional learning is primarily understood and experienced as an individual responsibility, with much of these kinds of activities undertaken outside of working hours and at personal expense. In Josie's case, this reality was exacerbated by the isolation of individual early childhood centres as locally managed entities. The importance of work-based learning is also strongly implicated, and Josie saw an important role for herself in developing high-functioning staff teams with highly developed early childhood pedagogies through workplace-based learning, building skills of critical reflection.

The experience of understanding one's practice in new ways through critical reflection on practice has been widely understood to be an important component of strengthening professionalism (Osgood, 2006). As Josie herself expressed this:

> In my opinion professionalism is also marked by the ability to first critically reflect on your own practice but secondly to make changes based on those reflections.

It is the integration of these two activities of reflection and action that emerged to characterise Josie's work in her centre.

2.4 Relationships, Reflexivity and Renewal

It is possible to discern some dominant themes related to professionalism emerging from this study. The first is the high value and importance that Josie placed on ongoing learning, both for herself and for the staff team that she led. Related to this is the emphasis on relationality in her discourse, which also related to both the practices and understandings of early childhood education – relationships with family and children, and the approach to working with staff teams to enhance pedagogical quality through establishing a relationship-focussed workplace culture. Finally, there was a strong articulation of the importance of reflexivity as a key strategy in ensuring relevance and resourcing renewal.

Despite, or perhaps because of, a long pathway to qualifications and an extended journey of professional learning, Josie remained committed and invigorated in her professional life. She also revealed a clear understanding about the important role of ongoing professional learning and reflection in achieving and sustaining a dynamic staff team.

2.4.1 Professionalism in Context

A small international literature describes and critiques constructs of professionalism and the many challenges to the development of robust professional identities in the field of early childhood. Many highlight the feminised nature of the profession (e.g., Moyles, 2001) and problematise the positioning of professional discourses within discourses of femininity and motherhood (Ailwood, 2007). Some have highlighted the difficulties associated with the hegemony of developmental discourses (Grieshaber, 2001; MacNaughton, 2001), particularly in relation to the formation and sustainability of activist identities. Others draw attention to the many competing discourses that frame early childhood work, claiming:

> The education of young children is deeply embedded in a range of complex and contradictory adult discourses and knowledges, including those of motherhood, politics, worker, citizen, and the economy. (Ailwood, 2004, p. 19)

Glimpses of contradictory discourses were revealed in this study, evident in the intersection of eclectic policy and practice discourses in the practitioner's work setting. This was particularly evident in how Josie privileged discourses of critical reflection, action, change and non-hierarchical leadership in discussions of professionalism. However, strong developmental discourses were juxtaposed alongside these more proactive pedagogical positionings when describing her rationale for the organisation of children's spaces for learning and descriptions of the curriculum. This perspective offers an interesting challenge to critiques of both eclecticism and developmentalism as paralysing professional discourses (Grieshaber, 2001; Woodrow, 2002).

This study highlighted an important role played by both formal and non-formal ongoing professional learning in sustaining Josie's professional life, enabling her to re-invigorate her teaching and respond positively to provocations of change, in the process of building resilience and maintaining a 'hopeful' commitment to the profession and the staff with whom she worked. Given the isolation in which many early years teachers work due to the typically stand-alone nature of many early childhood centres, it is understandable that opportunities to connect with others in communities of practice are highly valued and taken up by practitioners such as Josie. Here, her participation in multiple communities of practice (Wenger, 1998) emerges as potentially significant for future planning of professional learning and consideration of sustainability and change.

Perspectives on the socially situated nature of professionalism were also evident when Josie provided a critique on the nexus between professionalism and qualifications. In spite of her own journey of increasing credentialing through formalised study, Josie quite strongly asserted that professionalism:

> ... is not necessarily linked to qualifications and training; however, it's more the workplace culture, the overall community culture and yes of course government policy does set the mood and the context for feelings of professionalism.

Here Josie identified an affective and relational dimension to professionalism and located professionalism as a situated concept, rather than fixed, captured in time and space in a 'complicated nexus between policy, ideology and practice' (Stronach, Corbin, McNamara, Stark, & Warne, 2002, p. 109).

Josie adopted a position of critique of traditional constructions of professionalism, by alluding to what she called the 'trappings' of professionalism such as 'badging and branding' (increasingly adopted by the community sector and evident in, for example, branded clothing). She also included ethics, advocacy and traditional notions of leadership as potentially problematic dimensions to professionalism. Josie expressed a strong sense of moral purpose in her work, which was clearly guided by ethical principles associated with equity, justice and fairness, and a strong sense of her leadership responsibilities in her centre and the broader early childhood community. As she explained, qualifications (and by implication, associated elements such as codified ethics and hierarchical constructions of leadership) are only part of the professionalism story; it's the practices, and culture that produces and shapes those practices, and changes in practices and cultures, that really matter.

These perspectives resonated with an emerging literature about the importance of developing discourses of professional identity in the field in which community and collectivism are privileged over individualism and in which activism and leadership are robustly articulated (Goffin & Washington, 2007; Sumsion, 2006, 2007; Woodrow, 2008). These are also perspectives very consistent with the themes of Being, Belonging and Becoming, which form the focal point of the newly released national *Early Years Learning Framework for Australia* (DEEWR, 2009b).

2.5 Concluding Comments

The findings from this study highlighted the commitment and professional resilience of one early years educator working within a challenging micro context and ever-changing policy environment. In providing insights into the dynamics of early childhood professional practice and the associated challenges of resourcing professional growth, the study allowed the identification of significant themes implicated in discourses of professionalism. Themes of reflexivity, relationality and renewal emerged as particularly distinctive. The study findings signal possible avenues of further research incorporating these themes.

Equally significantly, the study facilitated the celebration of the work of one early years practitioner, bringing a practitioner's perspective into focus. This is particularly significant at a time when the field of early childhood is being reshaped through large-scale national reform agendas.

References

Ailwood, J. (2004). Genealogies of governmentality: Producing and managing young children and their education. *Australian Educational Researcher, 31*(3), 19–34.

Ailwood, J. (2007). Mothers, teachers, maternalism and early childhood education and care: some historical connections, *Contemporary Issues in Early Childhood, 8*(2), 157–165. http://dx.doi.org/10.2304/ciec.2007.8.2.1.

Anning, A., Cullen, J., & Fleer, M. (2008). *Early childhood education: Society and culture.* London: Sage.

DEEWR. (2009a). *Investing in the early years: A national early childhood development strategy: An initiative of the Council of Australian Governments (COAG).* Canberra: Department of Education, Employment and Workplace Relations. Retrieved July 13, 2009, from http://www.DEEWR.gov.au/EarlyChildhood

DEEWR. (2009b). *Being, belonging and becoming: A national learning framework for Australia.* Canberra: Department of Education, Employment and Workplace Relations.

DoCS. (2002). *The practice of relationships: The NSW curriculum framework for children's services.* Sydney: Office of Childcare, NSW Department of Community Services.

Early Childhood Australia. (2006). *Early childhood Australia's code of ethics.* Canberra: ECA Watson.

Fasoli, L., Woodrow, C., & Scrivens, C. (2007). Challenges for leadership in New Zealand and Australian early childhood contexts. In L. Keesing-Styles & H. Hedges (Eds.), *Theorising early childhood practice: Emerging dialogues* (pp. 231–253). Sydney: Pademelon Press.

Feiman-Nemser, S. (2001). From preparation to practice: Designing a continuum to strengthen and sustain teaching. *Teachers College Record, 102*(6), 1013–1055.

Fenech, M., Sumsion, J., & Goodfellow, J. (2006). The regulatory environment in long day care: A 'double edged sword' for early childhood professional practice. *Australian Journal of Early Childhood, 31*(3), 49–58.

Fenech, M., Sumsion, J., & Goodfellow, J. (2008). The regulatory environment: A source of job (dis)satisfaction for early childhood professionals? *Early Childhood Development and Care, 178*(1), 1–14.

Fleer, M., Edwards, S., Hammer, M., Kennedy, A., Ridgway, A., Robbins, J., et al. (2006). *Early childhood learning communities: Sociocultural research in practice*. Frenchs Forest: Pearson Education.

Goffin, S., & Washington, V. (2007). *Ready or not: Leadership choices in early care and education*. New York: Teachers College Press.

Grieshaber, S. (2001). Advocacy and early childhood educators: Identity and cultural conflicts. In S. Grieshaber & G. Cannella (Eds.), *Embracing identities in early childhood education* (pp. 60–72). New York: Teachers College Press.

Katz, L., & Chard, S. (2001). *Engaging children's minds: The project approach* (2nd ed.). Stanford, CT: Ablex.

MacNaughton, G. (2001). Equal opportunities: Unsettling myths. In T. David (Ed.), *Promoting evidence-based practice in early childhood education* (pp. 211–226). Oxford: JAI.

MacNaughton, G., & Williams, G. (2004). *Teaching techniques for young children* (2nd ed.). Australia: Pearson.

Moss, P. (2006). Structures, understandings and discourses: Possibilities for re-envisioning early childhood education. *Contemporary Issues in Early Childhood, 7*(1), 30–41.

Moyles, J. (2001). Passion, paradox and professionalism in early years education. *Early Years Education, 21*(2), 81–95.

Organisation for Economic and Co-operative Development. (2001). *OECD country note: Australia: Early childhood education and care policy in Australia*. Paris: OECD.

Osgood, J. (2006). Deconstructing professionalism in early childhood education: Resisting the regulatory gaze. *Contemporary Issues in Early Childhood, 7*(1), 5–14.

Press, F. (2006). *What about the kids? Improving the experiences of infants and young children in a changing world*. Sydney: Commission for Children and Young People.

Press, F. (2007). Public investment, fragmentation and quality care: Existing challenges and future options. In E. Hill, B. Pocock, & A. Elliott (Eds.), *Kids count: Better early childhood education and care* (pp. 181–198). Sydney: Sydney University Press.

Press, F., & Hayes, A. (2000). *OECD thematic review of early childhood education and care policy* (Australian Background Report). Canberra: Commonwealth of Australia.

Press, F., & Woodrow, C. (2005). Commodification, corporatisation and children's spaces. *Australian Journal of Education, 49*(3), 278–297.

Siraj-Blatchford, I., Clarke, K., & Needham, M. (2007). *The team around the child: Multi-agency working in the early years*. London: Trentham Books.

Stronach, I., Corbin, B., McNamara, O., Stark, S., & Warne, T. (2002). Towards an uncertain politics of professionalism: Teacher and nurse identities in flux. *Journal of Education Policy, 17*(1), 109–138.

Sumsion, J. (2002). Revisiting the challenge of staff recruitment and retention in children's services. *Australian Journal of Early Childhood, 27*(1), 8–13.

Sumsion, J. (2006). From Whitlam to economic rationalism and beyond: A conceptual framework for political activism in children's services. *Australian Journal of Early Childhood, 31*(1), 1–9.

Sumsion, J. (2007). Sustaining the employment of early childhood teachers in long day care: A case for robust hope, critical imagination and critical action. *Asia Pacific Journal of Teacher Education, 35*(3), 311–327.

Valentine, K., Katz, I., & Griffiths, M. (2007). *Early childhood services: Models of integration and collaboration.* Perth: Australian Research Alliance for Children and Youth. Australia: Part A, Final Report. Canberra: Lifelong Learning Network.

Wenger, E. (1998). *Communities of practice: Learning, meaning, and identity.* Cambridge: Cambridge University Press.

Woodrow, C. (2002). *Living ethics in early childhood contexts.* Unpublished PhD thesis, Central Queensland University, Rockhampton.

Woodrow, C. (2004). Contested territory: Early childhood curriculum in the Australian context. In W. Fthenakis & P. Oberhuemer (Eds.), *Fruhpadagogik international: Buildungsqualitat ImBlikpunkt (Early childhood curriculum issues: International perspectives)* (pp. 241–254). Munich: Staatsinstitut fur Fruhpadagogik.

Woodrow, C. (2008). Discourses of professional identity in early childhood: Movements in Australia. *European Early Childhood Research Journal, 16*(2), 269–280.

Woodrow, C., & Brennan, M. (1999). Marketised positioning of early childhood education: New contexts for curriculum and professional development in Queensland, Australia. *Contemporary Issues in Early Childhood, 1*(1), 79–95. www.triangle.co.uk/ciec

Chapter 3
Leading and Managing in an Early Years Setting in England

Linda Miller, Carrie Cable, and Gill Goodliff

3.1 Recent Developments: An Overview

3.1.1 Background

The chapter has been completed during a time of change and uncertainty in England where a Coalition Government replaced the former Labour Government (1997–2010). Historically, England has had a split system model of care and education services (Owen & Haynes, 2008); more recently the generic term 'early years' has been adopted because of a long-standing campaign to eliminate this false divide.[1] The Labour Government brought together services for children, young people and families under a new Department for Children, Schools and Families (DCSF) as part of a drive to unite these services. Under the new Coalition Government this department was renamed the Department for Education (DfE) in 2010, reflecting a change in policy and focus. Responsibility for children's health remains with the Department of Health.

The Labour Government had prioritised early years policy as part of the wider reform of Children's Services. A National Childcare Strategy released in 1998 (Department of Education and Employment [DfEE], 1998) gradually brought together early years services under the jurisdiction of local education authorities, and at a national level under the DfE. The strategy aimed to reduce child poverty and social exclusion and improve affordable provision for children and families.

---

[1] There are considerable differences between developments in ECEC across the United Kingdom (England, Northern Ireland (NI), Scotland and Wales). For example, in NI there is strong aspiration towards integrated services for young children and families as in England, but the reality across the United Kingdom is a 'split' system of provision and practitioner training. It is beyond the scope of this chapter to discuss these differences and indeed there are few texts that distinguish developments across the four countries. In this chapter we focus on developments specific to England.

L. Miller (✉)
Faculty of Education and Language Studies, The Open University, Milton Keynes MK76AA, UK
e-mail: l.k.miller@open.ac.uk

L. Miller et al. (eds.), *Early Childhood Grows Up*, International Perspectives on Early Childhood Education and Development 6, DOI 10.1007/978-94-007-2718-2_3, © Springer Science+Business Media B.V. 2012

The subsequent *Every Child Matters* report (Her Majesty's Treasury [HMT], 2003) provided a framework for the reform of children's services in England within an ethos based on children's rights and positive outcomes for children, and particularly for children at risk.

The Sure Start programme is a key arm of the National Childcare strategy. Based on the US early intervention programme, Head Start, and the more recent initiative *No Child Left Behind* (2001), Sure Start includes Children's Centres which offer holistic provision and multi-agency services (Department for Education and Skills [DfES], 2006). This legislation aimed at providing integrated early learning and care and better access for parents to high quality early years services. It set out what government perceives as all children's entitlement to five key outcomes: being healthy; staying safe; enjoying and achieving; making a positive contribution; enjoying economic well-being.

The OECD report (2006) noted 'significant progress' (p. 423) in England since its 1999 review, mostly in relation to government investment, expansion of Children's Centres, and extended schools which offer before- and after-school provision. It also noted that spending on children's services in the United Kingdom quadrupled between 1997 and 2007 from GBP 1.1 billion in 1996/1997, to GBP 4.4 billion by 2007/2008. This reform process continues to develop integrated services for children and young people and is attempting to break down organisational and professional boundaries in the children's workforce to encourage multi-agency working (DfES, 2006; DCSF, 2008a).

3.1.2 Early Years Provision

In England, early years provision is organised across the private, voluntary, independent and publicly funded sectors and ranges from short sessional to full day. There is part-time free nursery education for all 3- and 4-year-olds across all providers that meet nationally approved standards. All service providers are required to be registered and inspected against a set of common standards. The Office for Standards in Education (Ofsted) is an independent regulatory and inspection body, but is accountable to government; it inspects both childcare and early education provision through a common inspection process. There has been an increase in private-for-profit providers, in particular in full daycare, and a decline in sessional provision and childminding (Childcare and Early Years Providers Survey, 2007).

Government schemes assist families with childcare costs. There is a Minister for Children and Youth Justice, and a Children's Commissioner. At local authority level, Directors of Children's Services integrate planning and delivery of services. A key tool in the delivery of integrated services is the development of a Common Assessment Framework (CAF) (DfES, 2006) for early assessment and identification of children's additional needs. This framework is used by practitioners across all children's services.

3.1.3 The Early Years Curriculum

Since 2008 all providers of early years services are required to work to a curricular framework *The Early Years Foundation Stage* (EYFS), for children from birth to five (DCSF, 2008b). The EYFS is based on four guiding principles – A Unique Child; Positive Relationships; Enabling Environments; and Learning and Development. It sets out learning, development and welfare requirements and Early Learning Goals (ELGs) which most children are expected to reach by the end of the EYFS. These cover the six areas of learning and development of: personal, social and emotional; communication, language and literacy; problem solving, reasoning and numeracy; knowledge and understanding of the world; physical; and creative. Guidance documents provide support for practitioners (DCSF, 2008b). However, a framework that encompasses key learning areas, learning goals and a sequential approach to achievement has been criticised as the 'schoolification' of early childhood (OECD, 2006, p. 62), and for encouraging practitioners to focus on 'strategic compliance' with national requirements (Goouch, 2008, p. 93). The new government has commissioned a review of EYFS with the aim of making it less bureaucratic and more focused on young children's learning and development (DfE, 2010 http://www.direct.gov.uk/en/Nl1/Newsroom/DG_189908). However, recent research indicates that practitioners 'welcome the play-based and child-led nature of the guidance' (Brooker, Rogers, Ellis, Hallet, & Roberts-Holmes, 2010, p. 1).

3.1.4 The Early Years Workforce

The qualifications of the early years workforce range from unqualified to undergraduate/postgraduate degrees. A Children's Workforce Development Council (CWDC) is responsible for improving qualifications and training for all those working with children and young people. However, a change of government has resulted in most of the functions of this body being taken over by the new DfE in 2011, thus generating uncertainty in the sector. The skills and knowledge deemed essential for the workforce are set out in a document entitled *The Common Core* (DfES, 2005) and laid out in six areas of expertise: effective communication and development; child and young person development; safeguarding and promoting the welfare of the child; supporting transitions; multi-agency working; and sharing information. A review of the Common Core in 2010 (CWDC, 2010) broadly retained the six areas of skills and knowledge but aimed to strengthen some key areas such as early intervention and prevention and integrated working. As part of workforce reform, an Integrated Qualifications Framework (IQF) was developed for launching in 2010, listing approved qualifications and enabling progression across professional boundaries within the children's workforce. However, following a change of administration in May 2010, this initiative did not proceed (National Archives, 2011).

Graduate-qualified teachers work mainly in maintained (supported by government and local authority) nurseries and schools. A new graduate Early Years

Professional (EYP) role has been developed for those leading work with parents and children in full daycare settings and is proposed to have equivalence to qualified teacher status; however, equivalence has not been clearly defined and the lack of parity in status and pay between these two roles remains. To achieve Early Years Professional Status (EYPS), practitioners are required to meet a set of 39 national standards that cover the knowledge and skills deemed essential for those leading practice and supporting the practice of others in early years settings (CWDC, 2006); this status is achieved through one of four 'pathways'. The new government has committed to continued funding for the EYP role in the immediate future and also for *New Leaders in Early Years* pilot programme, a 2-year scheme for graduates outside the sector, both administered by CWDC. After completing this course, candidates are awarded EYP status and a Masters Degree in Early Years (http://www.cwdcouncil.org.uk/early-years/graduate-leaders-in-early-years/new-leaders-explained).

A major government-funded evidence-based study *The Effective Provision of Pre-school Education* (EPPE) (Sylva et al., 2003) has demonstrated the positive impact of staff with qualified teacher status on high quality pre-school provision. To date there is limited evidence of the impact of the EYP role, but a recent study suggests that 80% of the EYPs surveyed had increased their confidence as practitioners and more than three-quarters felt that that the EYP role enhanced their professional status (Hadfield, Jopling, Royle, & Waller, 2010).

3.2 The Day in the Life Project in England

3.2.1 The Setting

The English study was initiated in April 2007 when we first approached the management of a private (for profit) day nursery with which the project team was familiar to explain the project aims and to talk with key staff about what their involvement in the project would entail. The day nursery provides care and education for children aged 0–5 years in a converted watermill situated in a residential area of a small market town in the south east of England. The nursery closes for just 5 days each year and can provide for up to 66 children full time from Monday to Friday from 7.30 am to 6.30 pm. There were 154 children on the roll at the time of the visit.

The nursery director explained the philosophy of the nursery as providing a 'home from home'; she explained that this atmosphere was reflected through grouping the children into 'vertical' or 'family groups' so that children of different ages could spend time with siblings. The Ofsted inspection report at the time of the visit described the learning facilities at the nursery as good.

The nursery has three floors, each with a central area and 'quiet' bays for sleeping and quiet play, plus a 'sensory' room. All children sleep when they wish, and toys and equipment are freely available. The 'pre-school' children, aged 3–5, spend part of the day in a separate building with a qualified teacher. Julie, as nursery manager, has an office on the second floor of the nursery and is visible to children and staff as they pass the office to access the toilet and sink area. There is an outdoor fenced play area, and a large well-equipped indoor play hall in a separate building.

Organic meals are prepared by a resident cook. There is an information page for parents on the website and an information pack. Parents are able to talk to their child's key worker on a daily basis, share written records, and attend parent evenings. At the time of the study, the nursery was privately owned and fees were £47.20 for a full day with a 10% discount for siblings.

We were fortunate in having funding which allowed us to engage a professional film crew to video a working day for Julie. At the time of the filming there were 43 members of staff, including volunteers. Most staff were qualified or working towards a Level 3 (supervisory level) qualification with two qualified teachers holding post-qualifying diplomas, and many holding vocational qualifications; the nursery also operated a staff training programme. Staff roles included a nursery director and financial director (held by the owners), an administrator and cook, a nursery manager (Julie), an officer in charge, and deputy officer in charge, nursery nurses and nursery assistants. Full daycare is offered alongside part-time 'education' for 3- to 5-year-olds. At the time of filming the nursery was introducing the then new curriculum framework *The Early Years Foundation Stage* which aims to integrate the curriculum for children from birth to 5 (DCSF, 2008b).

3.2.2 The Practitioner: Julie

Julie was 26 and had worked in the nursery for 1 year as nursery manager. She had 7 years' previous experience in day nurseries. Her role involved extensive administrative duties alongside some work with the children and she worked from 10 am to 6 pm. She was supported by an officer in charge and her deputy. Julie was studying towards a Foundation Degree in Early Years (Level 5)[2] at the Open University to enable her to progress to the graduate EYPS. Julie's employers supported her studies through enabling her to take some study days.

3.2.3 Julie's Day

The account of Julie's day is based on the edited film data and subsequent interview. The filmed material was viewed by the co-researchers who identified, discussed and

---

[2] Foundation Degrees are recognised as an award equivalent to level 5 (of 8) within the National Qualifications Framework (Qualifications and Curriculum Authority, 2009). They are equivalent to the first 2 years of higher education study. A shared feature of all Foundation Degrees is a clearly articulated progression route that offers students the opportunity to 'top-up' with additional study and assessment in order to achieve a bachelor's degree with honours. It is this latter award that in Europe, under the terms of the Bologna declaration (Bergen, 2005), would represent the end of the first cycle of higher education qualifications.

Table 3.1 Timetable of Julie's day

Approximate time of day	Situation
10.05–	1. Working in the office
10.20–10.25	*Move from office*
	2. A group story reading with the children
10.35–10.40	*Back to office then move to pre-school*
10.45–10.57	3. Meeting with the pre-school teacher
11.12–11.15	*Walk back to main block*
11.30–11.47	4. Julie sitting with the children for lunch
11.55	5. Meeting with Senior Management team re rota planning
	Meeting with senior management team continued. Training planning for new curriculum
12.30–12.42	6. Sitting-in on pre-school story with children
12.42–12.50	7. Supervising pre-school children brushing teeth after lunch
12.50–12.56	8. At table playing with a group of children in pre-school
	Walk back to main block
13.00–13.20	9. Meeting with parent
	Lunch break
14.25–14.28	10. Assisting with the minibus departure – checking seatbelts (health and safety check)
	Walk to Play Hall
14.29–	11. Play hall: carrying out a health and safety check
14.35–14.40	12. With group of staff and children on the play hall equipment
	Walk back to main block
14.55–15.02	13. Discussion with key worker about a new child
15.07–15.14	14. Outdoor play, then supervising children back inside
	Return to office
16.20–5.30	15. Meeting with financial director
	The remainder of the day was used for the interview

analysed the various roles Julie undertook during the day (see Chapter 2). Table 3.1 presents key situations from her day selected from filming. Each situation refers to a temporal period and a significant event in the day, and shows some overlapping episodes (in italics).

3.2.4 Narrative Account of Julie's Day

In the following section we provide a narrative account of some of the main episodes within the main situations in Julie's day (see Table 3.1). Space does not permit us to expand on all the situations; instead, we have selected episodes to comment on which throw light on notions of professionalism and features of professional practice which this study sought to understand. Our comments on Julie's responses to our interview questions are guided by this same intention. Emergent themes are shown in italics and/or bold print, and the numbering of the selected situations reflects that in Table 3.1.

3.2.4.1 Situation 1: In the Office

Julie's day began in the office with administrative tasks. She made and received phone calls; for example, she phoned a colleague and arranged to see groups of staff and children later in the day. She sent and replied to e-mails and dealt with the mail.

Julie's Interview Comments

During the interview Julie gave an account of the usual timetable of her day which reflected what we had observed. On arriving at work she met with the officer in charge or her deputy about any major problems. She then dealt with paper work and organised her day. She checked for messages and e-mails from staff, parents and the nursery owners to make sure that everything was 'ticking along'. She dealt with anything 'really important' straightaway. Julie said she then tended to go down and see the nursery secretary to see if anything had 'come up' or arrived in the post that the secretary herself could not deal with, or something that needed an urgent decision.

On *professionalism* Julie said:

> ... professionalism really comes from that circle where I'm saying I'm in charge and I know what's going on. If you ask me how many children are in the building, I know. If you ask me how many are going home at lunchtime, I know. If you ask me how many staff are First Aid trained ..., I know where to get this training and I know where to get this funding from.

Commentary

These observations showed that a key part of Julie's role was '*managing*'. She ensured the nursery was running smoothly and had an overview of the day's events. With a large staff, changing numbers of children, a wide range of indoor and outdoor activities and community visits, keeping everything 'ticking along' is challenging. Julie therefore had *multiple demands* on her time and dealt with a range of *complex tasks* and *responsibilities.*

3.2.4.2 Situation 2: Group Story Reading

Julie moved from her office to the main area where a group of children seated on a mat were engaged in a 'big' story book about a farmyard. Julie joined the group at a point in the story where a fly had landed on the farmer's nose. The nursery assistant reading the story encouraged the children to point to their noses and join in with 'atishoo' as the farmer gave a loud sneeze. Julie joined in with the actions and encouraged the children to point to their noses.

Julie's Interview Comments

Julie said that in the mornings she spent time with the children and with more senior members of staff:

Something else I like to do, if I'm walking through a room is go in and interact with the children and spend a little bit of time with them. It means that my day doesn't then become just a big, long list of meetings. They see me around and the parents and staff then know that I'm quite accessible.

Commentary

Julie's interactions with the children were very brief – both in this second situation and throughout the day. The main focus seemed to be for Julie to have a monitoring role. It seems that as she has moved up the staffing hierarchy, her contact with the children has lessened.

3.2.4.3 Situation 3: Meeting with the Pre-school Teacher

Following the group story reading and a brief visit to her office, Julie met with the pre-school teacher, Pam, in the 'pre-school' building. They discussed plans for a 'Pet Day' where staff members would bring in animals. Julie suggested contacting a vet to talk to the children, a suggestion Pam welcomed. Pam asked Julie about any Health and Safety regulations that would need to be observed when the animals were within the nursery, and Julie said she would check these out. Julie said she would need to undertake a 'risk assessment' and contact parents to check that their children did not have any allergies to animals.

A key aim of Julie's day was to introduce the then new EYFS curriculum documents that had recently been distributed to all registered care/ education providers for children from birth to 5 years. Julie and Pam then looked together at these and Julie briefly explained some key changes.

Julie's Interview Comments

Julie explained that she met with Pam at least once each week to go through issues arising at the pre-school. The meetings enabled Pam to ask for any resources or help she might need. Julie referred to their discussion of the EYFS curriculum and how this would affect Pam's work with the children (for example possible higher child to adult ratios). Julie said she passes information to Pam so that Pam is aware of what is going on.

On professionalism Julie said:

Acting professionally could range from anything such as how I am within meetings. For example, I had a meeting with the pre-school teacher this morning and it may have been that we disagreed on something and I could have said to her 'actually, I'm not going to take your opinion into account and what I say goes', but I don't see that as a very professional approach. I see that, the way this nursery runs in particular, everyone should be able to be included and have their say.

I need to recognise that they are professionals too and that some of them have qualifications far above what I have and they have different experiences to me. We have to draw on that and use it to our advantage.

Commentary

Julie was *respectful* of Pam's position and showed *empathy* in this conversation. If Julie and Pam had been working in a school setting, Pam would have a much higher 'status' than Julie. As Julie acknowledges, Pam is more experienced and more highly qualified than her. Julie values what others bring to their role. She seems to act as a *'conduit'* for information and has responsibility for overseeing policy change and for the health and well-being of the children. The enormous scope and demands of Julie's role were beginning to emerge.

3.2.4.4 Situation 5: Meeting with the Senior Management Team

Julie met with the nursery director and officer in charge and briefed them about the new EYFS curriculum documents. Julie discussed the training that would be required and was keen to include part-time staff who would not normally attend training sessions. The nursery director suggested sharing the training provided by the Local Authority with other nurseries. She consulted Julie about when this should begin, and Julie said as soon as possible as staff can take a long time to 'get used to it'. The director asked for Julie's confirmation that the teachers should be involved in the training, which Julie provided. They discussed the need for the teachers to be involved in curriculum planning in the main nursery to ensure a smooth transition. They also discussed how the newly qualified EYP could take a leadership role in liaising between the pre-school and nursery on the curriculum. They went on to discuss the staff rota for the following week and the pending 'Fun Day'.

Julie's Interview Comments

Julie explained that the senior staff had regular meetings and that today's meeting was to discuss the EYFS and related training and to prepare for the coming weeks, *'For example, we have a Fun Day in June, we need to work out the logistics of that and plan everything'.*

Commentary

Julie took both a *leadership role* and *management role* in this meeting. For example, she asserted that the EYFS training should begin sooner rather than later. She also showed *empathy* and *awareness* of the training needs of different staff members.

3.2.4.5 Situation 9: Meeting with a Parent

Julie met with a parent to discuss the possibility of her child increasing his time in the nursery so that she could increase her work commitments. Julie used the notes from the child's key worker to tell the mother that he had been washing the dolls' clothes in the outside play area that morning. Julie reassured the mother that both she and the key worker felt that he was ready to stay for lunch and for the afternoon sessions.

Julie's Interview Comments

Julie explained that the parent felt that, 'He's got to that age now where she's finding he's not getting as much from being at home as he would from being at the nursery and she needs to work more'. She said the mother was worried about this change, 'So I was talking to her about that and reassuring her'.

On *professionalism* Julie said:

> The parents look to you and see that you are somebody who is at the forefront of the nursery and that you're setting an example for the staff. They're coming to you to look for answers and they want to make sure that you've got the answers and that helps them put their trust in you. Obviously, they're leaving their children with you everyday and trusting that you're going to look after them in the appropriate way and that you're going to follow all the guidelines and that you're going to adhere to Ofsted. That's the only way they can trust you, by seeing how you are and knowing that you do your job professionally, working with other parents and with the other practitioners out there. If they see you're doing that, it gives them confidence.

Commentary

Julie's statement here reveals that she sees her *management role* in the nursery as giving her external professional status with the parents. She is *accessible* to the parents and provides reassurance based on her *professional knowledge* of the child and of policy regulations and procedures, which she perceives as ensuring parents' *trust*.

3.2.4.6 Situation 13: Discussion with a Key Worker

Julie met with Lily, the key worker for Sarah (aged 4 months), to discuss how she had settled in. She sat informally on the floor with Lily as children played around them. Lily said Sarah was getting used to the routine of the nursery. They discussed Sarah's sleep patterns, and Lily explained they were trying to match the routine at home and that Sarah's mother thought she was getting used to other people feeding her. Julie said the mother was looking to increase Sarah's sessions in the nursery.

Julie's Interview Comments

Julie explained that staff try to settle in new parents, as well as the child, as parents can be worried and apprehensive. She said that parents can telephone at any time to check on their child through the key worker, 'Even if it's a case of the parents checking up on whether their child has had a sleep or how much lunch they've had, we can discuss that with them over the phone'. If the staff detect what Julie described as 'teething problems', then someone from senior management will talk to the key worker and then the parent, 'rather than the parent feeling that they've come to this brand new nursery and they don't know who anybody is and have to knock on a door to try and see somebody who is in charge. It can be quite worrying for them'. Julie explained that the nursery had recently put together a 'settling in' brochure for the parents.

On *professionalism* Julie said:

> Involvement with parents is the main key. It's really that, when you're working in the early years, it's always seen that the parents are the main carers and they are the people we have to refer to. Whatever we do here, we have to inform the parents and that's the basis we work on. We do it to make sure that the parents are confident in what we're doing.

Commentary

Julie again demonstrated her *profession*al knowledge, in particular in relation to Sarah's well-being and the importance of *parental involvement*.

3.2.4.7 Situation 14: Outdoor Play

Julie joined a group of children and staff outdoors who were tidying up playthings. She encouraged children to put the tubes in a storage box, then said, 'Well done'. She helped one child to put his shoe back on and said to another child, 'Your brother's just gone swimming'. The children then went over to the nursery door to go back inside.

Julie's Interview Comments

Julie explained that sometimes she stands back and at other times she will be quite involved with the children, and that sometimes she observed the practitioners interacting with the children and might make suggestions to them. She added that they (the senior management team) had been looking to plan, 'a bit more structure out there'; for example, in today's play, supplying cardboard tubes so that 'it's not the same sort of bats, balls and bikes for the children. They're having different experiences when they're outside as well as when they're inside'.

Commentary

Here Julie was involved in: *interacting with the children, monitoring staff and curriculum planning and leadership*. Being *visible, accessible* and offering *support* within the team are recurring themes.

3.2.4.8 Situation 15: Meeting with the Financial Director

Julie's day ended as it had begun, with administrative tasks in her office and also a regular meeting with the nursery co-owner and financial director. Julie explained the plans for staff training, discussed staff payments and also discussed a contract for a new staff member and details of a 'toy box' scheme offered by the Health Service to encourage children to play, which Julie said she would take forward.

Julie's Interview Comments

Julie explained that she met with the financial director at least once a week to go through any issues that may have arisen, such as parents who may have problems with payment, or to look at work schedules and salary payments.

On *professionalism* Julie said:

> Coming to a nursery like this I work quite closely with the owners. They say 'we were really pleased with the way you dealt with that situation. That's made us really happy with the way you've done that and we trust you'.

She gave an example:

> They (the owners) would normally run the (staff) training days. They said 'we actually feel that you would be best suited to do the training day and we've got confidence in the fact that you know what you're talking about and the staff respond to you very well. So please would you do it for us?' So when they come and say that to me I feel that I'm being a manager here and meeting those standards they've set for me.

Commentary

Julie is clearly proud of her management and leadership role in the nursery and in the trust and confidence the owners have in her. This role seems to 'frame' her professional identity. Does Julie see herself as a professional?

> Yes I do. I think that my role, especially because I am the manager here, and because I'm seen as a sort of head figure within this nursery, I do see myself as a professional. I think other people see me as a professional. I have to adapt myself to different circumstances. When I'm dealing with parents I'm different to when I'm dealing with junior staff and when I'm dealing with more senior practitioners. I think that what makes me a professional is the fact that I come in to do my job to the best of my abilities and I go home every day knowing that I've put in 110 percent into that day and I've done as much as I can do. I think that the responses I get from other people make me feel that they have trust in me and they've got confidence in me.

Commentary

Julie's position in the nursery was framed within her key role as a leader and manager. She was *confident* within this role and her *professional identity* derived from this status. We were struck by the *diversity*, *complexity* and *multiple demands* of Julie's day and the energy that her relentless schedule required. At the centre of all that was happening, Julie acted as a *conduit* for information and policy implementation. She appeared to have excellent *organisational skills* and a *detailed knowledge* of all that was happening, although multiple demands seemed to remove her from sustained interaction with the children.

3.3 Discussion

In this chapter we have considered the key aims of the project in relation to the English case study and explored what it means to act professionally in one particular early years context and through one specific workplace role. Alongside Julie's perceptions of what being a professional means to her, and also how she perceives others view her, we have also added our own interpretations of how Julie locates her professional identity. Table 3.2 below brings together some key themes and features of practice that emerge when these perceptions are considered holistically; these indicate that in the context of a private-for-profit situation Julie's professional role is primarily that of a management leader.

3.3.1 Managing and Leading

Julie's sense of professional identity seemed to be derived mainly from her status and position as a manager and member of the senior management team. Her credibility and confidence in this role were linked more closely to her previous work experience than to the level of qualifications she had achieved at the time of the study. According to Muijs, Aubrey, Harris, and Briggs (2004), leaders in early childhood have a multiplicity of roles which are context specific. Rodd (1997) identified the five most common management and leadership roles as: managing and supervising staff; making contact with parents and other professionals; supporting staff development; managing the budget; and co-ordinating what is happening in the centre. These roles would seem to capture Julie's professional practice. However, Hatherley and Lee (2003) see leadership as involving having a vision, and being able to articulate this in practice. Julie's role appeared to us to be more about managing the implementation of the vision of the nursery owners than her own.

Table 3.2 Key themes and features of practice

Themes and features of practice
The diversity, complexity and multiple responsibilities of Julie's role
Trusted relationships
Leading, managing and organising
Acting as a conduit for information
Availability, accessibility and visibility
Ensuring regulatory and policy compliance
Personal knowledge (of the setting, children and families)
Professional knowledge (child development, pedagogy, policy)
Empathy and respect for others
Commitment (to the children, the parents, the staff and the nursery owners)
Confidence (in her management role and skills)

3.3.2 Acting as a Professional

Julie's role as manager in the nursery is both demanding and complex. In co-ordinating provision she acts as a conduit for information and policy initiatives, which is dependent upon her professional knowledge base. Julie has an important role in ensuring 'strategic compliance' (Goouch, 2008, p. 93) with regulatory and policy guidelines as in situations 3 and 5 (Table 3.1), where she ensures staff are aware of the new curriculum documents. This applies also to situations 10 and 11 where Julie was ensuring compliance with health and safety regulations, thus ensuring the children's safety and well-being (HMT, 2003). Julie draws upon her professional knowledge in situation 9, where she meets with a parent to negotiate what is best for her child at a particular point in time. Communication and contact with parents is clearly important to her (see also situation 13).

In her discussions with colleagues, Julie demonstrated respect and empathy, for example in situation 3 where she recognised Pat's status and valued her contribution to the discussion. Similarly, in situation 13, Julie consulted Sarah's key worker before speaking to the parent. Pound and Joshi (2005) noted that when team members are treated with respect and empathy by their leaders, then they are much more likely to treat children in this way too.

3.3.3 Perspectives on Professionalism

In 2003 Moss argued for the reform of the childcare and early years workforce, noting that despite government reforms, the early years workforce remains a gendered and low-paid occupation and is still essentially understood as 'women's work'. As Moss then argued, 'women, it is assumed, have natural capabilities for caring, . . . if, for example, all women are natural mothers, so all women make natural workers with children . . .' (2003, p. 3). This construction of childcare as 'substitute mothering' rather than a profession which, Moss says, involves 'quite different relationships, practices and purposes to mothering' (p. 3), is reflected in Julie's comments about external perceptions of nursery workers:

> I think it (professionalism) isn't really valued as much in nursery nurses and nursery assistants – because people do see them as just carers for their children.

> Because child raising has always been a mother's role, they (i.e., external people) get this impression that it's always just women who work in nurseries. I think that people from outside do see that being in a nursery is 'playing with children' all day and just an extension of the mother's role.

Oberhuemer (2005) described 'democratic professionalism' (p. 13) as evidenced through: Interacting with children; centre management and leadership; partnership with parents and professional knowledge base, all of which feature in Julie's professional practice. For example in situations 10 and 14 Julie is demonstrating her *professional knowledge* of child development and pedagogy through her awareness of the importance of outdoor play and risk taking. She is exercising her *managerial* role in ensuring Health and Safety regulations are adhered to and so ensuring the children's well-being. Her practice is also reflected in Dalli's (2008) definition of *professional knowledge and practice* and *collaborative* relationships when she consulted with the key worker, parent and pre-school teacher in situations 3, 9 and 13.

Discussing professionalism in relation to early years workers in England is confounded by the creation of the EYP role, a graduate-level status but currently without equivalent status to that of a teacher in terms of pay or conditions. This raises the question of whether those practitioners, including Julie, who do *not* have this title are therefore not 'professionals', despite undertaking high levels of responsibility and demonstrating professional practice as defined in the literature cited above (see also Miller, 2008a, 2008b). In a discussion of power relations within early childhood services, Fenech and Sumsion (2007, p. 119) warn of the 'othering' of less qualified or non-accredited staff. In England, qualified teachers working in early years settings *are* regarded as professionals, whereas others working with young children are not. Julie shows awareness of this dilemma, as despite her management status, she confirmed that it was important to her that she is not seen as distanced from other staff: 'They know that, when I ask them to do something, I'm just as happy to go and do it myself. I think I'm very open to all of the staff . . . . we try to act as a team so that everybody is on the same level'.

3.4 Summary

Julie's view of her role and responsibilities is as a manager and leader with a strong emphasis on her ability to organise provision on a day-to-day basis. She has responsibility for ensuring that the day runs smoothly for children and staff and that any issues are dealt with promptly and effectively. Julie's day is characterised by busyness and complexity. She is constantly moving from one activity or task to another around the nursery. Despite this, she creates spaces for interactions with children, parents and colleagues. Aubrey (2010) noted that in a study of leaders working in multi-agency settings, they demonstrated and reported on 'a rich and varied range of activities' (p. 220) including meetings, telephone calls, staff interactions and communication with parents and children. It is clear from our interview discussions with Julie, and from the video data, that Julie views herself as a professional, and that the features of practice (see Table 3.2) that we have identified as emerging from the data accord with those identified by Rodd (1997). However, these features of practice lean more towards management than leadership, which is not surprising given Julie's job title as nursery manager.

The changing and diverse workforce role in the early years in England means that it is impossible to provide a simple characterisation of an early years practitioner's professional practice. It is therefore not possible to define Julie as a typical practitioner or her day as a typical day. Her situation presents as a microcosm of some workforce roles in early years settings in England in the independent, voluntary and private sector. The case study illustrates the challenges faced by practitioners such as Julie, who take on demanding roles in early years settings, requiring high levels of responsibility and professionalism, without corresponding recognition in the form of qualifications, status or commensurate pay (Miller, 2008a, 2008b). However, the variety and complexity of roles, frequent changes in activity and limited time to reflect during the working day can perhaps be said to be typical characteristics of the working days for many practitioners in the early years.

Acknowledgements The project was funded by the Practice Based Professional Learning Centre for Excellence in Teaching and Learning (CETL) at The Open University, UK.

References

Aubrey, C. (2010). Leading and working in multi-agency teams. In G. Pugh & B. Duffy (Eds.), *Contemporary issues in the early years* (5th ed., pp. 209–255). London: Sage.

Bergen Conference of European Ministers Responsible for Higher Education. (2005, May 19–20). http://www.enic-naric.net/index.aspx?s=n&r=ena&d=qf

Brooker, L., Rogers, S., Ellis, D., Hallet, E., & Roberts-Holmes, G. (2010). *Practitioners' experiences of the Early Years Foundation* Stage, DFE RB-029.

Childcare and Early Years Providers Survey. (2007). Retrieved December 14, 2009, from https://www.education.gov.uk/publications/standard/publicationDetail/Page1/DCSF-RB047

Children's Workforce Development Council (CWDC). (2006). *Early year professional prospectus.* Leeds: CWDC.

Children's Workforce Development Council (CWDC). New leaders in early years pilot. http://www.cwdcouncil.org.uk/early-years/graduate-leaders-in-early-years/new-leaders-explained. Accessed 16 October 2011.

Children's Workforce Development Council (CWDC). (2010). *Refreshing the common core of skills and knowledge for the children's workforce*. Leeds: CWDC.

Dalli, C. (2008). Pedagogy, knowledge and collaboration: Towards a ground up perspective on professionalism. *European Early Childhood Education Research Journal, 16*(2), 171–186.

Department for Children, Schools and Families (DCSF). (2008a). *2020: Children and young people's strategy*. Nottingham: DCSF.

Department for Children, Schools and Families. (2008b). *Statutory framework for the early years foundation stage*. Nottingham: DCSF.

Department for Education. (2010). *Review of the Early Years Foundation Stage*. Retrieved January 17, 2011, from http://www.direct.gov.uk/en/Nl1/Newsroom/DG_189908

Department for Education and Employment (DfEE). (1998). *Meeting the childcare challenge: A framework and consultation document*. London: HMSO.

Department for Education and Skills (DfES). (2005). *Common core of skills and knowledge for the children's workforce*. Nottingham: DfES.

Department for Education and Skills (DfES). (2006). *Children's workforce strategy: Building a word-class workforce for children and young people*. Nottingham: DfES.

Fenech, M., & Sumsion, J. (2007). Early childhood teachers and regulation: Complicating power relations using a Foucauldian lens. *Contemporary Issues in Early Childhood, 8*(2), 109–122.

Goouch, K. (2008). Understanding playful pedagogies, play narratives and play spaces. *Early Years: An International Journal of Research and Development, 28*(1), 93–102.

Hadfield, M., Jopling, M., Royle, K., & Waller, T. (2010). *First national survey of practitioners with early years professional status*. UK: Centre for Developmental and Applied Research in Education (CeDare), University of Wolverhampton. Retrieved January 27, 2011, from http://www.wlv.ac.uk/default.aspx?page=20748

Hatherley, A., & Lee, W. (2003). Voices of early childhood leadership. *New Zealand Journal of Educational Leadership, 18*, 91–100.

Her Majesty's Treasury. (2003). *Every child matters*. London: TSO.

Miller, L. (2008a). Developing professionalism within a regulatory framework in England: Challenges and possibilities. *European Early Childhood Education Research Journal, 16*(2), 255–269.

Miller, L. (2008b). Developing new professional roles in the early years. In L. Miller & C. Cable (Eds.), *Professionalism in the early years* (pp. 20–31). London: Hodder Education.

Moss, P. (2003). *Beyond caring: The case for reforming the childcare and early years workforce*. London: Daycare Trust.

Muijs, D., Aubrey, C., Harris, A., & Briggs, M. (2004). How do they manage? *A Review of the Research on Leadership in Early Childhood, 2*(2), 157–169.

National Archives (2011). "http://webarchive.nationalarchives.gov.uk/20100908154344/http:/ www.dcsf.gov.uk/everychildmatters/strategy/deliveringservices1/iqf/iqf/" (accessed 16 October 2011).

No child left behind (2001). Retrieved November 5, 2009, from http://www.ed.gov/nclb/overview/ intro/index.html

Oberhuemer, P. (2005). Conceptualising the early childhood pedagogue: Policy approaches and issues of professionalism. *European Early Childhood Education Research Journal, 13*(1), 5–15.

OECD. (2006). *Starting strong 11 early childhood education and care*. Paris: OECD.

Owen, S., & Haynes, G. (2008). Developing professionalism in the early years: From policy to practice. In L. Miller & C. Cable (Eds.), *Professionalism in the early years* (pp. 9–20). London: Hodder Education.

Pound, L., & Joshi, U. (2005). Management, leadership and teamwork. In L. Dryden, R. Forbes, P. Mukherji, & L. Pound (Eds.), *Essential early years* (pp. 153–157). London: Hodder Arnold.

Qualifications and Curriculum Authority (2009). http://www.courtauld.ac.uk/degreeprogrammes/ documents/NQF.pdf

Rodd, J. (1997). Learning to develop as leaders: Perceptions of early childhood professionals about leadership roles and responsibilities. *Early Years, 18*(1), 24–34.

Sylva, K., Melhuish, E., Sammons, P., Siraj-Blatchford, I., Taggart, B., & Elliot, K. (2003). *The Effective Provision of Pre-School Education (EPPE) Project: Findings from the pre-school period: Summary of findings*. London: Institute of Education/Sure Start.

Chapter 4
Acting as a Professional in a Finnish Early Childhood Education Context

Kirsti Karila and Jarmo Kinos

4.1 The Finnish Macro-level Context for Professionalism in Early Childhood Education

4.1.1 Organisation and Funding of Services

Daycare is a public and universal societal service in Finland with the promotion of the child's overall well-being as its principal target. It is the main institution providing early childhood education and care and also one of the main contemporary environments in which the majority of small children grow up. Finnish children, aged 0–6 years, have a subjective right to early childhood education regardless of parental employment. Currently, about 70% of 3- to 5-year-olds are in daycare and 99% of Finnish children go to pre-school at the age of 6 (Anttonen & Sointu, 2006). At the national policy level, pre-school is distinguished from daycare as a separate institution, but in practice it is often a part of the municipal provision of daycare services. According to the background report for OECD (2000), expenditure in Finland on 'preprimary educational institutions' as a percentage of GDP is 0.4%, and expenditure per child per annum is US$3929. For parents, affordability is not an issue because of the relatively small parent contribution of about 15% of costs, the rest being subsidised by state and local authority taxes. In addition, parents pay for only 11 months of attendance per year despite their child's place being available during holidays. No fee is charged for low-income families, while the highest fee cannot be more than EUR €200 (c. US$261) per month. Pre-school hours for the 6-year-olds are free.

Two tasks have been defined for the Finnish daycare sector in the legislation (Act on Children's Day Care 367/1973). They are the following: (1) the comprehensive support for the development of the child; and (2) support for the parents in nurturing

K. Karila (✉) · J. Kinos (✉)
School of Education, Early Childhood Education, University of Tampere, Tampere 33014, Finland
e-mail: Kirsti.Karila@uta.fi, jarmo.kinos@uta.fi

L. Miller et al. (eds.), *Early Childhood Grows Up*, International Perspectives on Early Childhood Education and Development 6, DOI 10.1007/978-94-007-2718-2_4,
© Springer Science+Business Media B.V. 2012

and educating their child. In legislation, these tasks have been defined in such a general fashion that they allow a variety of interpretations. Thus, in Finland, daycare has been considered a part of social and family policy and, only more recently, as part of educational policy (Hujala, Karila, Nivala, & Puroila, 1998). Legislative changes have also emphasised the child's subjective right to daycare and the municipalities' duty to make pre-school education available for all children aged 6 years. In the process, these changes have also highlighted the function of teaching and educating as part of daycare (Hujala et al., 1998). A working group set up in 2009 was tasked to review the daycare legislation. The working group worked with a view to foregrounding within it a children's rights perspective.

Recent policy documents stress the educational, reciprocal partnership between parents and professionals. In particular, the two documents, *Decision in Principle of the Council of State Concerning the National Policy Definition on Early Childhood Education and Care* (Ministry of Social Welfare and Health, 2002), and the *National Curriculum Guidelines on Early Childhood Education and Care in Finland* (National Research and Development Centre for Welfare and Health, 2003) highlight the obligation set by the *Act on Children's Day Care* (367/1973) to support parents in nurturing and educating their child through formally organised early childhood education services. Parents have a crucial role in ensuring the responsiveness of services to child interests and needs. *The National Curriculum Guidelines on Early Childhood Education and Care in Finland* (National Research and Development Centre for Welfare and Health, 2003) position care, education and teaching as an integrated whole.

At the national level, early childhood education falls under the administrative responsibility of four key government agencies with municipalities carrying responsibility for administering national policy at the local level. Responsibility for defining national policy for early childhood education and care (ECEC) for children aged 0–6 years rests primarily with the Ministry of Social Affairs and Health. This includes responsibility for policies surrounding allowances to parents and service providers, health care, child and family counselling, child welfare and home-help services. The National Research and Development Centre for Welfare and Health – abbreviated as STAKES in Finnish – has guided the formulation of the national curriculum guidelines in ECEC for children aged 0–6 years; this was put in place in 2003. The Ministry of Education has responsibility for pre-school education for 6-year-olds and morning and afternoon activities for school children. The National Board of Education has responsibility for the curricular orientation of pre-school education. This division of responsibility creates a certain bipolarity of mindset related to the functions of early childhood education which is also visible in the administrative solutions at the municipal level. From the beginning of 2007, municipalities became able to choose the administrative agencies under which early childhood education services were organised. Over 50% of all municipalities in Finland – which total over 400 – have placed children's daycare services under the same auspices as the pedagogical and educational services, while the remaining municipalities have located daycare with either social services or the social and healthcare services.

The municipalities have the obligation to organise daycare for all young children whose parents choose to use it. Provision, operating hours and the annual duration of services vary according to service type. Municipalities can opt for a mixed system of provision, combining public and private provision. In general, municipalities provide services directly through municipal daycare centres (päiväkoti), family daycare homes/places and the pre-school class (the main forms of provision). There are two types of private services in municipalities: firstly, the fully private services (7% of total) that parents can choose for their child, while accessing a private childcare allowance; and secondly, services outsourced by the municipalities to selected private providers. These outsourced services are considered as part of the municipal network and are partly administered by the municipality, e.g., in managing the delivery of places and in supervising quality. In addition, municipalities and voluntary organisations offer various open part-time or sessional ECEC services. Municipalities are fully responsible for the implementation and steering of the services in their own localities. The variations in municipalities' political, organisational and economical situations result in variations in the municipal-level solutions, and thus variations in the working environments for early childhood staff.

4.1.2 Professional Development

Finland has adopted a strongly decentralised style of regulation. At the same time, the legislation sets out strong and clear requirements, for example, for staff qualifications and adult–child ratios (1 trained adult for every 4 children under age 3 years; 1 trained adult for every 7 children over 3 years). These requirements apply to both public and private service providers.

In Finland, it has been broadly accepted that quality provision comes from well-trained staff with ongoing access to professional development opportunities. Therefore, the entrance into professional careers is controlled via qualification requirements; working as a professional in Finland requires an appropriate professional training. Finnish daycare centres are staffed by both teachers and nursery nurses. The Finnish regulations (Decree on Children's Day Care 239/1973; Act on Qualification Requirement for Social Welfare Professionals 272/2005; Decree on Qualification Requirement for Social Welfare Professionals 608/2005) specify that one (kindergarten teacher) in three of the staff in any daycare centre must have a tertiary education-level degree (Bachelor of Education, Master of Education, Bachelor of Social Sciences) and two staff members (nursery nurses) in three in any daycare centre are qualified with a secondary school-level qualification in the field of social welfare and healthcare. This means that key staff of the daycare centres (nurses, teachers and directors) are required to have the appropriate training. The requirement to train is not in question; however, the content of domain-specific knowledge required in the field is vigorously debated (see Karila, 2008, pp. 216–218). A 10% decrease in the number of early childhood staff with a kindergarten teacher's degree working in daycare centres (Unpublished statement for the Ministry of Social Affairs and Health by the representatives of the university-level early childhood education, 30.4.2005) also suggests that there are interesting dynamics going on among the early childhood workforce. (See also Karila, 2008, pp. 214–215.)

In the past, there were general recommendations on the roles and responsibilities of each occupational group defined by the state administration (National Board of Social Welfare, 1984). However, due to the decentralisation[1] process that occurred at the beginning of the nineties, decisions concerning the division of labour among different occupational groups working in the sector are now made in the daycare centres themselves (Hujala et al., 1998).

4.1.3 Multi-professional Working

Recent policy documents (e.g., Ministry of Social Welfare and Health, 2002; National Research and Development Centre for Welfare and Health, 2003) have also emphasised multi-professionalism. This term refers to both the co-operation of early childhood education and daycare centre professionals with professionals in other sectors (social work, comprehensive schools, maternity and child health), and to the multi-professional operations within daycare centres between kindergarten teachers[2] with varying educational backgrounds and the nursery nurses (National Research and Development Centre for Welfare and Health, 2003). Multi-professionalism has also emerged as an analytic concept in research on the work life of early childhood practitioners. In this context, multi-professionalism is seen as a solution for the increasingly complex problems faced by practitioners. The shared expertise of various occupations has been regarded as a possible solution as it suggests that professionals from various fields may contribute via their own expertise to shared problem-solving (Karila & Nummenmaa, 2001). In the working practices of early childhood education, however, internal multi-professionalism in particular has been interpreted in differing ways.

---

[1] In the early part of the 1990s, Finland went through extensive deregulation. Decision making powers were increasingly delegated to the local level (see OECD, 2000, p. 40). Furthermore, at the turn of the 1990s, regulations by the central government were reduced both in the educational and the social sector. Regulation was increasingly redirected towards guidance by information (see OECD, 2000, p. 62.). At the beginning of this period the information steering in the field of early childhood education was quite scanty. The national project of curriculum in ECEC (since the year 2003) has changed the situation and nowadays the *National Curriculum Guidelines on Early Childhood Education and Care in Finland* (2003) is a significant means of information steering.

[2] In Finland teachers working in day care centres and preschool settings are usually called *kindergarten teachers* (lastentarhanopettaja). The title comes from the Fröbelian tradition and has remained in use even after kindergartens were re-named *day care centres* in 1973 through the Act on Children's Day Care (367/1973). Nowadays the day care centres are sometimes called *early childhood centres*. The current names indicate the change in the cultural and historical interpretations of the functions of the centres.

4.1.4 Curriculum Guidelines

During the last decade the quality of daycare has also been addressed, specifically at governmental and municipal level. Following the suggestions of the OECD (2000), the National Curriculum Guidelines on Early Childhood Education and Care were published in Finland in 2003 (National Research and Development Centre for Welfare and Health, 2003). The guidelines cover the individuality of the child, the parent–practitioner partnership, and the child's right to participation as key principles for developing ECEC. As a means for development, they present a hierarchy of curricula to be enacted at the municipal level. Municipalities are required to draw up a local curriculum which is then complemented by the daycare centres' unit-specific curricula. Additionally, each child is provided with an annual individual educational plan that is drafted jointly with the child's parent(s). Finally, the activities of each group of children in a daycare centre are guided by a group-specific curriculum. The goal is to integrate the more general principles of the national, municipal and unit-specific curricula with the needs of individual children and with their educational objectives. Finnish daycare is usually appreciated as a high quality institution. Parents emphasise its importance in socialising the child and in supporting the child's development and learning (e.g., Alasuutari, 2003). Daycare also has an important role in supporting children with special needs or otherwise facing adversity and, hence, in preventing marginalised trajectories of growth and development in childhood. Recently, however, a critical tone has emerged in public discussions, suggesting a decrease in the quality of daycare services because of cuts in resources.

4.1.5 The Micro-level Context of the Practitioner

The practitioner at the centre of the Finnish case study worked in a daycare centre in a suburban area close to a major city in the south of the country. It provides public daycare services for over 200 children – full-time daycare centre services for 135 children, and part-time play group activities for 80 children. Twenty-five adults are employed in the centre – one director, seven kindergarten teachers, thirteen nursery nurses, two cleaners, and two trained staff members for the play group activities. The curriculum is based on the national and municipal-level curricula and emphasises a project approach in organising the activities for the children in the centre.

The case study practitioner was a female kindergarten teacher who finished her 3-year tertiary-level training in 1988 and had gone on to do further studies in education and pre-school education through the Finnish open university. She had worked in many daycare centres and had also been a teacher in primary school for a year. During the time of this study she worked as a kindergarten teacher with the 3- to 4-year-old age group within the centre. She also deputised for the centre director when the director was not available. During the interview, the teacher stated:

> I do see myself as a professional nowadays. Maybe that role has formed along with the experience and training, it's become clearer.

4.1.6 What Is Happening During the Typical Day of the Practitioner?

We began the study of a typical working day of our kindergarten teacher, Maija, by examining the daily schedule of the group of children she taught and subsequently interviewing her about her day. Using this preliminary information, we were able to plan the observation of the actual day when we were gathering a visual record of one day in the life of the teacher using a video recorder.

The teacher's day starts at half past seven.[3] When she arrives at the centre, her colleague, the nurse, is already in the classroom. The teacher begins to organise breakfast for the children in her group. At the same time she welcomes the children and their parents as they arrive.[4] After breakfast both the teacher and the nurse take their own group of children and have a learning session with them. As the children typically go outside after this session, the teacher helps them to put on appropriate clothing for outdoors. The teacher joins the children in the play yard, where she oversees their play. At the same time, she negotiates with her colleagues the future plans related, for example, to children's activities. Before lunch the teacher holds another activity session with the children. While the children are resting after lunch, the teacher holds meetings with other staff members. She also takes care of any administrative and co-operative tasks with other day-care centres. The tasks may deal with in-service training or with organising daycare places for new children. Her working day ends by organising the snack for the children and supervising them in the play yard in the afternoon. She also talks with the parents, updating them on their child's day when they arrive to pick up their child.

This brief description reveals that the day consists of multiple tasks and various encounters and interactions with other persons. In the following section we explore both the content of the events observed during the teacher's day, and the teacher's interpretations of the day alongside her view of the professionalism of these actions.

4.1.7 Meaningful Episodes Illustrate the Practitioner's Work and Professionalism

In analysing the teacher's day, we were able to see that the typical day for our practitioner, Maija, was constructed around a number of meaningful *episodes*. An episode here refers to an event, a situation, or a temporal period with a marked

---

[3] In full-time day-care services the staff members usually work different shifts, namely the morning shift, the middle shift or the evening shift. The teacher had the middle shift during the day we observed her.

[4] In full-time day-care services there are no particular times the children have to be at the day care centre. Children's arrival and departure times are mainly related to their parents' working hours.

beginning and an end. Each episode has its own goals and functions. The contexts of an episode may vary: some episodes have a social context (the parents, the children, the personnel), while others have a physical one (indoor and outdoor activities, the various rooms in the daycare centre).

As a result of the analysis, the events of the day were divided into *main episodes* and *sub-episodes*. A main episode is an independent entity that gives rhythm to the day. It does not overlap with another main episode. Main episodes follow each other in a consecutive order and are established work practices that are planned in advance by the working community. Main episodes recur at the same time each day and are usually marked on the bulletin board to notify the parents of the daily schedule.

The definition of a main episode was agreed during the various rounds of analysis of the videoed material, as all events in the data could not be classified merely as main episodes. To assist in this, the concept of a sub-episode was constructed. A sub-episode is a side event, a partial event or a middle event in the kindergarten teacher's work. It serves its own function, which is not the same as the function of the main episode that is temporally the nearest. A sub-episode may be very brief in duration. Sub-episodes overlap with, and/or are located in various ways within, the main episodes. They may be pre-planned or spontaneous in nature.

In our analysis we identified two types of sub-episodes (see Fig. 4.1). A *bridge episode* creates a bridge between two main episodes so that the operations proceed smoothly and logically (see a in Fig. 4.1). A bridge episode is thus a pedagogical concept. It starts towards the end of the previous episode and may end as a new episode begins. An *overlapping episode* is situated within a 'new' main episode (for example, the father and child entering the daycare centre during breakfast); thus, an overlapping episode requires the teacher to interrupt her actions in the main episode while she deals with the overlapping episode. The teacher then returns to the previous main episode when the overlapping episode is successfully completed (see b in Fig. 4.1).

A sub-episode differs from a main episode in that a sub-episode does not meet the main criterion for a main episode, that is, it is not independent without overlapping with another episode. Our key focus in analysing the data was to identify the essential thing that was going on within each episode and sub-episode. As we were interested in the teacher's perspective of her work, we defined the episodes from the perspective of the kindergarten teacher's work; we did not define them from the children's perspective.

Main episodes	-------------	-------------	-------------	-------------
Bridge episodes		----- a	----- a	----- a
Overlapping episodes	---b	---b	---b	

Fig. 4.1 The relationship of the episodes in a graphical presentation

4.2 Analysing the Data: The Teacher's Day as a Series of Different Episodes Reflecting Different Dimensions of Professionalism

Using the notion of meaningful main episodes, we were able to analyse the video data collected during one day in the life of our teacher in terms of the established daily schedule of the group of children. We then superimposed on these main episodes the spontaneous situations that arose in the day via the mechanisms of overlapping episodes and bridge episodes. Table 4.1 shows the episodes and sub-episodes that occurred during the observed day and the type and function of each episode. In combination, the episodes present a picture of the day that unfolded for our teacher.

As Table 4.1 shows, on the day we observed her, the teacher's day consisted of a total of 32 main episodes (ME) and sub-episodes. In coding episodes we distinguished three types of activities: those focusing primarily on work with the children (C); those with a primary focus on family (F); and those with a primary focus on daycare co-operation (D). Overlapping episodes (OE) were related to gathering/arranging the children (C = 3 episodes), co-operation with the family (F = 7 episodes), and internal co-operation within the daycare centre (D = 3 episodes). Bridge episodes (BE), in turn, were divided into organising the group of children and the 'direct' instructing of the children (3 episodes), and internal co-operation within the daycare centre (3 episodes).

Looking at the main episodes ($n = 13$), the distribution of episodes shows that Maija's activity was primarily focused on the children with nine main episodes recorded as activities involving children, two as involving family members (main episodes 1 and 11), and two other episodes focused on internal co-operation within the daycare centre (main episodes 9 and 10).

In the 19 sub-episodes, Maija's work emerged as divided into three nearly equal parts: co-operation with the family (7 episodes), internal co-operation within the daycare centre (6 episodes), and the activities with the group of children (6 episodes).

The analysis of the sub-episodes clearly illustrates that Maija's work involves substantial co-operation and interaction with adults. Considering the functions of the main episodes (with the exception of main episodes 1, 9, 10 and 11), it is interesting to note that work at the adult level takes up a significant part of the time during which the teacher, in our opinion, could have been interacting with the children. This is most clearly visible in outdoor activities. On the other hand, there was co-operation with the families (7 overlapping episodes) without specific time reserved for this purpose. It is typical that work with adults and work with children overlap during the day according to the defined schedule and via spontaneous situations. Overlapping episodes have two opposite consequences. The first is positive – it means flexibility; and the other one is negative – interruptions and fragmentation.

Table 4.1 also illustrates that various episodes overlap in the teacher's daily work, providing what could be said to be a fragmented-looking day. This provides a challenging context for implementing professionalism. We discuss this idea below.

Table 4.1   Episodes and activities in the teacher's day

The episodes as the result of the analysis	Type of episode			The function of the episode
	ME	OE	BE	
1. Encounter with the child and the parents[a]	[b]F			Welcoming the children and the parents and exchanging news
Gathering the children for breakfast		C		*Gathering the children for breakfast and preparing for breakfast*
2. Breakfast	C			Helping the children and organizing the meal
Encounter with the child and the parents		F		*Welcoming the children and the parents and exchanging news*
Team meeting[c]			D	*Agreeing on the usage of time and the work division*
Organizing the children's meeting			C	*Calming and motivating the children and arranging for the children's meeting*
3. Children's meeting	C			Strengthening the children's participation and presence
Encounter with the child and the parents		F		*Welcoming the children and the parents and exchanging news*
4. Operative situation	C			Instructing the children with various methods of working and operating
Administrative tasks		F		Co-operation with the family
Team meeting			D	*Agreeing on the usage of time and the work division*
5. Guiding the dressing	C			Dressing the children and going out in the yard
6. Playing out in the yard	C			Controlling and observing the children
Administrative tasks		F		*Co-operation with the family/meso-level co-operation*
Team meeting (extended)[d]		D		*Agreeing on the usage of time and the work division*
Administrative tasks		F		*Co-operation with the family/meso-level co-operation*
Team meeting (extended)		D		*Agreeing on the usage of time and the work division*
Guiding the undressing of the children		C		*Preparing the children for the activity period*
Team meeting			D	*Agreeing on the usage of time and the work division*
Team meeting		D		*Agreeing on the usage of time and the work division*
7. Activity period	C			Instructing the children with various methods of working and operating
8. Meal	C			Helping the children and organizing the meal

Table 4.1 (continued)

The episodes as the result of the analysis	Type of episode			The function of the episode
	ME	OE	BE	
Guiding the undressing of the children		C		*Preparing for the afternoon nap*
Activity			C	*Instructing the children with various methods of working and operating*
9. Personnel meeting	D			Discussing and agreeing on the common issues at the kindergarten on the level of the work community
10. Team meeting	D			Reporting personal issues to the team and discussing them
11. Various tasks[e]	F			Taking care of administrative and co-operative tasks (on the micro and meso level)
12. Snack	C			Helping the children and organizing the meal
Saying goodbye to the children		F		*Exchanging news with the parents, saying goodbye to the children*
Guiding the dressing			C	*Dressing the children and going out*
13. Playing out in the yard	C			Controlling and observing the children
Saying goodbye to the children		F		*Exchanging news with the parents, saying goodbye to the children*
A total of 32, of which	**13**	**13**	**6**	

[a] We use the singular form, as the goal of the episode is an individual encounter

[b] All the episodes are coded (and labelled) to show the type under which they were counted: C episode related to children, D episodes related to daycare centre and F episode related to family

[c] A team meeting, a situation with the practitioners working with the group of children

[d] A team meeting (extended), a situation with practitioners working with the other groups of children and/or experts working outside the kindergarten

[e] Various tasks: e-mailing, phone calls, pedagogical planning, etc.

4.3 The Diversity and Complexity of the Work

On the basis of the episodes, Maija's day emerges as extremely varied and as requiring her to be very versatile; there are numerous tasks and responsibilities that Maija has to deal with including physical care. In fact, educating and instructing appear to be only one main area of work. As mentioned earlier, Maija's work consisted of working with the children and carrying out various co-operative tasks with other professionals and with the parents. In the observation data we noticed that Maija often acted in these fields simultaneously.

4.3.1 Educare-Thinking Forms a Basis for the Teacher's Pedagogical Expertise

During the interview the teacher highlighted the integration of care, education and teaching. She emphasised ideas of the so-called educare-thinking which is considered a strong characteristic of public early childhood education in Finland and which is also emphasised in the key policy documents. She said

> Well, our daycare and early childhood education are, well, we provide physical care and nurturing and we are also professionals of education, we provide pre-school education and early childhood education and care here on the same premises. Yes, every single encounter and the children's everyday experiences in the daycare centre contain aspects of both childcare and education, and we try to support the children's development and growth in every situation.

4.3.2 Co-operation and Working with Others

Our case study shows that Maija operated in a professional relationship with a number of people: children, parents, colleagues and other professionals; so professionalism in this context means working together with other people. This issue is linked to the idea of democratic professionalism discussed by Oberhuemer (2005).

When asked about her own understanding of professionalism in the early childhood education sector, Maija divided professionalism into four types of relationships: (1) the relationship with the children, (2) the relationship with the parents, (3) the relationship with the work team, and (4) the relationship with other expert groups. She said

> The professionalism of an educator is visible from the perspective of various people. One has a relationship with the parents, with the children, with colleagues, the working community, and other expert groups with which we interact. That [characteristic of having to interact with many groups] may be the role that makes a professional.

Clearly, Maija saw the maintenance of professional interactive relationships as a marker of professionalism. The teacher is not alone in her interpretation. The same interpretation is highlighted by many researchers (see, for example, Dalli, 2008). The teacher saw the tools for maintaining a professional stance as including the optimal balance of remoteness and closeness, the control of one's moods, and an attitude towards one's work that is based on skills and awareness of one's actions. What also seemed essential is the fact that each relationship is formed in the context of its tasks. In relation to the children, the teacher is a leader, the organiser of target-oriented operations, but also a warm empathiser. The teacher described her relationship as a professional with the children as follows:

> When I'm with the children, as the leader of a group of children, I'm not their mother, and I'm not some friend of theirs, and I don't act like children. When you're in such a situation, you need to think carefully about everything in you that conveys the message of a professional educator. You must hold to your task and be an authority with credibility, yet warm and empathetic. So you must combine your personality and the awareness of how an educator behaves.

The teacher also commented on the need to pay individual attention to each child:

> ... paying attention to each child individually in a big group of children means of course
> that one thinks of this particular day, of how you can make each day safe and good for each
> child.

In relation to parents, the teacher noted that professionalism entailed listening and sharing the educational task with the parents whom she described as her 'clients'. The role of a guide and the conveyor of professional knowledge was also implicated in how the teacher saw her relationship with the parents. In explaining the parent–professional relationship, the teacher emphasised the importance of retaining a professional role:

> Sometimes I'm in close contact with the same family for ten years. But I need to separate
> the listening and talking with the family, so that they have the main role as clients, not the
> other way around; I don't bring in my experiences, let alone my moods.

The teacher's relationship to the other members of the team is clearly that of a leader. The concept of pedagogical responsibility includes the idea of leading the pedagogical actions of the team. According to the teacher, working with a team provides a professional with the responsibility for the atmosphere and for one's own behaviour. Skills, knowledge and open discussion about issues also emerged as important components of professional responsibility:

> .... [in] the team and the overall work community, a professional has an important role in
> those. Again when you work with people, you're responsible for the atmosphere. A profes-
> sional takes care of noticing others in team work. You're consciously thinking about your
> interactive skills all the time. Do I know how to listen well enough, do I know how to
> encourage, do I take criticism, and do I give feedback? One evaluates one's work, and with
> the people one works with, it means talking about things and knowing what you're saying.

4.3.3 Appropriate Knowledge Is a Key Dimension of Finnish ECEC Professionalism

The teacher considered pedagogical and interactive knowledge and skills as important tools to be able to maintain a professional touch when interacting with others at work:

> When working with another person, whether a child or an adult, for example, your own
> feelings are not involved and you act on the basis of listening to the client. But also we
> have the principle that the client is not always right because we have our own knowledge
> and skills that we can and will use. But expertise means that you are aware of the areas of
> knowledge required by the task, that is, pedagogical knowledge and interactive knowledge.

In this statement it is clear that professional knowledge and skills are perceived by this teacher as a key dimension of professionalism which in this context are manifested as *interactive and pedagogical knowledge* (Karila, 2008) in particular.

Additionally, knowledge of the context (Karila, 2008) is seen as important. This became evident when Maija spoke about being accountable for implementation of policies and guidelines. The teacher seems to be well aware of the content of both the national key policy documents and the municipal-level alignments as key factors guiding the work:

> We're not allowed to invent things; we must abide by the commonly agreed rules. So it's documents that guide our work: it's the national principles of early childhood education and pre-school education, they've been agreed upon on the national level. And the quality of daycare and early childhood education and pre-school education in all of Finland is based on those documents.

So, acting as a professional involves being aware of, and acting in ways that are consistent with, established policies and principles of practice. Therefore, it is easy to share Urban's (2008) idea that professionalism can be understood not only as a feature of an individual practitioner but as an attribute of the entire system, to be developed in its reciprocal relationships (Karila, 2008).

4.3.4 Professionalism Becomes Evident in Various Interactions with Other People

Meetings seemed to be significant arenas for exhibiting professionalism. In meetings with the parents, other team members and also with the children, Maija was observed to negotiate and discuss what was going on and what would happen next. Awareness as a key factor characterising professionalism also clearly emerged in the interview with the teacher when she noted:

> When you work with people, the role of a professional is a big thing, because you have your entire personality at stake there. But I think being professional first and foremost means being aware.

Maija also associated awareness with reflecting on one's work:

> When one is constantly making choices and interacting with people and doing things with the children, deciding on various solutions, you know, pedagogically and otherwise, it's good that you can use your previous experience and knowledge, to reflect on your action.

4.3.5 The Practitioner's Roles and Responsibilities Are Constructed in the Context of Multi-professionalism

Multi-professionalism is strongly emphasised in Finnish policy documents and guidelines, and our observation data also strongly emphasised issues of multi-professionalism. But the constant negotiations between the kindergarten teacher and the nursery nurse raised the question that even when co-operation is flexible, constant negotiations of situation-specific agreements are surely socially cumbersome and time-consuming. It also often seemed to steal the attention away from the main function of the situation. Within the multi-professional team of the daycare centre, the participating kindergarten teacher had the main pedagogical responsibility. This, however, is not always the case in all Finnish daycare centres. In their working cultures, multi-professionalism seems to have generated a unique interpretation. In other words, instead of clarifying the special expertise of the professionals working in daycare centres and developing a new kind of shared expertise based on it (Karila & Nummenmaa, 2001), we have reached a situation where using special expertise in work is not taken for granted (Karila, 2000). Kinos (1997, 2008) has argued that this has resulted in territorial fights between the occupations which may even lead to the disappearance of specialist pedagogical expertise, in particular from daycare centres. Where previously the job descriptions, the responsibilities, and the obligations of professionals were defined on the basis of the qualification of the occupational groups, during the last decade, we have experienced a shift from clearly defined tasks for different job roles in early childhood settings to an increasing 'everybody does everything' work distribution (Karila, 1997).

Maija expressed her view about the implementation of multi-professionalism in everyday practices in the following way:

> In a multi-professional team, the kindergarten teacher is the one who runs the show. She has the pedagogical responsibility and she informs and allocates the tasks together with the nursery nurses. But she does that professionally, so that everything has a pedagogical idea. So that in whatever we do it does not matter which team member carries out the event with the children, but the training of a kindergarten teacher makes her most skilled and aware of early childhood education and pedagogy. The content and the aim, and the good planning of the event are the kindergarten teacher's task. So when we plan these things together and everybody contributes to the planning, the overall systematic alignment is the responsibility of the kindergarten teacher.

4.4 Conclusions

The Finnish case study only tells the story of one early childhood education professional's 'typical' day. Nonetheless, our long experience in the field gives us some confidence in stating that the experience of this teacher is also fairly typical of the experience of other Finnish early childhood teachers. We would suggest that the data discussed in this chapter do indeed illustrate significant elements of being an early childhood professional in Finland.

Our case study illustrates that being an early childhood professional at the current time in Finland is rather challenging. There are new expectations for professionalism in the early childhood field due to the changes in society and work life. Multi-professionalism and ideas of partnership and educare are strongly emphasised in the key policy documents. Recently, also, the individuality of the child has been emphasised in policy guidelines. These ideas can be considered to have become the new ideals of professionalism in Finnish early childhood education. They also form an important cultural context for the practitioners to construct their professional identities. The everyday working contexts in which the practitioners are facing the new expectations seem to be fragmented. Obviously, they do not offer supportive environments to renew professional identities and develop everyday practices based on the new expectations. In future, more discussion is required about the resources practitioners need when implementing new expectations and requirements, and also about their own reflections related to their working practices so that their voices are clearly heard.

References

Act on Children's Day Care 367/1973.

Act on Qualification Requirement for Social Welfare Professionals 272/2005.

Alasuutari, M. (2003). Kuka lasta kasvattaa? *Vanhemmuuden ja yhteiskunnallisen kasvatuksen suhde vanhempien puheessa. [Who is raising the child? Mothers and fathers constructing the role of parents and professionals in child development].* Helsinki: Gaudeamus.

Anttonen, A., & Sointu, L. (2006). *Hoivapolitiikka muutoksessa [Care Policies in Transition]: A Comparison of 12 European Countries.* Helsinki: Stakes.

Dalli, C. (2008). Pedagogy, knowledge and collaboration: Towards a ground-up perspective on professionalism. *European Early Childhood Education Research Journal, 16*(2), 171–185.

Decree on Children's Day Care 239/1973.

Decree on Qualification Requirement for Social Welfare Professionals 608/2005.

Hujala, E., Karila, K., Nivala, V., & Puroila, A.-M. (1998). Towards understanding leadership in Finnish context of early childhood education. In E. Hujala & A.-M. Puroila (Eds.), *Towards understanding leadership in context of early childhood: Cross-cultural perspectives.* Acta Universitatis Ouluensis. E35 (pp. 147–170). Oulu: Oulu University Press.

Karila, K. (1997). *Lastentarhanopettajan kehittyvä asiantuntijuus: lapsirakkaasta opiskelijasta kasvatuksen asiantuntijaksi. [The developing expertise of kindergarten teacher]* Helsinki: Edita.

Karila, K. (2000). Esiopetus työyhteisöjen ja työntekijöiden oppimismahdollisuutena. [Preschool education as a learning possibility for the early years professionals] In M. Kangassalo, K. Karila, & J. Virtanen (Eds.), *Omat opetussuunnitelmat* esiopetukseen (pp. 99–147). Helsinki: Tammi.

Karila, K. (2008). A Finnish viewpoint on professionalism in early childhood education. *European Early Childhood Education Research Journal, 16*(2), 210–223.

Karila, K., & Nummenmaa, A. R. (2001). *Matkalla moniammatillisuuteen. Kuvauskohteena päiväkoti. [On the way to the multi-professionalism. Day care center at glance].* Helsinki: WSOY.

Kinos, J. (1997). Päiväkoti ammattikuntien kamppailujen kenttänä. [Kindergarten as a field for struggle]. *Turun yliopiston julkaisuja, C,* 133.

Kinos, J. (2008). Professionalism – A breeding ground for struggle: The example of the Finnish day-care centre. *European Early Childhood Education Research Journal, 16*(2), 224–241.

Ministry of Social Welfare and Health. (2002). *Decision in principle of the Council of State concerning the National Policy Definition on Early Childhood Education and Care.* Helsinki: Publications of the Ministry of Social Affairs and Health, p. 9.

National Board of Social Welfare. (1984). *Children's day care.* Circular A3/1984/pe Helsinki: National Board of Social Welfare.

National Research and Development Centre for Welfare and Health. (2003). National curriculum guidelines on early childhood education and care in Finland. Available at http://www.stakes.fi/varttua/english/e_vasu.pdf

Oberhuemer, P. (2005). Conceptualising the early childhood pedagogue: Policy approaches and issues of professionalism. *European Early Childhood Research Journal, 13*(1), 5–16.

OECD (2000). *Childhood education and care policy in Finland.* Background Report prepared for the OECD Thematic Review of Early Childhood Education and Care Policy.

Urban, M. (2008). Dealing with uncertainty: Challenges and possibilities for the early childhood profession. *European Early Childhood Education Research Journal, 16*(2), 135–152.

Chapter 5
The Uncertain Expert: A Case Study from Germany

Mathias Urban

5.1 Background

With a population of approximately 80 million, Germany is the most populous country of the European Union. It gained its present form of statehood in 1990, when the former German Democratic Republic (East) joined the Federal Republic of Germany (West) to form what is now the unified German state. Although widely referred to as *re-unification*, the political reality of the process that led to the formation of post-1990 Germany had little to do with a sovereign decision of two equal partners. Not least due to the overwhelming economic dominance of the west and the perceived failure of the socialist alternative in the east, East Germany formally *joined* the Federal Republic of Germany and, with only minor alterations, the West German legal system was extended to former East Germany.

Over the following two decades, this was to have major consequences for many areas of public life, including education, and for early childhood education and care in particular. On a structural level, the *unified socialist education* – a key feature of the East German education system – was practically abandoned overnight and the West German education and welfare system introduced to what had become the five new länder (states). But 40 years of separate development had created more than structural differences between the two countries. During the peaceful demonstrations in Leipzig in 1989, and later all over East Germany, protesters chanted 'Wir sind das Volk' (we are the people) as they demanded civil rights and democracy in their country. After the fall of the Berlin Wall, the slogan was slightly but significantly altered as it entered the political debate of the reunited Germany: 'Wir sind *ein* Volk' (we are *one* people); this became the slogan for the electoral campaign of the Christian Democrats, the conservative party led by then Chancellor Helmut Kohl. This apparently subtle change was indeed a successful attempt to blur the differences between East and West, two countries which, during the 40 years of their separate existence, had developed distinct *cultural scripts* (Goddard & Wierzbicka,

M. Urban (✉)
Cass School of Education and Communities, University of East London, London E15 4LZ, UK
e-mail: m.urban@uel.ac.uk

L. Miller et al. (eds.), *Early Childhood Grows Up*, International Perspectives on Early
Childhood Education and Development 6, DOI 10.1007/978-94-007-2718-2_5,
© Springer Science+Business Media B.V. 2012

2004). As Fulbrook (1991) observed in an early analysis, the slogan 'Wir sind ein Volk' was central to the unification rhetoric of the 1990 election campaign. But it was a '*consequence*, not a *cause*, of the coming down of the Berlin Wall; and it was a key factor in the drive towards electoral success of conservative forces in the spring 1990 elections' (p. 389). The notion of a common German national identity 'played little part in the origins of the East German revolution' (p. 389). Two decades after the re-unification, policy analysts had turned the slogan of unity into an obvious question. Citizens of former East and West Germany, they argued, were living in one State – but in two different worlds and they asked: Are we one people? (*Sind wir ein Volk?* (Falter, Gabriel, Rattinger, & Schoen, 2006)).

There are many possible readings of the impact of German macro-politics, during and after the re-unification, on the local micro-practices of early childhood education. As I have argued elsewhere (Urban, 2007), reasons for the rushed shift from one education and welfare system to another – a colonisation, as some would argue – were primarily ideological, not based on rational considerations of actual performance of either of the approaches. In the context of this chapter, I take them as an exemplar of Paolo Freire's (2000) analysis of the relationship between education and politics – that there is no such thing as un-political education.

5.2 The Context: Early Childhood Education in Germany

Germany, like Australia, Canada and the United States, is a federal State that comprises 16 *länder*. Political and administrative responsibilities are spread over three layers of government, at the municipal, state and federal level. Both education and social welfare are governed mainly at the *länder* levels. There is only a framework legislation for social welfare (including children's welfare) at federal level and the federal government has almost no responsibility for education. As a result legislation, regulations, curricula and, not the least, funding for early childhood services vary widely across the 16 German states, causing, or at least contributing to, remarkable inequalities for children and families living in different parts of the country. The 'inequality of condition' (Baker, Lynch, Cantillon, & Walsh, 2004), which is a structural feature of the German education system, consequently results in stark 'inequality of outcome' for children and families. In recent years, this has been widely criticised, not least by international observers (e.g., OECD, 2008).

Germany today has one of the lowest birth rates in the world. The OECD (2004) states: 'Germany, in short, is aging and more rapidly than most other countries' (p. 9). The per capita GDP is about average for the European Union, and slightly above OECD average. Germany has rather low-income inequality compared to other western countries, but has a 14% rate of child poverty (i.e., unacceptably high), with long-term unemployment being the most important cause (OECD, 2008). There is a significantly higher unemployment rate in the eastern *länder*.

International organisations criticise a lack of public investment in early childhood services with an average public expenditure of 0.4% of the GDP, compared to 2.0% in Sweden and an OECD average of 0.6%. Germany's lack of recognition of the early childhood workforce, and failure (of the education system in general) to compensate for inequalities, especially for children from minority, migrant and disadvantaged backgrounds (OECD, 2006, 2008, 2009), also draw international criticism.

There are marked regional differences in early childhood provision across all 16 *länder*. The main gap, however, still exists between the former eastern and western parts of the country, with the western part of the country struggling to increase provision, in particular for children under the age of three. An entitlement to a place in a publicly funded *kindergarten* for children from age three has been in place since 1996. While in West Germany this has been praised as an important achievement, the introduction of this entitlement also conceals the fact that there had been a 100% coverage in East Germany long before the re-unification. From 2013, the entitlement to a place will be extended to children under the age of three and again, especially in the western part, the country is struggling to meet the target.

Several initiatives and pilot projects to raise the quality of provision have been launched by non-governmental research institutions, supported by the federal government. This includes the *National Quality Initiative*, a major concerted effort to develop quality criteria and evaluation procedures across the wide range of public, private-non-profit and denominational service providers (Bundesministerium für Familie, 2007). While the results of the initiative have been influential in the sector, they are not mandatory and quality varies between providers and regions.

In recent years, concerns have been raised that the qualification of the workforce at post-secondary vocational level is no longer adequate to meet the actual requirements of the increasingly challenging work context. Diversity has always been a reality in German society but has only recently entered the public and political consciousness. Equal access to *kindergarten* provision is increasingly seen as important for tackling social exclusion and for supporting equal educational achievement. Changes for the workforce are underway and university colleges have begun to offer a fast growing number of early childhood degree programmes at bachelor level. Yet, it remains unclear what the role of the new graduates will be and a coherent policy towards re-structuring the workforce is lacking. Recent reforms of the distribution of responsibilities within the federal system (*Föderalismusreform*) have further weakened the central government, and inequalities, caused by the lack of a coherent approach to public education, are likely to increase.

5.3 Bildung, Erziehung, Betreuung – Purpose and Conceptual Foundations of Early Childhood Institutions in Germany

There are two distinct historical roots of German early childhood institutions – education in its broadest sense in Fröbel's kindergarten and care for disadvantaged and impoverished children in the *kinderbewahranstalt* (for a more detailed discussion see Urban, 1997). The tensions between these roots remain unresolved. The optimistic reading of the distinct tasks given to early childhood institutions in policy documents and legal frameworks is that German kindergartens, today, genuinely integrate different social functions and serve multiple purposes. This view is reflected in the wording of official documents as well as in the self-image of the sector: The purpose of early childhood institutions is to provide the triad of *bildung, erziehung* and *betreuung* which are seen as inseparable.

From a less enthusiastic perspective, it could be argued that the triad is little more than an umbrella for three distinct approaches, which, in consequence, lead to different, often contradictory practices.

While *betreuung* easily translates as *care*, it is interesting to see the conceptual distinction between the first two aspects of the triad – *bildung* and *eziehung*. Educationalists from English-speaking countries with a strong tradition of schoolified early childhood institutions (*pre*-schools) still struggle to understand the concept of *bildung*. Rooted in the tradition of *humanism* and *enlightenment*, and often linked to eighteenth century educational theorist Wilhelm von Humboldt, *bildung* refers to the *process* of an individual striving to reach their full potential as well as to an *ideal* – having, for instance, reached a state of reflexivity towards one's self, others, and the world (Luth, 1998). In German, the verb to the noun *bildung* is *bilden*. It is a transitive verb, i.e. the action of *bilden* always has an object, a *something* or *someone* it is directed to. Moreover, in the context of educational philosophy and debate, *bilden* is almost exclusively used as reflexive verb (*sich bilden*), meaning the object of the process of *bildung* can only be oneself. Hence, as a philosophical concept, *bildung* is inseparable from the individual; it began as an individualistic, not a communal, public project. Needless to say, historically, the individuals in question were usually male, well-off members of the *bourgeoisie*.

In current German early childhood discourses, however, *bildung* largely represents the holistic, reformatory side of the early childhood tradition, and understandings of children as active learners and meaning-makers. It is increasingly conceptualised in a social-constructivist and socio-cultural frame, linking humanistic *bildungstheorie* to Deweyan and Vygotskyan theories.

While there has been a renewed interest in the re-interpretation of *bildung* in early childhood in recent years (Laewen, 2002; Laewen & Andres, 2002), there has been little debate about the second conceptual pillar of the German early childhood system – *erziehung*. The term translates as *education* and, if placed in a continuum with *bildung*, would represent the societal or adult aspects of the triad. Education is to do with generational processes of transmitting cultural norms and values, transfer of curricular content and so on. It is, in short, what adults do *to* children in a purposeful way, usually in institutions set up to serve exactly this and no other purpose.

To summarise – and to use an overly simplified picture for the last time – *bildung* comprises the entirety of children's physical, emotional, cognitive, creative activities of *making sense of their world*; *erziehung* refers to children as recipients of what adults do *to* them, purposefully, in educational settings. *Betreuung*, then, could be understood as providing secure spaces in which – at best – *bildung* and *erziehung* can unfold.

What it means to be – and to act – professionally in early childhood settings in present day Germany is determined by all three conceptual foundations of the system. It is reflected in the layout of the institutions, the regulations and the programmes. It is reflected, too, as this case study shows, in the professional self-perceptions of practitioners and in the dilemmas they find themselves in.

5.4 The Day in the Life Project in Germany

Data collected in the German study consist of a video observation of an entire working day of the practitioner (4 July 2007), followed by an interview conducted on 11 July 2007. The video data were collected by two research assistants working with the author at Halle University. Both research assistants were present at the interview and participated in analysing the data.

5.4.1 The Setting

The setting for the German case study is a *kindertagesstätte* in a small town in the state of Saxony-Anhalt, in the eastern part of the country. It is part of a network of early childhood centres that co-operates closely with a group of researchers and trainers at Martin-Luther-University Halle-Wittenberg. This network originated in a participatory action research project, directed by the author, which developed the now mandatory early childhood curriculum for the State of Saxony-Anhalt (Ministerium für Gesundheit und Soziales des Landes Sachsen-Anhalt, 2004).

Like many early childhood centres in Eastern Germany, the setting is a former public institution, now run under the trusteeship of a welfare organisation as a non-profit (but publicly funded) service. The provider – the German *Red Cross* – is a non-denominational organisation.

Places are offered for 112 children from birth to six (compulsory school age) 5 days per week. Opening hours are 6 am to 6 pm. Children are organised in six groups: two groups for the youngest children (0–2 years) and four groups of children with an age range from 3 to 6 years. Three of these groups offer places for children with special educational needs (SEN). At the time of the study, 15 *erzieherinnen* (early childhood educators) were employed at the *kindertagesstätte* including one male.

The centre has two purpose-built buildings on a shared playground designed according to the philosophy of the centre which emphasises children's own activities, playful and experimental learning, and social interaction.

In their documentation (e.g., written philosophy) and in discussions during the curriculum project mentioned earlier, *erzieherinnen* at the centre described their educational task as supporting children's activities as they develop individual personalities and self-confidence. The role of the educator is understood as accompanying children rather than leading, or *teaching* them. The centre's daily curriculum, and the activities offered to children, aim at incorporating children's real-life experiences (inside and outside the centre) into pedagogical practices. The centre follows a child-centred approach which is widespread in German ECEC and is referred to as *situationsansatz* (contextually appropriate approach) (Preissing, 2003).

Like any publicly funded early childhood setting in the state of Saxony-Anhalt, the setting's pedagogical activities are framed by the mandatory early childhood curriculum *Bildung:Elementar* (Ministerium für Gesundheit und Soziales des Landes Sachsen-Anhalt, 2004; Urban, Huhn, & Schaaf, 2004). Unlike early childhood curricula in other German states, *Bildung:Elementar* is not built around learning goals for children but provides a framework for early childhood professionals to explore, critically question and develop their attitudes towards, and their interactions with, children in their processes of *Selbst-Bildung* (see above). Working within the curricular framework of *Bildung:Elementar*, therefore, requires constant re-invention, adaptation and evaluation of day-to-day practices and close relationships with children's worlds outside the centre. Joint planning and reflection as a team of educators, as well as parental involvement, are key activities in which all practitioners are involved (Ministerium für Gesundheit und Soziales des Landes Sachsen-Anhalt, 2004).

A typical day at the centre consists of a combination of *open* and *structured* times. Meal times are an important part of the fixed structure of the day as they offer the opportunity to engage with the entire group. Breakfast, lunch and afternoon snack are offered; children participate in preparing the meals. *Circle time*, just before lunch each day, is another fixed point for whole-group activities and discussions. Topics for circle time are usually brought up by children; sometimes they are prepared by the practitioner together with a group of children. The practitioners talk to each child at the end of their day about what has been important for them. Children's comments and reflections are documented and displayed in the hall.

5.4.2 The Practitioner: Frau Müller[1]

There is no *typical* German early childhood educator – we made this clear in the methodological approach of this project – and therefore this project is not concerned with comparisons between individuals, settings, let alone countries. There are, however, a number of experiences shared by practitioners working in a specific socio-cultural and socio-historical context, in this case in a small town in the eastern part of Germany, some 15 years after the re-unification. It is the 'historical concreteness' (Freire, 2004) of life experiences that shapes practices and understandings of a generation of early childhood professionals.

The collapse of the East German economy, and that of municipal funds in its wake, contributed substantially to the collective experience of East German early childhood educators. In the years preceding the *Day in the Life* study, for instance, huge numbers of educators had been made redundant or forced out of full-time into

---

[1] The name has been changed.

part-time employment. The resulting staff shortages in almost every early childhood centre practically eliminated any time for collaborative planning and reflection.

Frau Müller, who like many East German early childhood educators prefers to be addressed by her surname rather than her first name, had been working as an educator for 20 years, the last 12 years in the present setting. Like most members of her team, she had received her initial qualification in the pre-1990 GDR system. After the abolishment of the unified education system, and the introduction of the West German split system, each educator was required to undergo re-training in order to be allowed to continue working as an educator in the new system. As part of the unified socialist education system, early childhood education had a relatively high status in the GDR, and the formal qualification of practitioners was at a higher level compared to that of early childhood practitioners in West Germany. GDR-trained educators were used to working to a national curriculum, something that did not exist in West Germany. Considering these differences in professional status, the re-qualification was seen as de facto *de-qualification* by many practitioners. Even today, there remains a collective sense of professional and personal humiliation among this generation of East German practitioners. There is also, unlike among the majority of West German educators who qualified in the 1990s, a widespread self-perception by practitioners as competent early childhood experts, well able to communicate and collaborate with primary school teachers at eye-level.

5.4.3 Professional Perspectives

5.4.3.1 The Image of the Child

Frau Müller's perception of her own role as an early childhood professional, of the social and educational function of early childhood education in general, and her setting in particular, is closely related to her understanding of childhood, children, learning and upbringing. There is an underlying image of the child that orients Frau Müller's thinking and acting in her day-to-day practice. Frau Müller's image of the child is very much that of a child as *actor* in, and *constructor* of, their own learning and development. Coming from this perspective, children's interests and their existing knowledge and experiences are key to developing Frau Müller's practice with children.

In her interview, Frau Müller reflected about how her professional role and her practices derived from her image of the child and that her emphasis on interactive processes between children and child-initiated activities did not mean an absence of planning. Frau Müller's day with the group was highly structured and thought-out. The focus of the planning, however, was on initiating situations that allow for, encourage, or even provoke, the conversations and interactions she saw as key to children's learning in social contexts. Explaining a sequence during morning circle time, Frau Müller addressed how her image of the child related to her understanding of planning for the day:

It is important to me to ensure every child has an experience of success each day. The children were active and their views were taken into account, and for me, it was important to ensure the day passes harmoniously. . . . I want to emphasise children's strengths and provide secure spaces for them to experiment. And I take up children's ideas, which I keep in mind, or take notes, to bring them back to the group at a later stage.[2]

Children had the opportunity to share their knowledge, to communicate . . . at the same time they felt challenged. Although the day was planned, children had the opportunity to pursue their own interests and I supported them in doing so. I also referred to a few things that had happened the day before.

Acting professionally, for me, means to be aware of children's interests and wishes, and to incorporate them into my planning.

All this requires providing *time* and *space* for experimentation and communication with individual children as well as with groups of children. Communication *between* children is seen as important as communication between herself and children. It became clear at an early stage of the observation, as well as in the interview, that Frau Müller developed her interactions by deliberately and constantly shifting – or balancing – her attention between individual children and the group. In line with her understanding of children as actors of their own learning, Frau Müller was convinced that learning takes place through collaboration between children and group interaction. Thus, Frau Müller's image of the child shaped an important part of her professional self-perception – as a facilitator, rather than a teacher.

Frau Müller developed her concept of supporting children from her image of the active child. From this perspective, even *not* engaging with children in a particular situation can be a deliberate act of support. Staying out of the action, for instance, opens opportunities for children to *make sense* of situations, negotiate their own rules and relationships for interaction, and actively arrange their environment:

As I said before it is important because it is an appreciation I can show toward the child, and because children feel they are taken seriously in what they do.

Taking children seriously appears to be a key characteristic of Frau Müller's professional self-description in her day-to-day practice. Children are active members of the group, co-creators of situations, instead of recipients of Frau Müller's pedagogical programme. During the interview, she gave several examples to illustrate the extent to which the children's interests and questions contributed to shaping the course of the day at the centre, and how she referred to what children said or did in her planning:

. . . so I provide spaces and opportunities for children to realise [their ideas], provide material, and demonstrate possibilities . . . I support children's strengths and accept their weaknesses, too. It is all about the development of personalities.

Referring to children's developing personalities, Frau Müller used the German term *entfaltung* (the verb being *entfalten* – to unfold). Using the concept of *unfolding*, Frau Müller suggested that the child's personality is already there; it exists from

---

[2] As the original interview was conducted in German, all passages selected for this chapter have been translated by the author.

birth and is brought forth, rather than produced in social interaction. It is a complex image of the child that underpinned Frau Müller's actions: it brings together the acknowledgement that each child *is* a personality that has to be respected and taken seriously, and the belief that this existing personality can only reach its full potential through social interaction and experience – which it is the role of the early childhood professional to facilitate. Children, in Frau Müller's view, are *beings* as much as they are *becomings*.

This understanding was an important factor in Frau Müllers's self-perception as a professional. Building on a clear understanding of children as personalities, she could construct herself as *different-but-equal* in relation to children. Acting professionally, from her perspective, could be done without having to emphasise a *professional distance*, or a superiority of the adult in relation to the child. As a professional, Frau Müller aimed at establishing equal relationships between individuals who are different. In her practice, she meets children at eye-level, not to make them *the same* but to find out who they are:

> As an educator, I always see myself as a learner, as the one who learns from children, and who also gives something to children, but it is reciprocal.

This reciprocal relationship, in which learning takes place and personalities *unfold* is built on trust, rather than on the authority of the adult educator:

> Children meet my expectations towards them, and I try to meet their expectations towards me, and I find this all is based on a trusting relationship.

It could be argued that Frau Müller's self-concept as a learner and equal partner almost necessarily leads to an image of the child that is not static. Instead, it is transient, has to be constantly reflected upon and reconstructed, and, as she stated, would be influenced by the children's own action as active partners in the process of re-constructing her image of the child:

> I have to constantly re-think my image of the child.

> Yes, it has changed over time, for instance I have much more confidence in children now . . . I provide much more resources (material) for them.

A key element that linked Frau Müller's image of the child and her actions as a professional educator seems to be the way both were placed in the present, in the *here and now*. She hardly ever talked about her practice being oriented towards the future. Education, from her point of view, is not about teaching children what they need to know for the future. Professional practice is about engaging with children in present life situations in which learning occurs; it is not about guiding children through predefined developmental steps or towards achieving predetermined outcomes.

5.4.3.2 Understandings of Professionalism in Early Childhood

> Yes, I see myself as a professional . . .

As shown above, Frau Müller's view of professionalism is very much built on *respect for children, relationships between equals* and *reflection*. While being *situational*, Frau Müller's description of her professional practice also displays a specific relationship to professional knowledge. It is not surprising that this relationship is not a hierarchical one, where professional knowledge (e.g., acquired in training and professional preparation) is *applied* in order to solve problems or achieve specific, predetermined outcomes. Rather, it is a constant negotiation between knowledge and action; something that could be described as an informed *conversation with the situation*, to borrow Donald Schön's (1983) term. The two sides, knowledge and action, are inseparable and, similar to the way Frau Müller described her relationship with children: They are linked together by trust and confidence. It is this trusting relationship that enables the professional to act in, and productively deal with, *uncertain situations*:

> Acting professionally requires a high degree of knowledge that has to be applied to every new situation in a new and different way ... it only works in a special relationship, a relationship you also need to have with children, in a certain intimacy ... the relationship must be built on trust, yes .... Still I have to be aware that my actions are grounded in uncertainty ['ungewissheit'], they are always guided by expertise on the one hand and an understanding of the present situation on the other.

There is clearly an acknowledgement of the importance of a body of *professional* knowledge ('a high degree') in Frau Müller's conceptualisation of professionalism. But this body of knowledge has to be interpreted, made *actionable* (Argyris & Schön, 1996) by the professional who acts in ever-changing and uncertain situations; these situations are shaped by children and their real life in the here and now, as much as they are influenced by the educator.

5.4.3.3 A Team of Professionals – A Learning Community

Frau Müller's self-conceptualisation as a professional working with young children was very much based on the immediate interaction with children, individuals and groups. She described the core of her activities as something she developed in highly complex, ambiguous and *uncertain* situations which had to be negotiated anew every day. Acting in these contexts was not spontaneous but required profound knowledge, experience and constant reflection at a personal level. Nevertheless, as the following quote illustrates, her individual professionalism also required the context of the team, which provided a reflective, supportive and critical learning community.

> First of all I think the arguments and discussion that have taken place in our team, for a number of years, contributed a lot to a different understanding of our roles, for each of us ... I find it important to say that educators, today, need to have a different understanding of themselves and of children.

Together, the educators at the centre discussed and developed their interpretation of the curriculum, their understanding of children's and families' changing life-situations in the local community, and what this might mean for everyday pedagogical practices. Thus, conceptualisations of professionalism were constantly reflected upon and further developed at team level. Shared understandings, developed in a team of equally qualified (and experienced) educators, contributed to each individual's self-perception of *being professional* in their everyday activities.

> In the past, the image of society was different, and goals of society were different. Looking at economic developments, globalisation, people are facing different challenges today.
>
> In the past everything was, how to say that . . . certain and predetermined.
>
> It's a difficult but appealing world that poses different challenges to people, compared to fifteen years ago.

In this sequence, Frau Müller linked the changes in her professional self-conceptualisation to societal, and even global, processes of change. The place where the link between the *macro* and the *micro* context of professional practice was created, debated, reflected upon and, most likely contested, was the learning community of professionals. Conceptualisations of *childhood, professionalism*, and its *transformation* were understood as being connected to the transformation of society. Frau Müller and her colleagues were aware of the *embeddedness* of conceptualisations of professionalism. Frau Müller did not devalue her former professional self-conceptualisation. Rather, she talked about its *transformation*, and how the critical discussion in a team of professionals contributed to changing her understandings.

Professional development, from this point of view, becomes a continuous process of 'creating understandings' (Urban, 2008) and, for Frau Müller and her colleagues, seemed to enable them to productively deal with the ambiguities and uncertainties arising from their practice. Frau Müller repeatedly talked about her practice being grounded in uncertainty, but she didn't seem to see this as overly burdensome in any way.

> It was a process of development, of experimentation, of debate with the public and with parents.
>
> Constantly having to explain ourselves is difficult for educators undergoing such a process of transformation.
>
> Since not every step forward turns out to be a success, [this is]something you have to be aware of . . . two steps forward, one step back.

This is an important sequence of statements because it signals another link between day-to-day professional practices with children, and the expectations and understandings of a wider society towards these practices. *Constantly having to explain*, on the one hand, may signal an increasing public interest in early childhood practices. It may, on the other hand, point to a general lack of understanding in the wider public. From Frau Müller's point of view, acting professionally required embracing uncertain outcomes. It was about experiments, which might not always be an immediate success, but might require a step back and a new start. This process had to be reflected upon continuously in a critical learning community.

Frau Müller's conceptualisation of early childhood professionalism and its relationship with societal processes is in stark contrast to any *expert* model of professionalism, built on certainties about children, development and learning. Although acting professionally, for her, would be unthinkable without a profound knowledge, there was no top-down relationship between theory and practice in her model. Professionalism was not about *applying* scientific knowledge to achieve specific, predetermined outcomes. On the contrary, professional practice was constantly re-constructed and negotiated by professionals, in situations 'which are puzzling, troubling, and uncertain' (Schön, 1983, p. 40). Frau Müller's knowledge and experience enabled her to *make sense* of, and act in, uncertain situations. By doing so, it can be argued that she constantly co-produced actionable knowledge (Argyris & Schön, 1996).

5.4.3.4 The *Outside World*

How does Frau Müller's conceptualisation of the early childhood profession fit into (perceived) external expectations of this profession? First of all, Frau Müller did not assume a universal external perspective. Her statements suggest that notions of professionalism, of parents and the wider public depended on a variety of factors.

> I believe people regard us differently, depending on how old they are, and on their own expectations and experiences in their families.

> how they look at the world, and how they live their lives, and yes, what do they want for their child?

Assuming an outside perspective on her practice, Frau Müller again situated professionalism in a societal and biographical context which is fluid and changing. She saw public notions of early childhood professionalism as largely influenced by life experience in a society under transformation. She also saw a close relationship between notions of childhood and expectations about the practitioner. However, this acknowledgement of the embeddedness, and the transitory nature of professional images, did not mean there was no conflict between society's external and Frau Müller's internal perspective on what was achievable, or even desirable in educational practice.

> I believe many parents define our role [as professionals] as removing obstacles in children's development and as compensating for children's deficits.

Describing her relationships with children, Frau Müller repeatedly talked about her necessary acceptance of children's strengths and weaknesses; she clearly did not see herself as *compensating for children's deficits*. Instead of *removing* obstacles for children, she would rather confront children with challenges arising from real-life situations, and explore possible ways of dealing with them.

Discrepancies in expectations about professional practice were identified at various levels. The mismatch of expectations between primary school and her own practice as an early childhood educator, for instance, was a recurring issue for Frau Müller:

> School expects a child who is well prepared. It is about being able to sit still, put one's hand up, write your name.

Different images of the child, underlying the two institutions (kindergarten/primary school), lead to different conceptualisations of early childhood practice and its desirable outcomes. While Frau Müller and her team valued children's individuality, curiosity, and their ability to experiment, she also expected schools to prioritise conformity and obedience.

5.5 Conclusion: The Uncertain Expert in a Professional Dilemma

Frau Müller's perception of what primary school required of children may or may not reflect actual expectations of primary school teachers. Her perception was, however, important for her construction of early childhood professionalism as it points to a fundamental dilemma. Reflecting on Frau Müller's experience, there are at least two competing and, I want to argue, contradictory aspects that characterise her profession into being what I call an *uncertain expert*.

The first aspect is that early childhood practitioners act in complex situations with individuals and groups (children and adults). They engage in processes of joint *meaning making* and they unfold their practice *with* children (as opposed to acting *upon* them). It is a relational practice, where themes, the actual content, and the eventual outcomes depend on children as much as on the practitioner's planning. Early childhood practice is a constant co-construction which requires *shared thinking* (Siraj-Blatchford & Sylva, 2004) and, as Rinaldi (2005) argued, is best developed as a 'pedagogy of listening'. The shift towards what Margaret Mead has called 'post-figurative upbringing' (Mead, 1978, p. 83) necessarily removes any certainty about the outcomes of educational practice – which is not to say there are no outcomes. There are many: some of them expected and planned for, others most likely surprising and unexpected. What is required, in these contexts, is permanent attention to *what is actually going on*, an attitude (an ethos) of enquiry rather than a mind-set of assessment. Uncertainty, surprise and curiosity, from this perspective, are at the very core of professional early childhood practice. It can be argued, from Frau Müller's case, that reflective practitioners not only *cope* with the uncertainties of their practice; they actively build their professional practice on it. By taking children's interests and ever-changing life situations seriously, and as starting points for open ended interaction, they embrace what Paolo Freire has called *untested feasibilities* (Freire, 2004).

The second aspect of early childhood practitioners' fundamental dilemma is that institutional contexts for these relational, uncertain professional practices are limited and clearly defined. They are confined by external expectations from the profession that quite often contradict the necessary openness and uncertainty of practice with young children. Instead, practitioners are expected to know what is *right*, to perform *best* practice, and to *achieve* externally determined outcomes. From this external perspective (which can be the perspective of parents, teachers or the wider public) professionalism is expected to be demonstrated as *expertise* in order to avoid uncertainty.

This leaves practitioners with a fundamental dilemma: the impossibility of matching their internal self-perception with the external expectation of what it means to be a professional in early childhood education and care. They live and act an open, relational practice with children and yet, in order to be recognised as professionals (by parents, teachers, and the public etc.), they feel they have to construct and communicate their professional identity *against* the key characteristics of their practice.

Reflective practitioners, like the one portrayed in this chapter, are well aware of this dilemma and, as illustrated by Frau Müller, are seeking strategies to balance the two sides, knowing they cannot be brought together. Frau Müller provides an articulate self-description of a professional whose actions are necessarily *grounded in uncertainty* and experimentation. She is well aware of the constraints of her work context and the external expectations that, by contrast, seek certitude. Her account supports what I have argued elsewhere (Urban, 2008), that early childhood practitioners are regularly expected to act professionally in a system that, concerning the key characteristics of their practice, is largely *unprofessional*. Being able to acknowledge the different *ways of knowing* and *being* in the early childhood professional system, and to manage this dilemma in everyday work is undeniably a tribute to their professionalism. There is a risk, however, that practitioners who are not as critically reflective as the one portrayed in this study will internalise the problem and assume a personal insufficiency. Not being in control of a situation, not knowing the *right* answer or the *best* practice may then be seen as a personal failure. Practitioners unaware of the inherent dilemma of early childhood professionalism may seek to *solve* the problem (e.g., by relying on external expertise, ready-made solutions) rather than developing confidence in their ability to deal with ambiguity and uncertainty. Personally and professionally, it takes a lot of self-confidence to embrace 'difference, diversity, and the messiness of human life rather than seeking . . . to resolve it' (Schwandt, 2004, p. 40) – in other words, to become confident as an *uncertain expert*.

References

Argyris, C., & Schön, D. A. (1996). *Organizational learning II: Theory, method and practice.* Reading, MA: Addison-Wesley.

Baker, J., Lynch, K., Cantillon, S., & Walsh, J. (2004). *Equality: From theory to action.* New York: Palgrave Macmillan.

Bundesministerium für Familie, Senioren, Frauen und Jugend. (2007). *Nationale Qualitätsinitiative im System der Tageseinrichtungen für Kinder.* Retrieved September 18, 2009, from http://www.bmfsfj.de/bmfsfj/generator/BMFSFJ/kinder-und-jugend,did=97482.html

Falter, J. W., Gabriel, O. W., Rattinger, H., & Schoen, H. (Eds.). (2006). *Sind wir ein Volk? Ost- und Westdeutschland im Vergleich.* München: C.H. Beck.

Freire, P. (2000). Cultural action for freedom. *Harvard Educational Review. Monograph series, no. 1.*

Freire, P. (2004). *Pedagogy of hope: Reliving pedagogy of the oppressed.* London: Continuum.

Fulbrook, M. (1991). 'WIR sind ein Volk'? Reflections on German unification. *Parliam Aff, 44*(3), 389–404.

Goddard, C., & Wierzbicka, A. (2004). Cultural scripts: What are they and what are they good for? *Intercultural Pragmatics, 1*(2), 153–166.

Laewen, H.-J. (2002). *Bildung und Erziehung in der frühen Kindheit: Bausteine zum Bildungsauftrag von Kindertageseinrichtungen.* Weinheim [u.a.]: Beltz.

Laewen, H.-J., & Andres, B. (2002). *Forscher, Künstler, Konstrukteure: Werkstattbuch zum Bildungsauftrag von Kindertageseinrichtungen.* Weinheim [u.a.]: Beltz.

Luth, C. (1998). On Wilhelm von Humboldt's theory of bildung dedicated to Wolfgang Klafki for his 70th birthday. *Journal of Curriculum Studies, 30*(1), 43–60.

Mead, M. (1978). *Culture and commitment: The new relatuionships between the generations in the 1970s.* New York: Columbia University Press.

Ministerium für Gesundheit und Soziales des Landes Sachsen-Anhalt. (Ed.). (2004). *Bildung: Elementar. Bildung als Programm für Kindertageseinrichtungen in Sachsen-Anhalt.* Magdeburg: Ministerium für Gesundheit und Soziales.

OECD. (2004). *Early childhood education and care policy in the Federal Republic of Germany.* Paris: OECD.

OECD (2006). *Starting strong II: Early childhood education and care.* Paris: OECD.

OECD (2008). *Growing unequal. Income distribution and poverty in OECD countries.* Paris: OECD.

OECD (2009). *Doing better for children.* Paris: OECD.

Preissing, C. (Ed.). (2003). *Qualität im Situationsansatz: Qualitätskriterien und Materialien für die Qualitätsentwicklung in Kindertageseinrichtungen* (1st ed.). Weinheim: Beltz.

Rinaldi, C. (2005). *In dialogue with Reggio Emilia: Listening, researching, and learning.* London, New York: Routledge.

Schön, D. A. (1983). *The reflective practitioner: How professionals think in action.* New York: Basic Books.

Schwandt, T. A. (2004). Hermeneutics: A poetics of inquiry versus a methodology for research. In H. Piper & I. Stronach (Eds.), *Educational research: Difference and diversity* (pp. 31–44). Aldershot: Ashgate.

Siraj-Blatchford, I., & Sylva, K. (2004). Researching pedagogy in English pre-schools. *British Educational Research Journal, 30*(5), 713–739.

Urban, M. (1997). *Räume für Kinder: Pädagogische und architektonische Konzepte zur kooperativen Planung und Gestaltung von Kindertagesstätten.* Frankfurt am Main: Dt. Verein für Öffentliche und Private Fürsorge.

Urban, M. (2007). *The discovery of East German early childhood education: A post-colonial perspective.* Paper presented at the International conference: What is Quality Care? Cultural Assumptions in Institutions of Early Childhood Education, The Hebrew University of Jerusalem.

Urban, M. (2008). Dealing with uncertainty: Challenges and possibilities for the early childhood profession. *European Early Childhood Education Research Journal, 16*(2), 135–152.

Urban, M., Huhn, N., & Schaaf, M. (2004). *Bildung:Elementar. Bildung als Programm für Kindertageseinrichtungen in Sachsen-Anhalt. Integrierter Abschlußbericht.* Halle: Martin-Luther-Universität Halle-Wittenberg.

Chapter 6
A Constant Juggle for Balance: A Day in the Life of a New Zealand Kindergarten Teacher

Carmen Dalli

6.1 The Early Childhood Education Context in New Zealand

In recent years, New Zealand has acquired a reputation as a leader in professionalising its early childhood workforce. In large part this is due to policies introduced in 2002 as part of a 10-year strategic plan for early childhood education, *Pathways to the Future: Ngā Huarahi Arataki* (Ministry of Education, 2002). The plan described early childhood services as the 'cornerstone of our education system' (p. 2) and introduced the requirement that 100% of the workforce in teacher-led services would be qualified at the benchmark level of a 3-year degree or diploma by 2012. The strategic plan also introduced professional registration for all teachers in teacher-led early childhood services. A change of government, and of policy priorities, in 2009 resulted in the lowering of the qualification requirement to 80% of the workforce. This has stalled the momentum towards achieving a fully qualified workforce (e.g., Dalli, 2010; Smith, 2009), but not before transforming the professional habitus of the sector and bringing it closer to the goal of being a teacher-led profession (Dalli, 2008a). By 1 July 2009, 64% of teaching staff in teacher-led early childhood services were qualified and registered, an increase of 14.3% from the previous year (Ministry of Education, 2010).

Until the requirements of the 10-year strategic plan started to take effect, staff employed in early childhood services traditionally had a very diverse training and qualification background. This ranged from untrained staff, to staff holding qualifications such as a 1-year childcare certificate, a 3-year diploma, a 3-year Bachelor's degree, a 4-year conjoint BA/B.Tech degree, or a postgraduate degree. There are seven main types of licensed early childhood services – kindergartens, education and care centres (formerly known as childcare centres), playcentres (voluntary parent-run early childhood centres), ngā kōhanga reo (indigenous Māori language nests), home-based (family daycare) networks, correspondence school (an early childhood

C. Dalli (✉)
Institute for Early Childhood Studies, Victoria University of Wellington, Wellington 6140, New Zealand
e-mail: carmen.dalli@vuw.ac.nz

L. Miller et al. (eds.), *Early Childhood Grows Up*, International Perspectives on Early Childhood Education and Development 6, DOI 10.1007/978-94-007-2718-2_6, © Springer Science+Business Media B.V. 2012

programme within a distance education service), and casual education and care centres (in shoppers' malls and recreation centres); of these only the kindergarten service has had an unbroken record of employing fully qualified staff.

The origins of kindergartens and childcare services can be traced back to the late 1870s (May, 1997). In 1948, kindergartens became fully state-funded and kindergarten teachers became state employees. By contrast, childcare centres, together with other forms of early childhood services that emerged in later years (e.g., family daycare, indigenous kohanga reo, Pacific Island language groups and so on), continued to depend on part funding from government and other sources till the late 1980s; parental fees provided the shortfall. For many years this differential funding history contributed to a perceived division between preschool or *education* services (such as kindergarten) and other early childhood services considered as providing custodial *care* rather than educational benefit.

The false dichotomy between education and care services persisted until the transfer of administrative responsibility for childcare services from the Department of Social Welfare to the Department of Education in 1986 (Dalli, 1990; Meade & Podmore, 2002). A review of early childhood education at the end of the 1980s led to a comprehensive plan, *Before Five* (Lange, 1989), to rationalise early childhood policy, including the introduction of 3-year integrated training and degree qualifications for work across the full range of early childhood services. Today, all early childhood services come under the responsibility of a national Ministry of Education. A policy advantage in New Zealand is that there is no municipal or regional layer of decision-making for educational provision; this avoids the complexities of implementation that often accompany local body politics in other countries (e.g., Finland and Sweden).

6.1.1 The Early Childhood Curriculum: Te Whāriki

New Zealand introduced its first curriculum document for early childhood education in 1996. Entitled *Te Whāriki* (Ministry of Education, 1996), the document is a bicultural and bilingual statement that defines the curriculum as the 'sum total of the experiences, activities, and events, whether direct or indirect, which occur within an environment designed to foster children's learning and experiences' (p. 10). *Te whāriki* is a Māori word meaning a *woven mat*. This metaphor signifies that the curriculum is understood as a weaving (whāriki) of experiences that are not subject-bound but arise when professional early childhood teachers, soundly grounded in the traditional specialist knowledge bases of child development and early childhood curriculum studies, are able to draw knowledgeably on insights from multiple disciplines.

The curriculum is based on the four principles of empowerment (*whakamana*), holistic development (*kotahitanga*), family and community (*whānau tangata*) and relationships (*ngā hononga*). The five strands of well-being (*mana atua*), belonging (*mana whenua*), exploration (*mana aotūroa*), communication (*mana reo*) and contribution (*mana tangata*) are embedded within these principles, and each is explained by a set of three or four goals (18 goals in total). The principles, strands and goals thus create a statement about the purpose of early childhood education. New Zealand's aspirations for its youngest citizens are summarised as follows:

> to grow up as competent and confident learners and communicators, healthy in mind, body and spirit, secure in their sense of belonging and in the knowledge that they make a valued contribution to society. (Ministry of Education, 1996, p. 9)

6.1.2 Funding, Quality Assurance and Monitoring

A subsidy model of state funding, as opposed to full state responsibility, applies in the early childhood sector. Early childhood services wishing to receive government funding have to meet licensing and chartering standards, paid out as a bulk grant-in-aid. Alongside this, a targeted childcare subsidy is available to some families through the Department of Work and Income. It is generally stated that government and parents fund most out-of-home early childhood services on a roughly 50:50 basis. Thus, affordability remains an issue. A response by government has been to introduce a policy of 20 free hours a week for all 3- to 4-year-olds; this policy came into effect on 1 July 2007 for teacher-led services and was subsequently extended to playcentres and kohanga reo from July 2010 (Bushouse, 2009; Dalli, 2010).

As recipients of government funding, licensed early childhood services are subject to audit reviews by the Education Review Office (ERO) on a 3-yearly cycle. ERO audits are based on standards in the *Revised Statement of Desirable Objectives and Practices* (Ministry of Education, 1998), and on indicators developed from the principles of the early childhood curriculum, *Te Whāriki*.

6.1.3 Access for Parents

Early childhood teachers are expected to work in partnership with parents in all early childhood services, and some services are fully run by parents or whānau (family) (e.g., playcentres and kohanga reo). In community-based education and care centres, which make up 42% of all education and care centres (Ministry of Education, 2008), parents are responsible for the governance of the centres alongside teacher representatives.

6.1.4 Multi-agency and Multi-disciplinary Work

Collaboration across the various services that support children and their families is increasingly becoming a focus of government policy. As a response to the 1997 report from the United Nations Committee on the Rights of the Child, in 2002 Government launched the document *Agenda for Children* (Ministry of Social Development, 2002). This included a set of principles for a *whole child* approach to all government policies that affect children. An example of this approach within the 10-year strategic plan policies is a Parent Support and Development programme, initiated in 2006, and piloted in 18 sites as a collaboration between early childhood services and health and social services. The programme was targeted at vulnerable parents and delivered through existing early childhood education services (Bellett, Sankar, & Teague, 2010).

6.2 The Setting for the New Zealand Case Study

The New Zealand case study was conducted in a kindergarten situated in an old coastal suburb of Wellington, the capital city of New Zealand. Following the methodological protocol established for the overall project, a video record of one full day in the life of a kindergarten teacher, Bette, was made on one clear mid-winter day in July 2007 with a follow-up interview held 4 days later.

The case study kindergarten was purpose-built in the 1980s and forms part of the *Wellington Region Free Kindergarten Association*. Established in 1902, the Association is the employing body for all the region's kindergartens for which it provides guidelines, policies and administrative support. The Association also provides a teacher support structure via a small team of senior teachers who regularly visit kindergartens in a professional supervisory capacity. The Association is governed by an annually elected board accountable to the kindergarten community. Each kindergarten has its own management committee responsible for the day-to-day management of the kindergarten. Traditionally, kindergartens have enrolled children aged 3–5 years, offering an early childhood service with daily morning sessions for the older 4- and 5-year-olds, and three afternoon sessions for 3- to 4-year-olds. On two afternoons (Wednesdays and Fridays), kindergarten teachers have traditionally had *non-contact* (or child-free) time, to facilitate activities such as curriculum planning, administrative tasks and professional development. This long-standing feature of the employment conditions of kindergarten teachers is valued as a formal recognition of the need for teachers to have reflective planning time about their work. Non-contact time is not uniformly available to other members of the early childhood workforce; it is one of the characteristics that has given the kindergarten service a reputation as the *flagship* of high quality service of the early childhood education sector (Davison, 1997).

In recent years, demographic trends and changes to government funding policies have put pressure on kindergartens to keep rolls full and maintain eligibility for maximum funding. As a result, many kindergartens have been enrolling a wider age group of children and implementing changes that are transforming the way that kindergartens have traditionally been run, including going from a sessional to a full-day structure (Duncan, Dalli, & Lawrence, 2007). By July 2010, 84% of all kindergartens were operating on full-day licences.

The case study kindergarten still operates on a traditional sessional structure. Morning sessions are 3 hours long and run from 8.30 am to 11.30 am, while the afternoon sessions on Mondays, Tuesdays and Thursdays are 30 minutes shorter and run from 12.45 pm to 3.15 pm. Children arrive for each session over the initial half hour period, and a typical session consists of children then moving to a range of activities that are set up around the kindergarten. Children have free access to the outdoor area which is equipped with a range of climbing, sand and water equipment. A morning or afternoon snack is offered about one and a half hour into each session with children sitting down as two groups with one of the teachers inside the kindergarten over a flexible period of half an hour. Another period of self-chosen activity follows; after a short tidy-up time, each session ends with a group mat-time during which the teachers and the children briefly review the day, read stories and do action songs. Parents often arrive to pick up their children during this part of the session and some join in with the activity. Goodbyes are said individually as children leave the group mat-time to go home with their parents or other home adults.

The kindergarten serves a highly diverse community with a very mixed socio-economic and ethnic background. It has a full roll of 43 children in each of the morning and afternoon sessions. On the day of data gathering, 37 children attended the morning session and 36 were present for the afternoon session. The children ranged in age from 2 years 10 months to 5 years.

Three full-time qualified teachers work at the kindergarten during both the morning and the afternoon sessions; this includes the head teacher who was the participating practitioner in the case study. Kindergartens work with a staff:child ratio of 1:15. During each session, the three teachers occupy one of three roles: the *inside teacher* who works with children who choose to be inside; the *outside teacher* who is responsible for the outdoor curriculum areas; and the *resource teacher* who moves between the pre-arranged activities in the curriculum areas indoors and outdoors and has oversight of the day's flow of activities. The *inside* and *outside* teachers swop over during each session after the first teacher has finished snack time with the indoor group of children. On the day of the study, one additional educational support worker attended the morning session to work with a child classified as having special learning needs.

6.2.1 Selecting the Case Study Teacher: Bette

The teacher at the centre of the New Zealand case study, Bette, was one with whom I had worked as a researcher in an earlier research project at a different kindergarten. Bette had been teaching for 8.5 years and, at the time of the case study, was in her second position as a head teacher. Bette had graduated 9 years earlier with a 3-year diploma of teaching. Prior to that, while her own children were preschoolers, she had been a playcentre mother and trained as a playcentre supervisor.

6.3 Data Gathering: Videoing Bette's Day and the Follow-up Interview

The videoing of Bette's day was done by a professional cameraman who accompanied me for the day of data gathering; his instructions were to film all the teacher's activity throughout the day. On arrival at the kindergarten, Bette was *mike-d up* and video-ed continuously between 8.30 am to 11.30 am and again from 12.45 pm to 3.15 pm. The lunch period between 11.30 am and 12.45 pm, during which no children were present, was not videoed. This yielded just under 6 hours of film footage. As the writer–researcher, I remained on site throughout the day and made pen-and-paper notes to record the overall structure of the day's activity. Four days after the day of videoing, I interviewed Bette around the four foci of interest within the overall project (see Chapter 1), and with reference to the data gathered during the day of observation. The interview lasted 90 minutes. In the following week all the verbal interactions captured on film, as well as during the interview, were transcribed.

6.4 Analysis

Consistent with the overall project design, the analysis of the data was broadly thematic and involved developing codes for segments of the video data, relating them to other segments from the interview data, and inspecting, interrogating and interpreting the connections to establish themes (Richards, 2009) and thus open up meanings and understandings around the research questions.

This chapter focuses on key understandings about how Bette 'acted as a professional' in her specific context. An early image for the teacher's day as a 'buzz of activity' was used to capture the overall sense that emerged from the initial coding of the video data. Subsequent re-visiting of the video footage in the light of data from the interview resulted in a more refined set of themes that linked the initial image of a *buzz of activity* to multiple layers of meaning below the surface of the observed day. Four of these themes are discussed in this chapter with the aim of illuminating Bette's understanding of the nature of her professional practice:

1. 'We are all part of each other's life': professional practice as relational involvement
2. Keeping in touch with colleagues: professional practice as team work
3. Curriculum plans as open possibilities
4. The ethics of relational work: acting professionally in complex situations.

In exploring the connections that were initially hidden to this writer/researcher between what could be observed from the outside, and reference points in Bette's shared history with the children, as well as with her reflections on her practice, a different image for the teacher's day as 'a constant juggle for balance' became increasingly meaningful. The juggle was between the demands that flowed from the necessity of working with a group of children while also attending to children's individual interests; from taking forward a curriculum that was planned but also open to the spontaneity of the day that unfolds; and maintaining relationships in complex situations. 'Balance' was achieved when multiple layers of thinking were brought together in a moment of professional judgment.

These ideas are explored further in the following sections.

6.5 The Initial Image: Bette's Day as a 'Buzz of Activity'

Bette's day with the children started at 8.30 am with greetings to children and parents followed by settling down in the reading corner with a collection of books that various children asked her to read. The kindergarten pet rabbit also joined the group, tickling one girl on the nose as she stroked him and sparking a conversation about his habits, including that he possibly wanted to be in the research video. At 9.00 am, Bette moved to the dough table where she made some playdough and divided it up among the children at the table. Within the next half an hour, Bette had:

- taken one child to the bathroom;
- resolved an issue that had reduced another child to tears;
- cleared the equipment that she had used to make the playdough;
- answered a phone call;
- returned briefly to the dough table;
- sorted out a paint spill and helped wash-off two pairs of pink and purple arms; and
- welcomed Kenneth, who was in his first days at the kindergarten and had arrived for the session accompanied by his grandparents.

Throughout these activities, Bette maintained a constant flow of conversation addressed both to the group of children around her, as well as to individual children within the group. The short excerpt below, which occurred soon after Kenneth's arrival, is one illustration of the multiple threads of conversation that Bette regularly maintained at any one time.

It was 9.30 am and Bette was now in the kitchen area cutting up fruit for morning tea surrounded by helpful children. The kitchen was linked to the collage area via an open window on one side of the room, and to the main room via a counter.

Bette: *Is it turned on?* [addressed to Kenneth who has brought over the glue gun from the collage area]. *I don't think it is. I'll turn it on for you Kenneth. Jasmine!* [Bette calls out across the room to a child who is running inside from the outdoor area; Jasmine slows down and walks over to Bette who now turns to another girl beside her]. *Right, Rebecca can you go and get this* [gluestick] *on the other side of the window for me? Can you stand out there?*

Rebecca: *Why?*

Bette: *I'm going to pass this* [holding up the gluestick] *out there to put on the table for the glue gun. Okay?* [Bette now turns to another girl beside her.] *Oh that's a big cough Amy.*

[Bette looks out the kitchen window into the collage area where Rebecca has taken the gluestick as Bette had requested]. *Pop it on the table. Thanks.*

[Now addressing Kenneth who has gone back to the collage area and is attempting to use the gluegun]. *It's not hot yet Kenneth, I just turned it on love.*

[Jasmine has now reached the kitchen, having slowed down from her running]. *Jasmine, when you come inside love, remember to walk to make it safe. Do you think you could try and remember?*

These multiple threads of conversation, layered on top of the base task of preparing fruit for morning snack-time, give a glimpse into the complex multi-tasking that characterised Bette's day as captured on the video footage.

6.6 Themes of Professional Practice

6.6.1 'We Are All a Part of Each Other's Life': Professional Practice as Relational Involvement

Observed from the outside, Bette's day could easily appear as a collection of *trivial* momentary encounters between the teacher and the children, or between the teacher and her colleagues and parents. The substance behind the trivia, however, was very visible when Bette spoke about her day during the interview:

> I felt, looking back on the morning that there had been a whole lot of trivial conversation... but it's like, with each child you are in a conversation that has taken days and weeks. You know, you are all part of each other's life,... to the extent that... they notice if we have a new pair of shoes and we notice if they have a new pair of shoes. We are all a part of each other's life...

This assessment by Bette opens up one of the core themes in Bette's reflections about her professional practice: In her view, a teacher becomes a part of the children's lives just as they become a part of hers. Bette's example of the details observed by both children and teachers about each other signals not only passing attention but also intimate knowledge of each other's habits. The knowledge grew through conversations that spanned days and weeks; they established relationships with a joint history and shared reference points. In later describing the afternoon session, Bette's account again started with a focus on the personal involvement in children's lives that she felt characterised professional practice:

> [the structure of the afternoon] is similar. Although in the afternoon we are more likely to have more of our personal time and space – our body – more taken up with the comforting of children who are separating from their parents.

With the younger children who attended the afternoon sessions, Bette highlighted that:

> ...you're kind of more involved in their personal lives... More involved with their bowel habits and undies and... it's just so open, you know. You have this lovely talk: 'have you got nappies on today or undies?' {Bette changes voice affectionately to sound like a child} 'Oh, I don't have to have undies today, I've just got my nappy'. And they're all quite happy to be on a continuum of learning about toileting.
>
> ...different children develop a relationship with you – as teachers you have to be open to that. ...There's one little guy and if he needs to go to the toilet he gets me. So the other

teachers know – If they see me and this child running towards the bathroom – to check where I was at, and cover for me ... So you don't say: 'no, I'm the outside teacher' in that case. You go to the toilet: it's urgent.

These verbal cameos offered by Bette vividly captured the type of responsiveness that Bette felt was appropriate when a teacher perceived her professional practice in relational terms. Being professional is personal: the teacher's body is part of what is offered in creating a comforting space, particularly for younger children as they learn to stay at the kindergarten and separate from their parents; being professional is intimate: it involves learning – and teaching – about bodily functions and looking after very personal needs; and being professional means dropping everything and accompanying a child to the bathroom, thus privileging a child's need for support over other demands. In this way, being professional is about intimate involvement in the immediacy of children's lives and responding attentively to children's overall well-being – a key strand in the New Zealand early childhood curriculum.

6.6.2 Keeping in Touch with Colleagues: Professional Practice as Team Work

In the third cameo in the preceding section, Bette notes that her responsive attention to the child (whom she accompanied to the bathroom) was possible because her colleagues were also responsive, not only to the child and his relationship with Bette, but additionally to Bette to whom they extended professional support as a member of the teaching team. This example of collegial responsiveness to Bette's need for pedagogical 'cover' brings forth a second important theme in Bette's account of her day: To act as a professional means to work as part of a team.

In turn, working as a team entailed being responsive to the overall relational context of the kindergarten, and to what was needed to enable particular relationships between teachers and children, and teachers and teachers, to take their course. Early on in our interview, Bette explained that responsiveness to colleagues started at the beginning of the day:

We set up any things that we didn't set up the night before and check in with each other and grade each other's wellness . . . .

The attunement to colleagues' well-being implied in this statement was clearly an important consideration in planning the day. Thus, team work was something that occurred not only at the structural level of agreeing who was the indoor or outdoor teacher, or other roles for the day, but also at the level of day-to-day negotiation of human relationships.

Further insights into the ways that team work functioned emerged later in the interview. For example, discussing the difficulty encountered by some children in sitting in a circle for mat-time, Bette noted that this was 'a matter of ongoing discussion within the teaching team' and that various options were being discussed as they 'worked around that one'. Team work also meant that information about children was shared so that 'you would then include that in your consciousness as a team'. This latter statement is interesting because it adds the further dimension that professional action was not seen as dependent solely on individual action but as a feature of the professional habitus within the kindergarten which Bette called 'team consciousness'.

For Bette, team consciousness required regular communication. She emphasised that 'acting as a professional' with colleagues meant:

> ... keeping in touch during the day and communicating enough: that's a constant issue in a three-teacher team – to make sure that you communicate equally, or that all of you know [Bette's emphasis]. You have a personal relationship with your colleagues individually but then you have a collegial responsibility to share a certain amount of information about the children and about their needs and when you're making the transition between parts of the day, about how that's going to go.

> ... or making sure that the necessary apologies are made – you know, like somebody might ring and say 'make sure somebody doesn't get their left foot wet' and then you get called away to the toilet and you come out and you find that the person's got their left foot wet! And you know, saying: 'There was a phone call about that; I'm so sorry I didn't get out here in time and communicate that to you. . . . dealing with the consequences of miscommunication is part of it as well.

In both instances the focus on team work is related to collegial collaboration as well as to ensuring personal relationships continued to work well.

6.6.3 Curriculum Plans as Open Possibilities

When discussing Bette's day from the point of view of programme planning, Bette provided an explanation which started with the statement: 'I didn't have any particular plans'. Pausing for just one moment, Bette then continued:

> ... what happens in our programme planning cycle is that ... we observe the children, and take photos and write up what they're interested in doing, ... and then we talk about that maybe on a Friday afternoon or a Wednesday afternoon [non-contact time]. ... So ..., you'd have maybe ten or twenty things in your head about what could happen and you're not able to ever do all twenty, but it may be that you can see bits of them happening around the place and you could either just throw a supportive comment towards a child who is, again [Bette's emphasis], doing something or . . . . a child who has been practising writing a lot comes to you, or their friend comes and says 'could I have a pen?' You might say, 'And here, take one for Sam too'. . . so it's actually part of the plan, and it's part of an ongoing thing that you have all discussed together and put into your head for development . . . fortunately plans are not an aligning – I mean plans are much more of a question mark – and you have to have an open mind about where any bit of any interest might go . . . . So, . . . just taking opportunities to include them in things – it's just a huge, vast amorphous bunch of things that might [happen] – possibilities really. So as you say 'did what you planned happen?' Yes. [Bette's emphasis]

This detailed explanation of how the teachers at Bette's kindergarten managed the curriculum again illustrates the theme discussed earlier that behind the apparent serendipitous happenings of the day, there was a layer of purposeful teacher action that enabled the substance of the day to unfold. Bette's likening of curriculum plans to a 'question mark' is particularly powerful: It suggests that instead of channelling the curriculum into pre-designed directions, the teachers' purposeful actions created space for 'possibilities', the unexpected, a 'vast amorphous bunch of things that might happen'. In this way the teacher's role in the curriculum emerges as a 'finely balanced role, an intuitive role that sees each teacher making decisions 'in the moment' poised as provocateur, as listener, as learner, as teacher, ever vigilant for opportunities to widen and deepen knowledge' (Sands & Weston, 2010, p. 15). This way of imaging the teacher as programme planner also constructs the teacher's professional action as creative and agentic rather than as reactive and prescribed by narrow curriculum goals.

6.6.4 The Ethics of Relational Work: Acting Professionally in Complex Situations

Bette reflected that acting professionally regularly required decision-making about complex situations:

> ...where you have to judge, how urgent is this, how is the session going, how are my colleagues coping today, can I say: 'come in later, after work and I'd love to talk to you some more about this', or is it a person that's really needing you right then and how are you going to tell your workmates? And how much are you going to tell your workmates, and is it something that needs to be recorded and are you going to then have to pass that on to... our [Association] senior teachers?[1] You know, all those kinds of things have to go through your mind at the same time that you're even getting the telephone call.

In this statement, the issues identified by Bette as creating complexity are issues of timing, of weighing up priorities, of balancing confidentiality with the need to keep team members informed, and of deciding accountabilities to professional supervisory staff at the Kindergarten Association. Bette's reflection makes clear that professional decisions require keeping in mind multiple layers of thinking and inevitably impact people and their relationships. The following additional list of difficult situations described by Bette elaborates on the contextual and relational complexities implicated in professional decision-making:

> we have parents with post-natal depression;...we have families where the children have been taken off parents and are in custody; we have children who have got significant health problems; we have got parents who have got significant health problems. Sometimes you also have the main relationship with the caregiver of the child, and you have to still try and make a relationship with the parents, and the caregiver might have a different view of the child than the parent:...and balancing all those different facets of information you might be given. For example, we have a child who is brought [to kindergarten] by a caregiver – we have not met the mother; we have met the father – and the caregiver thinks that the child needs a special needs assessment. But the parent has not agreed. So, we have to...remember that this is this person's personal – in their professional role – view of the child that they are caring for, but that it need not be ours. That we need to meet the child, and consider what the parent sees in their child; and how they [the parents] interact with the

---

[1] Each Kindergarten Association employs a small number of senior teachers who provide advisory support to the kindergartens within the Association on any aspect of professional practice.

child may be entirely different from how the caregiver does. So it can be quite complex in that respect, those relationships . . . .

A little later, Bette added the further example:

. . . .and we don't always know the relationships between different parents in the community . . . who may be on opposite sides of a criminal court . . . we have a number of children who, if a policeman comes into the kindergarten they are scared . . . so all these people are expected to come into your building and be in quite close proximity to each other and leave their children together . . . .

The difficulties described in these examples illustrate that, as I have argued elsewhere, 'early childhood professional practice is troubling, complex, and embedded in relationships' (Dalli & Cherrington, 2009, p. 76). Reflecting on what helped her act as a professional in such contexts, Bette listed a range of influences including lectures during her training:

. . . where we talked about becoming a professional, and international concepts of professionalism and codes of ethics . . . . . and then you have to personally take ownership of it and accept that you are in that role . . . .

To illustrate this point, Bette drew on her observation of her mother whom she described as a community midwife who 'took responsibility for maintaining her professionalism' and 'managed to let it be more personal and still professional'.

Additionally, Bette emphasised that to act professionally as a teacher, including in dealing with complex situations, it was necessary to:

keep abridge of research in your field, . . . to keep learning . . . [to have] mentoring or . . . relationships of accountability, to invest in ethical practice, to be aware of what ethics are and take part in discussions, to be part of a professional community where there is discussion and debate.

6.7 'A Constant Juggle for Balance': What Meanings Have Been Opened Up? Concluding Comments

In bringing this chapter to a close, I highlight one final statement Bette made in response to the question of how she acted as a professional in interactions with children:

. . . while being fully present with a child you still have to access things you've learnt, and things that you have studied, and things you've planned, and you have to access your conversations with the parents, your conversations with the other team members – and bring it with you . . . . There is the concept of what the child, right then, needs, as well as this other stuff that's in your head . . . .

So you have your knowledge of that child, and you have the knowledge of the other children, and then you have to look and see what's happening at the table and work out what you're going to do professionally. That's the whole **balancing** [Bette's emphasis] of ethics between what needs to be said, to whom and how . . . You kind of say, I know her and I know him, and I can see probably what's been happening, and the other children are looking all a bit confused. So what needs to happen? . . . . . Yeah, **balance, balancing** [Bette's emphasis].

This statement draws together many of the threads of Bette's thinking about the nature of professional action discussed in this chapter. It also indicates Bette's awareness that when she acted as a professional, her actions were informed by multiple layers of thinking, experience, understandings and knowledge that came together in a moment of professional judgment. Bette described that professional judgment as a moment of 'balancing', thus contributing to the image of a *constant juggle for balance* used in this analysis.

The profile of the teacher that emerges in this chapter is that of a practitioner who is reflective and highly articulate about her practice. As head teacher, Bette led a small team of two other qualified teachers with whom she planned a curriculum that, consistent with the open-ended ontology of the early childhood curriculum, *Te Whāriki,* opened up 'possibilities' where 'any bit of interest might go'. To achieve this *curriculum of possibilities*, Bette's planning was informed by ongoing observations of children and 'conversations that take place over days and weeks'. Her view of professional practice accepted intense involvement in children's lives as part and parcel of pedagogical relationships. It also included team work, *team consciousness* and attention to colleagues' well-being, as tools of practice. Finally, Bette's practice further took account of relationships in its focus on ethical decision-making when dealing with complex and troubling situations – all characteristics which are consistent with the principles and strands of *Te Whāriki*, and in particular the principle of relationships (ngā hononga).

Considering these findings in the context of the small but growing body of research on New Zealand teachers' views of their practice, these findings indicate an emerging consensus on what it means to act professionally within the local early childhood setting. For example, childcare respondents to a national survey on professionalism in the early childhood sector (Dalli, 2008b) described professional behaviour in terms of: (i) a distinct pedagogical style that values respectful relationships, engagement with children and an ethics of care approach to practice; (ii) collaborative relationships with colleagues, parents and management marked by respect, open communication and sensitivity to others' points of view; and (iii) professional knowledge, including knowledge of the curriculum, regulations and specialised knowledge through qualifications alongside a reflective stance to practice. Respondents from other parts of the early childhood sector (Dalli, 2008a), including kindergarten and home-based network co-ordinators, reported similar views including widespread support for the qualifications and teacher registration policies that had not long been introduced as part of the 10-year strategic plan (Ministry of Education, 2002).

This emerging consensus about a particular form of professionalism – that is articulate about its practice, agentic in curriculum planning, and focused on relationships and ethical practice – is interesting to reflect on in the overall policy and pedagogical context described earlier in this chapter. In particular, it would seem that the reflective, articulate and agentic style of professional action articulated so clearly by Bette has been enabled by: (i) the New Zealand curriculum document, *Te Whāriki*, which encourages autonomy in programme planning, and defines learning in wholistic, open-ended terms as opposed to pre-determined outcomes; and (ii) the policy focus on enhancing the quality of early childhood services through improving the overall policy infrastructure of the early childhood sector, including through requiring higher qualification levels of all practitioners. As noted at the start, New Zealand early childhood policy is currently undergoing renewed scrutiny with the final phase of the introduction of the qualification requirements in the 2002 strategic plan stalled. It will be important over the next few years to monitor the impact of the stalled policies on the emerging consensus within the sector about what it means to act professionally as an early childhood teacher in New Zealand.

References

Bellett, D., Sankar, M., & Teague, M. (2010). *Early childhood education centre-based parent support and development. Final report.* Wellington: Ministry of Education. Retrieved from http://www.educationcounts.govt.nz/__data/assets/pdf_file/0003/74919/ECE-Final-15-Feb-06072010.pdf

Bushouse, B. (2009). The 20 hours free early childhood education programme: A USA perspective. *New Zealand Annual Review of Education, 18:2008,* 143–158.

Dalli, C. (1990). Early childhood education in New Zealand: Current issues and policy developments. *Early Child Development and Care, 64,* 61–70.

Dalli, C. (2008a). The new teacher in New Zealand. In L. K. Miller & C. Cable (Eds.), *Professionalism in the early years* (pp. 142–153). Abingdon: Hodder Arnold.

Dalli, C. (2008b). Pedagogy, knowledge and collaboration: Towards a ground-up perspective on professionalism. *Special edition of the European Early Childhood Education Research Journal: Professionalism in Early Childhood Education and Care, 16*(2), 171–185.

Dalli, C. (2010). Towards the re-emergence of a critical ecology of the early childhood profession in New Zealand. *Contemporary Issues in Early Childhood, 11*(1), 61–74.

Dalli, C., & Cherrington, S. (2009). Ethical practice as relational work: A new frontier for professional learning? In S. Edwards & J. Nuttall (Eds.), *Professional learning in early childhood settings* (pp. 60–81). Rotterdam: Sense.

Davison, C. (1997). *The sinking of the early childhood education flagship? Government's plan to privatise kindergartens: The bulk-funding story* (Occasional Paper 3: 33). Wellington: Institute for Early Childhood Studies, Victoria University of Wellington.

Duncan, J., Dalli, C., & Lawrence, J. (2007). The changing face of kindergarten: A national picture of two-year-olds in kindergartens. *New Zealand Annual Review of Education, 16:2006,* 119–140.

Lange, D. (1989). *Before five.* Wellington: Government Print.

May, H. (1997). *The discovery of early childhood: The development of services for the care and education of very young children.* Auckland & Wellington: Auckland University Press & NZCER.

Meade, A., & Podmore, V. N. (2002). *Early childhood education policy: Coordination under the auspices of the Department/Ministry of Education: A case study of New Zealand* (UNESCO early childhood and family policy series, 1). Paris: UNESCO.

Ministry of Education. (1996). *Te Whāriki: He Whāriki matauranga: Early childhood curriculum.* Wellington: Learning Media.

Ministry of Education. (1998). *Revised statement of desirable objectives and practices for chartered early childhood services in New Zealand.* Retrieved from http://www.lead.ece.govt.nz/~/media/Lead/Files/DOPsForCharteredEarlyChildhoodServicesInNewZealand.pdf

Ministry of Education. (2002). *Pathways to the future: A 10 year strategic plan for early childhood education.* Wellington: Ministry of Education.

Ministry of Education. (2008). *Prior participation in early childhood education: New entrants.* Retrieved April 9, 2008, from http://www.educationcounts.govt.nz/publications/ece/2507/27456/5

Ministry of Education. (2010). *Annual ECE summary report.* Education Counts. Retrieved July 9, 2010, from http://www.educationcounts.govt.nz/statistics/ece/55413/licensed_services_and_licence-exempt_groups/65543

Ministry of Social Development. (2002). *Agenda for children.* Retrieved from http://www.msd.govt.nz/documents/about-msd-and-our-work/publications-resources/planning-strategy/agenda-children/agendaforchildren.pdf

Penn, H. (1998). Comparative research: A way forward? In T. David (Ed.), *Researching early childhood education: European perspectives.* London: Paul Chapman.

Richards, L. (2009). *Handling qualitative data: A practical guide.* London: Sage.

Sands, L., & Weston, J. (2010). Slowing down to catch up with infants and toddlers: A reflection on aspects of a questioning culture of practice. *The First Years Nga Tau Tuatahi New Zealand Journal of Infant and Toddler Education, 12*(1), 9–15.

Smith, A. B. (2009, November). *Implementing the UNCRC in New Zealand: How are we doing in early childhood?* Paper presented at the New Zealand Association for Research in Education, ECE Special Interest Group Hui, Rotorua.

Chapter 7
Working with a Democratic Curriculum: The Swedish Case Study

Marja Kuisma and Anette Sandberg

7.1 The Swedish Macro-level Context for Early Childhood Education Provision

Within the Swedish educational system, the child is seen as having the right to high quality education from the beginning of his/her life (www.skolverket.se). Childcare in Sweden is mostly public and available to children aged 1–12 years starting at the end of the parental leave period when children turn one, and including the leisure-time centres in schools. Most 1- to 5-year-old children spend 3–10 hours every weekday at pre-school, while their parents are working or studying, or if the children have special needs (Swedish National Agency for Education, 2008). Local authorities have an obligation to provide pre-school activities for all children within 3 months of the date that parents ask for this service. If the parents do not work, or are on parental leave, the child has a right to pre-school education for at least 15 hours a week.

Independent childcare became more common in the 1990s, accounting for 15% of enrolments. The 1990s also saw a substantial increase in group sizes. Between 1990 and 2000 the average group size in pre-school increased from just below 14 children per group to more than 17 per group (Swedish National Agency for Education, 2008). In 2001 and 2003 several reforms were introduced to increase access to pre-school. A reform called the 'maximum fee' provided access to government-supported pre-schools for all 4- and 5-year-old children, thus giving pre-school the same status as the compulsory school.

More recently, with economic assistance from government to the local authorities during 2005 and 2006, there has been a trend to focus on creating smaller group sizes for children in early childhood education (ECE) settings. At the same time there has been a rise in the birth rate (Swedish National Agency, 2009) resulting

A. Sandberg (✉)
School of Education, Culture and Communication, Mälardalen University, 721 23 Västerås, Sweden
e-mail: anette.sandberg@mdh.se

L. Miller et al. (eds.), *Early Childhood Grows Up*, International Perspectives on Early Childhood Education and Development 6, DOI 10.1007/978-94-007-2718-2_7, © Springer Science+Business Media B.V. 2012

in 432,600 children enrolled in pre-schools during autumn 2008, an increase of 4% over the previous year. Similarly, in 2008, 81% of all 1- to 5-year-old children were in pre-schools, compared to 80% in 2007 and 61% in 1997. The increase of children in ECE has affected the adult:child ratio in some localities, though overall it has remained at two adults per five children.

Early childhood education became the responsibility of the Ministry of Education and Sciences in 2007 when it took its place as an integral part of the overall education system. ECE has its own curriculum, a document in the form of an ordinance, *Lpfö98/06* (Swedish Ministry of Education, 1998/2006). This marks the importance of the pre-school as the first step in life-long learning.

7.2 The Early Childhood Curriculum

The school system in Sweden is goal-based with a high degree of local responsibility. Overall, national goals are set out by the Swedish Parliament in the Education Act, and the national curricula and the different levels of school are linked to each other by fundamental values and tasks. Each of the three curricula (pre-school, primary and secondary) in the educational system has the same status and structure, and is written in the form of goals and guidelines. However, these guidelines are not teaching guidelines in a strict sense. Rather, they describe three different kinds of goal areas:

- *values and norms*: as the basis for the staff to develop and form how they work with children and parents
- *goals for development and learning*: detailing what to strive for in all activities
- *influence of the child in the pre-school context*: recognising children's rights and establishing a democratic base in working with children.

Across all three levels of the curriculum, guidelines are formulated for every goal area, thus allowing an incremental deepening or widening of each content area. Within the overall educational system, the three curricula create a sequenced and secure approach to build up a child's learning and knowledge. The child is described in terms of being an individual with competencies, and the child's rights are a key focus.

The origins of the Swedish pre-school curriculum lie within a progressive paradigm of pedagogy with key influences being Dewey (2004) and Vygotsky (1986). Pre-schools are founded on democratic values, and the first national and compulsory curriculum introduced in 2006 (*Lpfö 98/06*) specifies desired quality targets that are of a social nature, with some focussing on personality development. A minority of the goals relate to more traditional academic abilities. This clearly reveals the democratic mandate as prescribed in the Swedish curriculum (*Lpfö 98/06*) about how people should approach each other, and about knowledge; learning how to act in society is given priority. The academic skills of learning to read, write and mathematics are emphasised, but the curriculum does not describe the aims related to these areas as necessary outcomes. Rather, children's own ability to create meaning in interaction with the surrounding world is given prominence as a life-long learning process. The activities in the Swedish pre-school are intended to stimulate play, creativity and enjoyable learning. Pre-school staff use different kinds of documentation to record learning, for example child observations, individual plans for every child, and portfolios.

Underpinning the curriculum is the view that the pre-school should supplement the home by creating the best possible conditions for ensuring that each child's learning and development is rich and varied. The curriculum for the pre-school (*Lpfö 98/06*) states 'The parents or guardian are responsible for their child's upbringing and development' (p. 12), and this includes showing respect for parents and responsibility for developing good relationships between staff and children's families.

7.3 The Early Childhood Workforce

There are two staff categories in Swedish pre-schools: pre-school teachers and day-care attendants. About half of all pre-school employees have university degrees in early childhood education, while just over 40% of staff are daycare attendants. Pre-school teachers have completed a 3.5-year pedagogical training programme at university level, while daycare attendants have upper-secondary qualifications. In Sweden, pre-school teachers work with children aged 1–12 years. Pre-school is for children between the ages of 1–5 years; at the age of 6 children then attend 'pre-school class', and compulsory school starts at the age of 7. Almost all leisure-time centres are included on the grounds of compulsory schools.

Pre-school teacher education has been at university level since 1977, as a 2-year programme. In 2001 the programme was extended to a 3.5-year programme (210 ECTS or European Credit Transfer System credits). The university degree qualifies teachers to work in the lower school years of the compulsory school system as well as in leisure-time centres. The teacher training programme includes three areas:

1. *General field studies*: common for all student teachers, 90 ECTS including at least 15 ECTS as practicum experience
2. *Major orientation studies*: study of a particular field of knowledge (at least 60 ECTS including 15 ECTS gained from practicum experience)
3. *Specialisation*: with several options to choose from either for the depth or widening of content area that the student already knows (30 ECTS).

All students write an independent dissertation (15 ECTS). The teacher education programme emphasises a scientific approach in teachers' work, and links between research and practical work.

The training of daycare attendants takes place in upper-secondary schools. The programme is 3 years long and includes general academic studies, study of a foreign language, and mathematics. Students can choose a major orientation within the programme called 'Children, culture and recreation' (www.skolverket.se). This major orientation is very wide-ranging and focuses beyond working with children and adults in pre-school settings to even include work in recreational institutions like being a guardian in the public baths.

There is currently a movement to reform the pre-school teachers' education programme in line with the Bologna model which comprises a total of 210 ECTS (3 years of training) with the first of the reforms taking effect from 2011.

7.4 The Micro-level Context of the Swedish Case Study

7.4.1 The Setting of the Case Study Pre-school

The pre-school in which we conducted our case study is located close to a forest on the outskirts of a town in the middle part of Sweden and is under the responsibility of the local authorities. The pre-school is divided into six units: three units are for 3- to 5-year-olds, two units for under-3-year-olds and one unit for children aged 1–4 years.

The pre-school provides daycare for 108 children and is open from 6.30 am to 6.00 pm. All children have access to a play area in the yard. Meals are prepared three times a day by a resident cook: breakfast, lunch and an afternoon snack. In the unit where the observation took place, nineteen 3- to 4-year-old children were enrolled and there were three staff: two full-time pre-school teachers and one full-time daycare attendant.

The pre-school teacher in the study, Anna, is an experienced 59-year-old who has worked in several pre-schools since gaining her degree in 1972. Anna had worked in the pre-school since 2005. Each semester, with the support of her head of school, she has the possibility of in-service education from a free choice of optional courses offered by the Local Authorities.

7.4.2 A Typical Day for Anna

Our video observations were conducted during one day and illustrate Anna's work with the children. The researchers were aware that as the observations were only taking place during one day, the staff may not have been acting 'typically'. Problems were encountered in video-ing free play and outdoor activities in the afternoon when, due to a shortage of staff, all the activities took place out in the pre-school yard with the whole group of pre-school children. As we did not have approval for video recording from all the parents, we were limited in the data we could collect outdoors. Consequently, the video observations are mostly of planned activities and meal times indoors. Video recording included all staff members but the focus was on one pre-school teacher.

The day began with welcoming each of the children and their parents. The staff team had responsibility for different activities. The daily routines aimed to create a predictable environment for the children and security in knowing what possibilities were available. Activities within a topic started out of children's interests. Flexibility was very important and the structure of a day could easily be changed, depending on the children's interests and wishes. The pre-school had both indoor and outdoor activities. The outdoor activities took place in the play yard just outside the door or in the forest nearby for up to 3 or 4 hours a day, depending on the weather.

Once a week the staff have a team meeting or other meetings, for example with other professionals and/or parents. These are usually held during the outdoor play time in the morning; staff also do some administrative tasks in this period.

Some examples of the work of the pre-school teacher are described in more detail below, focusing on specific video-ed examples of circle-time, guiding dressing, laying the table for the meal, and storytelling during rest time. The subsequent Table 7.1 shows a typical daily schedule at the case-study preschool; the time periods are approximate.

7.4.2.1 Circle-Time

All the children and Anna sat in a circle on the floor. Anna held their attention by talking about the children who were away from pre-school on that day. She called out the children's names and when they responded she asked questions such as: 'What month is it now? What day is it today? What letter does the weekday begin with? Do you know someone whose name starts with the letter (t)? What date is it today?' Two children counted how many children and adults there were that day. Anna picked up a box of marbles and poured them on to the floor. One child counted all the marbles to see how many days were left in the month (i.e., 24). After singing the alphabet song the children asked for another song, they wanted to sing. Then it was time for an action song. The circle-time ended with a plate of fruit being passed around and free discussion to which each child made a contribution.

7.4.2.2 Guiding Dressing

Dressing for outside activities took place in the hall. All the children had to have waterproof trousers because it was wet outside. The majority of the children could put their clothes on by themselves, but some needed help from Anna, for example with the waterproof trousers. Anna constantly praised the children for being proficient in dressing.

7.4.2.3 Laying the Table

Tables needed to be laid before lunch time. Anna and one child talked to each other about how to lay the table and what was needed for the lunch. The child laid out the plates and glasses. Anna often knelt next to the child and praised the child. The child counted the glasses. Anna asked questions about what should be on the table. As the child responded with 'knives and forks', Anna presented them, asking if the child knew which side the cutlery was to be placed. Anna gave the cutlery to the child. Then they collected the food from the kitchen and together they brought the bowls of hot food to the table. The milk in the refrigerator was not enough for everyone so the pre-school teacher said that some more milk must be retrieved from the kitchen.

Table 7.1 The day's schedule and its content

Daily schedule	Content
Parents leave the children at pre-school (c. 6.30–9.00 am)	Welcoming the children and parents. Staff, parents and children exchange information. Before breakfast one staff member lays the table while the children have free play in different rooms
Breakfast (c. 8.00 am)	The majority of children and staff have arrived and have breakfast at pre-school. Children who had already eaten their breakfast at home sat on a sofa and read a book or played in another room. When parents arrive to drop off their children during breakfast, one of the staff members welcomes them and looks after the family in the cloakroom where the children leave their bags
Free play (c. 8.30 am)	After breakfast the children have free play with various play materials before moving to circle-time in different rooms
Circle-time (c. 9.00 am)	During circle-time discussions about children's experiences take place. One staff member is responsible for the content in circle-time which usually involves singing, rhymes, movement, counting children, and talking about those who are absent
Guiding dressing (c. 9.30 am)	The children dress themselves to go outside. Those who were unable to do this by themselves were guided by staff or other children with help or instructions
Outdoor play (c. 9.45 am)	The children go out to the yard or forest to play. The pre-school teacher observes and helps the children, for example to swing. She also plays with children. Sometimes the children go on visits to the public baths or library
Laying the table (c. 11.00 am)	One pre-school teacher and one child lay the table before lunch
Guiding dressing (c. 11.00 am)	The children are divided into different groups when they return from outdoor play. Children who cannot get their clothes off get help from the staff or other children
Circle-time (c. 11.15 am)	While they are waiting for lunch, a short circle-time occurs with songs chosen by the children
Lunch (c. 11.30 am)	Each staff member has responsibility for one table with some children during lunch. They sit and eat with the same children every day and have their own regular place at table
Rest (c. 12.00 am)	Rest with storytelling in different groups. One of the staff in each group reads a book
Free play indoor or outdoor (c. 1 pm)	Children use the resources in the environment for free play in different rooms and outdoors. Some children and staff also have activities or work with the topic
Snack-time (c. 2.30 pm)	By now some children have been picked up by their parents and one staff member has finished work for the day. A light meal is organised out of children's choices and children can choose where to sit
Free play (around 3.00 pm)	Free play until the remaining children are picked up by their parents. The pre-school teacher observes and helps children
Co-operation with parents (around 4–6.30 pm)	Teachers exchange information with the parents and goodbyes are said

The child offered to get more milk and did so. When the child came back, Anna knelt next to her and prepared her to be ready to inform the other children about the kind of food they would eat that day. Anna did this by asking the child some questions to which the child responded: 'potatoes, meat, vegetables and milk'. Then she and the child went hand-in-hand to where the other children and staff were having circle-time and the child told the other children and staff what they would have for lunch.

When everyone was sitting at the lunch table, the children chose an English nursery rhyme to sing. They served their own food by themselves and passed on the bowls to the child next to them. One child did not want any vegetables. Anna urged the child to have a taste, which made the child say that it tasted good. Anna and the children sat and talked throughout lunchtime.

7.4.2.4 Storytelling During Rest Time

The children were divided into different groups after lunchtime. Anna read a book to three children. One child leaned against Anna as he listened. Other children also sat by and listened; they had a doll sitting on their knees. Anna read and held up the book to each child to show them the pictures.

7.5 The Pre-school Teacher's Thoughts About Her Work

The interview questions arose from the project as detailed in Chapter 2. The interview was audio recorded and transcribed.

7.5.1 The Pre-school Teacher's Role and Contact with Colleagues and Outside Agencies

When we asked Anna how she saw her role, she said that her main responsibility was for the 5-year-old children. She emphasised that, 'children are the most interesting people in the world that exist. ...It is a big, big challenge to know how to approach children'. Anna emphasised that she saw her key role as providing a good role model in co-operation with the children. She explained that her main task was the responsibility she took for the pedagogical work:

> To be an adult and a role model, to use my competencies and to send out a positive spirit.

An important task for Anna was to lead and allocate tasks to a group of children; she also emphasised the importance of children acquiring knowledge through the experiments that they naturally carried out, including all aspects of development such as language, movement skills and emotions.

Anna had a holistic vision of learning and development and wanted to create a pedagogical context where children could learn how one becomes a human being.

She said the social developmental area was the most important area to work with during the pre-school years. One part of this was to teach the children how to cope with conflicts, and to value and support each other.

Anna also noted that constructing and reflecting on knowledge with colleagues were important aspects of her work, for example, talking about the in-service training they had gone through and discussing and sharing working tasks on a weekly basis. Anna said that she wanted to be a good role model and was 'not afraid of conflict' as this provided an opportunity to influence others. Flexibility was an approach she valued in team work with her colleagues. Co-operation with other supporting agencies in the broader community was not a feature of this pre-school teacher's view of her role, apart from the local librarian whom she mentioned as a source of good advice.

Quality for our pre-school teacher was when 'all the children feel good, are happy, learn and develop'. Quality became visible in work which stimulated children in their development and in listening to the parents and children. It was difficult for Anna to describe precisely how quality could be guaranteed and she explained 'I do not know if I can say that exactly'.

7.5.2 Parental Involvement

Involvement with parents was an area that was included in the pre-school teacher's working tasks. Each morning the important task was to welcome the parents when they arrived to drop off their child at the pre-school, and when they came back to pick up their child in the afternoon, the important task was to inform them about the child's day. She considered parent participation to be an important part of her pedagogical work. Anna believed this was the way to meet and learn to know each other and share information. The parents were invited to participate in a developmental dialogue about their child once per semester. Anna emphasised 'I like parents and it is fun to talk with them and I think they feel the same'. Co-operation with the parents could give: '. . . more security for the children, when they know that adults like the same thing and all want the best for the child'. She explained that parents had the possibility to influence but not to determine the pedagogical work: 'The developmental dialogue and the daily contacts give opportunities for parents to influence'.

7.5.3 The Curriculum

Anna referred to the guidelines in the pre-school curriculum, *Lpfö98/06* (Swedish Ministry of Education, 2006), as supporting her own values; she felt they gave her enough support in her pedagogical work. She spoke in this way about the most important aspect of her work:

> . . . for myself to take children seriously and see them, listen to what they say and do. It is important to confirm the child in what she/he says and does all the time.

Anna found it difficult to describe how the curriculum was used in the concrete and practical work with children, parents and together in teamwork; she explained that 'the curriculum is in the background in all that I do'. But on the other hand, she was clear that 'the curriculum gives status' for her in her profession.

7.6 Discussion

7.6.1 What Does Being a Professional in Early Childhood Education Mean in Sweden?

According to the Swedish National Agency for Education (2005), university-educated pre-school teachers are essential in the professionalisation of the Swedish pre-school workforce. As discussed earlier in this chapter, being a pre-school teacher within the Swedish early childhood education system demands both the ability to analyse, and work within the national curriculum guidelines as well as the ability to document the work in the pre-schools back to society. Society monitors whether the pre-schools are living up to the curriculum guidelines, and teacher education is seen to provide the tools for the pre-school teachers to be able to do a high quality job within the curriculum guidelines. It is also seen as important for pre-school teachers to constantly review and develop activities to suit children's interests and needs, and for this to happen it is necessary for pre-school teachers to have good quality education and in-service training. The Swedish National Agency for Education (2004/2005) places responsibility for the quality of pre-school education on the pre-school teachers and the ways in which they use their knowledge. A clear leadership role is assumed to rest with pre-school teachers, and 'a teacher-led profession' is promoted similar to that described by Dalli (2008, p. 173).

7.6.2 What Does It Mean to Act Professionally in This Particular Swedish Context?

In exploring the questions of what it means to act professionally in this particular Swedish pre-school, we have identified a number of key themes as discussed in the following sections.

7.6.2.1 Working from an Ethical Base of Respect for Children

Earlier in this chapter we noted that the ethical base of the Swedish early childhood curriculum is clearly written in the first goal area of norms and values in *Lpfö98/06*, the pre-school curriculum that provides the foundation for the whole school system. Commenting on the values inherent in the practice of New Zealand early years teachers, Dalli (2008) identified a pedagogical style based on respectful practices and a valuing of collaborative relationships. In our study, the ethical base that the pre-school teacher worked from was similar, and clearly articulated and demonstrated in the way that the pre-school teacher acted in the group of children: the pre-school teacher respected children and strove to establish equality within her relationships with them as was evident in her efforts to find the child's level in her interactions with them. For example, the pre-school teacher was careful to identify the level of independence, security and self-confidence shown by the children in the various activities and then build on these to extend the children's level of performance. This was clear when, after having laid the table, a child was encouraged by Anna to describe the lunch they were going to have to the other children in the group. Through this coaching by the pre-school teacher, the child was able to rehearse what to say and find the courage and confidence to address the group.

7.6.2.2 Children's Development and Learning

The pre-school teacher's work in the curriculum goal area of development and learning (*Lpfö98/06*) was illustrated mostly through the pre-school teacher's work in the content areas of language development and mathematics. For example, during circle-time Anna asked children to mention the name of the month and the letter with which the actual month began:

Child:	March
Pre-school teacher:	March, do you know with which letter the word can start?
Children:	M
Pre-school teacher:	Does anyone have a name beginning with M? What is your name?

The child says his name beginning with M.

Pre-school teacher:	Are there any more names that start with M here?
Children:	Malcolm
Pre-school teacher:	Good.

Other content areas such as play, creative activities, science and so on, and how the pre-school teacher worked to develop children's knowledge and actions within these areas, were not illustrated or verbally mentioned during this one-day observation study. Arguably, it is difficult to illustrate all areas of the curriculum in such a short timeframe. Additionally, one could argue that the pedagogical strategy and style of the pre-school teacher can be demonstrated quite unselfconsciously (see Dalli, 2008), while the specialist knowledge required to work with the traditional academic areas of language, reading, writing and mathematics may need to be more consciously drawn on by teachers when they are asked to talk about professional practice. This raises the question of whether pre-school teachers might perceive this academic knowledge as giving professional status in the pre-schools. Traditionally, academic knowledge has been the area for compulsory school education in Sweden. It would be interesting to ask these questions more broadly of the Nordic model of educare than was possible in the present study.

7.6.2.3 Democratic Values

The third area of goals in *Lpfö98/06*, the pre-school curriculum, includes the democratic values of making space for the child to be able to influence the pre-school
context in line with the child's right to be listened to, and to influence her/his
daily life in the pre-school. In this study the time schedule for the day was set,
but children's interests were allowed to change this schedule. Even within the
planned schedule Anna made space for children to make their own suggestions
and bring their interests to the structure of the day. In this way, the pre-school
teacher was 'acting in the child's best interest' (Dalli, 2008, p. 174). In the interview, Anna emphasized the importance of listening to every child and to affirm
her/him.

7.6.2.4 Interacting and Communicating Actively with Children, Colleagues and Parents

The collaborative relationships between the pre-school teacher and the children
were clearly demonstrated. The structure of the day included activities in which
children were active participants as a matter of course, for example when they laid
the table for lunch. Within the staff team, having common goals was seen by the
pre-school teacher to lead to joint action work with other professionals and parents.
Anna explained

> Co-operation provides greater security and confidence for children. Children need to know
> that parents and pre-school staff think the same way and they both want the best thing for
> the child.

Anna emphasised good collaboration and communication with parents with
whom she had almost daily contact. She believed this led to a good and natural
connection developing between them. At the same time, Anna perceived the parents
as not having many opportunities to influence the content of pre-school activities.
She explained

> Parents only concentrate on their own child but the pedagogical activities in the group
> must work for the whole group of children. Developmental dialogues and daily contact
> give parents a chance to influence the curriculum.

Anna considered it important that the parents had confidence in the staff; she
saw the 'developmental dialogues' held once per semester as a way of developing
this confidence and giving parents the opportunity to discuss their child and their
thoughts about the pre-school. Sandberg and Vuorinen (2008) also reported similar
findings in another Swedish study that looked at co-operation between pre-school
and home. This study showed the varied and rich forms of co-operation that are
possible and that different types of co-operation appeal to different parents' needs.
From the parents' perspective, the key concern is that their own children get the best
from pre-school; they, therefore, are interested in having well-qualified pre-school
teachers and good resources in every other respect. Other studies have also shown
that parents see the pre-school teacher's education background, and how she/he uses

it in their daily work, as key factors that influence quality in the early years (see also Asplund-Carlsson, Pramling-Samuelsson, & Kärrby, 2001; Gustafsson & Myrberg, 2002).

7.6.2.5 Communication with Children

The pre-school teacher valued communication with children including as a way of evaluating their learning, and enabling them to participate in decisions. For example, when the child was setting the table for lunch, Anna knelt next to the child so as to be at eye level with the child when speaking to her. Anna gave responsibility to the child to get more milk from the pre-school kitchen. She showed flexibility in her work and adjusted the situation to the children.

7.7 Concluding Comments

Teachers in early childhood education in Sweden work mostly in public pre-schools. Their responsibility is to work actively with children, parents, colleagues and the school system. ECE in Sweden is regulated by the state in terms of an ordinance, the curriculum, *Lpfö98/06* (Swedish Ministry of Education, 1998/2006). This demands that the pre-school teachers interpret the curriculum and conduct their work according to the guidelines described in the curriculum. The pre-school teachers' professionalism thus demands both the ability to analyse and work according to these guidelines, but also to communicate their work in the pre-schools back to society. Teacher education gives pre-school teachers tools to be able to do high quality work of this nature, including developing the ability to implement pedagogical strategies, and respecting children's democratic rights by taking account of the children's interests with their good in mind. Furthermore, reflecting individually and collectively on curriculum experiences, and learning to document these, is considered important.

Reflecting on our study within these contextual parameters, we noted that although as researchers we were able to identify key themes in the pre-school teacher's practice, in the interview the pre-school teacher struggled to articulate what the day consisted of, and the reasons for her actions and decisions. For example, Anna said that the curriculum played an important role in her pedagogical work, but had difficulty in describing how this influenced her practice. It seems to us that a professional teacher should be able to describe her work with a language that can reach other professionals, politicians and parents, and make her work accessible to others in the society.

We also note that it is possible that the teacher was feeling tense and self-conscious under observation and that her practice on the day was not typical, as it was clear to us that the teacher had the necessary knowledge to articulate her practice and used this in her interactions and relationships.

Furthermore, we reflected also that the pre-school teacher's most obvious pedagogical engagement with the children during the day of observation was mainly in the areas of language and mathematics (see Table 7.1, circle-time and laying the table). However, the curriculum encompasses many other areas. Language and mathematics are two areas currently being highlighted by government policy, and the pre-school teacher was perhaps focusing on these rather than the more traditional areas such as play and creative activities. Staff did not actively participate in the children's free play but rather stood back and allowed it to happen; by contrast, within other activities Anna was interacting and communicating with the children to develop the content area further.

Finally, we note that the study showed some discrepancy between the thoughts expressed in the interview and the actions recorded in the observations of Anna; and that it was difficult for Anna to define what she wanted to achieve in her work.

These observations raise a number of issues that would seem worthy of further investigation. Firstly, while accepting that one's professional self-awareness, or mindfulness, can never be complete, our small study suggests that a deliberate focus on discussing curriculum content within pre-school teaching teams might be expected to enhance teachers' ability to be articulate about their practice. Secondly, we wonder whether the situation would be different if the pre-school teacher's background had been different, for example, if she had gained her qualification more recently. And thirdly, we also wonder whether the findings in this one case study would be similar across a greater number of settings.

These issues would make useful foci for future research agendas as interest in the nature of professional practice in early childhood settings continues to broaden.

References

Asplund-Carlsson, M., Pramling-Samuelsson, I., & Kärrby, G. (2001). *Strukturella faktorer och pedagogisk kvalitet i barnomsorgen och skola; en kunskapsöversikt. [Structural factors and pedagogical quality in pre-school education and school]*. Stockholm: Skolverket.

Dalli, C. (2008). The new teacher in New Zealand. In L. K. Miller & C. Cable (Eds.), *Professionalism in the early years* (pp. 142–153). Abingdon, Oxon: Hodder Education.

Dewey, J. (2004). *Individ, skola och samhälle; utbildningsfilosofiska texter*. Stockholm: Natur och Kultur.

Gustafsson, J.-E., & Myrberg, E. (2002). *Ekonomiska resursers betydelse för pedagogiska resultat; en kunskapsöversikt. [Economical resources and their importance in the educational result]*. Stockholm: Skolverket. Liber Distribution.

Sandberg, A., & Vuorinen, T. (2008). Preschool-home cooperation in change. *International Journal of Early Years Education, 16*(2), 151–161.

Swedish Ministry of Education. (2006). *Curriculum for the pre-school, Lpfö 98*. Stockholm, Sweden: Fritzes.

Swedish National Agency for Education. (2004/2005). *Förskolan i brytningstid. Nationell utvärdering av förskolan. [Pre-school in the changing period. A National assessment of the pre-school]*. Stockholm: Skolverket, Nr 239.

Swedish National Agency for Education. (2005). *Kvalitet i förskolan. [Quality in pre-school]*. Stockholm: Skolverket: Fritzes förlag.

Swedish National Agency for Education. (2008). *Descriptive data on pre-school activities, school-age childcare, schools and adult education in Sweden*. Report no. 320.

Swedish National Agency for Education. (2009). *Statistics, PM*. 2009-04-02.

Vygotsky, L. (1986). *Thought and language*. Cambridge, MA: MIT Press.

Part II
International Perspectives
on Professionalism

Chapter 8
Radical Reconstructions? Early Childhood Workforce Profiles in Changing European Early Childhood Education and Care Systems

Pamela Oberhuemer

8.1 Introduction

Although the qualifications and working conditions of personnel[1] in early childhood centres are recognised as a significant contributory factor towards achieving and maintaining high quality services (see e.g. Barnett, 2004; EACEA-Eurydice, 2009; Kelley & Camilli, 2007; OECD, 2006; Siraj-Blatchford, 2004), little is known about the current staffing situation in early childhood centres in Europe, particularly in the newer European Union countries. Between 2007 and 2009, the SEEPRO project (*Systems of early education/care and professionalisation in Europe*), a study on the early childhood education and care workforce in 27 countries, aimed to redress this knowledge gap.[2]

In Germany, where the project was based, the rationale for carrying out this study included the following:

- Although student and early childhood practitioner mobility in Europe is steadily increasing, there is limited knowledge among those involved in early years training, field support and administration about current qualification requirements, professional profiles and workplace settings of ECEC staff in different countries.
- Although professional circles show a keen interest in European developments as a frame of reference for critical analyses of the system of ECEC professionalisation

---

[1] In this chapter I use the term "core practitioner" to refer to those with group or centre leadership roles, "early childhood professional" or "practitioner" interchangeably for staff with a professional qualification, and "personnel" or "workers" as a more generic term for all staff working in early childhood centres.

[2] The SEEPRO project (2007–2009) was based at the State Institute of Early Childhood Research (IFP) in Munich and funded by the German Federal Ministry of Family and Youth Affairs. Members of the research team were Pamela Oberhuemer (IFP, lead researcher) and Inge Schreyer (IFP), in collaboration with Michelle Neuman (external researcher based in Washington, DC).

P. Oberhuemer (✉)
State Institute of Early Childhood Research (IFP), 80797 Munich, Germany
e-mail: pamela@oberhuemer.com

L. Miller et al. (eds.), *Early Childhood Grows Up*, International Perspectives on Early   119
Childhood Education and Development 6, DOI 10.1007/978-94-007-2718-2_8,
© Springer Science+Business Media B.V. 2012

in Germany, available resources (particularly in German) for these reflexive processes are few and far between.

• Although a number of higher education institutions in Germany are now offering first-time degree-level qualifications in early childhood education beyond the stipulated post-secondary level of training, the required and desired professional profile is far from clear.

The initial research focus of the project was the ECEC workforce in the 12 countries to join the European Union in 2004 or later: Bulgaria, Cyprus, the Czech Republic, Estonia, Hungary, Latvia, Lithuania, Malta, Poland, Romania, the Slovak Republic and Slovenia. Within the SEEPRO framework, the project team also fully revised relevant data from an earlier State Institute of Early Childhood Research (IFP) study on work with young children in the former EU15: Austria, Belgium, Denmark, Finland, France, Germany, Greece, Ireland, Italy, Luxembourg, the Netherlands, Portugal, Spain, Sweden and the United Kingdom.

Research methods for the 12 post-2004 countries included commissioned reports by national experts as a background resource for 5-day research visits. During these field trips arranged by a country co-ordinator, the research team conducted semi-structured, context-relevant interviews with a range of representatives and stakeholders in each country (ministry officials, researchers, professional education/training specialists, personnel in early childhood settings). For the former EU15 countries, national experts were commissioned to provide contributions on identified gaps in the available data on specific aspects of staffing and the ECEC system. Document analysis and the utilisation of international resource banks such as Eurostat, Eurydice and OECD were part of the research procedures for each country. Each of the SEEPRO country profiles was validated by a national expert. Leading research questions in the 27 countries were the following: What are the qualification requirements for work in early childhood settings? What are the main professional profiles for core practitioners? What are current workforce issues within and across countries?

8.2 Sites of Change: Early Years Work Contexts Across Europe

Early childhood professionals in Europe are experiencing rapidly changing work contexts, both at the macro and micro level. Whereas in the eastern European countries the system changes at governance level during the early 1990s led in most cases to both a devaluing and re-structuring of public services – including early childhood services – in many western European countries, early childhood education and care have been accorded more public and policy attention than ever before. The forces which have increased politicians' and policy makers' awareness of the advantages of a well-resourced system of early childhood services have been primarily driven by demographic, economic and social pressures, with beneficial effects seen in terms of family and employment policies, long-term education policy and even economic policy. The research-backed argument for this has been that investment in the early years brings "greater returns" than funding targeted at later stages of education. As a consequence, expectations directed towards early childhood professionals are both increasing and intensifying.

One current issue of concern across countries centres on provision for the under-threes. In the eastern European countries, rebuilding the levels of provision to meet strong demand while developing more flexible systems attuned to the changing, and more varied needs of families are a challenge both for policy makers and practitioners. In the western European countries it is the fast-paced expansion of services for under-threes (e.g. in Germany) which is generating concern about the quality of places provided. These various changes both at macro and micro level have also been impacting on the national qualifications systems.

8.3   National Qualification Systems and European Goals and Targets

Alongside these challenges on the ground, goals and targets at the European level both for higher education and vocational education are impacting on national qualifications systems, including those for the early childhood profession. According to our study, the most immediate influence up to 2009 seems to have been the Bologna Process. This higher education strategy, agreed in principle by 29 European Ministers of Higher Education in 1999, and endorsed in the meantime by a further 17 European states, aimed to create a transparent European Higher Education Area by 2010. A major goal is to enhance student mobility and mutual recognition of awards through the introduction of similar two-tier study routes (usually implemented as Bachelor's and Master's degrees) and an agreed system of credit transfers (ECTS) and diploma supplements (Hechler & Pasternack, 2009). As a result, in nearly all countries, professional study routes and pathways at higher education level have been undergoing considerable change. Our interviews showed that these and other developments have also impacted on the early childhood qualifications scene, which in many countries has been in a constant state of re-construction over the past few years, as the SEEPRO research team quickly discovered. We were interested in the directions being taken and how these are related to the new European Qualifications Framework for Lifelong Learning adopted by the European Parliament in 2007. The Framework aims to combine vocational, professional and higher education qualifications and competencies. However, national strategies for including the early years in this particular Framework are mostly at a very early stage, and currently only a relatively small number of countries appear to have fully developed National Qualifications Frameworks which could feed into a European one.

I shall now turn to different groups of countries in order to trace some of these developments and will start by looking at the situation in the English-speaking and mainly English-speaking countries in the EU.

8.4 English-Speaking/Mainly English-Speaking Countries: Ireland, Malta, United Kingdom (England, Wales, Scotland, Northern Ireland)

In the United Kingdom, the Republic of Ireland, and Malta, the history of early childhood provision and professionalisation reads like a collection of unfinished stories, of fragmented and un-coordinated initiatives. In none of these countries has there been a tradition of a highly professionalised early years workforce for work with children *across* the age-range of birth to school entry. Instead, there have been historically ingrained divisions between the education and welfare/care sectors, with only limited publicly funded nursery provision within the education system.

Until recently, a Bachelor-level qualification (ISCED[3] Level 5) has only been required for work in the mainly state-maintained pre-primary education provision (although not for work in the kindergarten centres in Malta, where the requirement is an upper-secondary-level qualification, ISCED 3B/C). Provision for children below statutory school age – officially 4 years in Northern Ireland, 5 in England, Scotland, Wales and Malta, and 6 in the Republic of Ireland – has been predominantly in the private-independent and voluntary sector. Qualification requirements for work in the various forms of private provision have traditionally been at a much lower formal level than those for working in the education system. For example, in Ireland and Malta there have been no specified requirements at all for work in the largely privately run early childhood provision outside the school system. At the same time Irish teachers working with 4- and 5-year-olds in the (non-compulsory) infant classes in primary school are primary-trained, but usually without a strong speciali-sation in early years pedagogy. A recently completed survey of the Irish workforce confirmed that 12 per cent of the childcare workforce does not have any accred-ited childcare-related qualification (OMCYA, 2009), whereas earlier estimates were around 30 per cent (Donnelly, 2007). The recent formulation of a set of occu-pational profiles linked into the National Qualifications Framework of Ireland is expected to make it possible for early childhood practitioners in Ireland to acquire an award as Basic Practitioner in Early Childhood Education/Care at Level 4 of the National Qualification Framework (ISCED 3A/C) through modular courses. Following on from this initial award, practitioners can then progress through var-ious stages to becoming an Advanced Practitioner at NQF Level 7 (ISCED 5B) or Level 8 (ISCED 5A), or to complete postgraduate studies for the award of Expert Practitioner (ISCED 5A and 6). These profiles for career progression currently have the status of non-binding recommendations. However, this is expected to change in the wake of a new policy initiative which since 2009 has entitled a fee-free year of pre-school provision for all 3-year-olds. The entitlement policy additionally requires that the leader of settings offering this provision holds a certificate in childcare/early

---

[3] ISCED – International Standard Classification of Education – an instrument for comparing levels and fields of education across countries, developed by UNESCO in the 1970s, and revised in 1997. http://www.unesco.org/education/information/nfsunesco/doc/isced:1997.htm

education at a minimum of Level 5 (equivalent to ISCED 4C) on the Irish National Framework of Qualifications, or an equivalent nationally recognised childcare qualification, or a higher award in the childcare/early education field. It is also expected that in the reasonably near future, the required qualification for staff in this position will be a Level 6 major award (OMCYA, 2009).

The restructurings in England are even more fundamental (see also Chapter 3, this volume). Graduates with a one year postgraduate qualification or a three or four year undergraduate degree leading to Qualified Teacher Status account for only around 11 per cent of the workforce in early years provision for children from birth up to school entry. Up to 2005, this Bachelor-level qualification was required only for those working as teachers in state-maintained provision in the education sector (*nursery schools, nursery classes*), but not for those working in the private, voluntary and independent sectors, where requirements traditionally have been much lower, even for those leading a centre. However, according to government proposals, by 2012 there is now to be at least one graduate-level early years worker in each children's centre, a fairly new form of community-based integrated service for young children and their families being established in all boroughs. Building on research evidence from the influential EPPE study[4] and driven by goals to create conditions for the successful implementation of the recent (2008) statutory curricular framework for 0–5 year olds, the *Early Years Foundation Stage*, a new graduate qualification has been introduced for work in these multi-professional centres. The *Early Years Professional Status* (CWDC, 2008) is part of the *Children's Workforce Strategy*, which envisaged a major restructuring of qualification pathways for all child-related professions. The vision of the Children's Workforce Strategy is to achieve an Integrated Qualifications Framework that would allow for horizontal and vertical movement both within and across professions. As yet there are no evaluation studies available which scrutinise the quality of the multiple pathways available for gaining EYP status. It is also not clear how this new qualification will sit alongside the award of Qualified Teacher Status. However, the declared political goal is clear: the proportion of graduates with a pedagogical qualification working in the early childhood sector is to be significantly increased. The qualifying courses are fully funded for those working in the non-statutory sector. By 2009, 3000 persons had gained this new qualified status.

In terms of the professional profiles for early years workers in these countries, the following pattern can be construed: in the United Kingdom and Ireland, those working in state-maintained settings before compulsory primary schooling are generally trained as primary school teachers, either with a specialisation in the early years (possible in England, Scotland, Wales) or not (generally the case in Northern Ireland and Ireland). It is a profile strongly linked to the logistics of the education system and excludes work with the under-threes. In the case of the wide variety of vocational qualifications for work in the non-statutory sector, the training is on the

---

[4] EPPE – Effective Pre-school and Primary Education 3-11 project. http://www.ioe.ac.uk/schools/ecpe/eppe/eppe3-11pubs.htm

whole fairly specialised towards working with young children across the age range of birth to 5, or birth to 8.

In these countries the two-tier route of undergraduate and postgraduate studies proposed in the Bologna Process documents has long been in place in higher education institutions (in general and also in the case of teacher education). Therefore, there has been no need to introduce newly structured degree courses, as is the case in many other European countries. In this respect, the Bologna Process can be seen as only a peripheral influence on structural developments at the higher education level, including qualification pathways for the traditional teaching profession leading to Qualified Teacher Status. However, the moves at European level to include both higher education and vocational education within one single framework, combined with the need to accommodate quite radical changes in the field – such as the commitment in England to country-wide expansion of children's centres and the *Every Child Matters* agenda – are leading to changes within the qualifications systems. None of these changes, however, seem to be attracting a large number of men into the early childhood professions. In the United Kingdom around 2 per cent of the centre-based early years workforce are male, in Ireland and Malta the proportion is under 1 per cent (Oberhuemer, Schreyer, & Neuman, 2010).

8.5 The Nordic EU Countries: Denmark, Finland, Sweden

In contrast to the fragmented landscapes in the mainly English-speaking countries, the development of qualification routes for early childhood staff in the Nordic EU countries – Denmark, Finland and Sweden – has been contextualised within a co-ordinated approach towards early childhood services. In Sweden this has been under the overall auspices of the Education Ministry, while in Denmark and Finland responsibility lies with the national Social Welfare Ministry – although in Finland there are current moves in many local authorities to transfer this responsibility to the education office at the regional level (Onnismaa, 2009). This has led to a single structure qualification for the core practitioners in early childhood settings, with no dividing lines between "education" and "care", and in all three countries the higher education study route leads to a Bachelor degree (of 3 years' duration in Finland and 3.5 years in Denmark and Sweden). Sweden has the longest tradition, with higher education courses at universities or university colleges starting in 1977, whereas the first university-level study routes in Finland leading to the award of "kindergarten teacher" (*lastentarhanopettaja*) commenced nearly 20 years later, in 1995. All three countries adapted their degree qualifications (BA/MA) to the Bologna requirements at an early stage. However, even in these neighbouring Nordic countries, the focus of the core qualification for work in early childhood settings varies considerably (Oberhuemer, 2009). In Denmark the profile is that of a social pedagogue (*pædagog*) with a broad qualification for social work and pedagogical settings *outside* the education system and *including* early childhood institutions. In Sweden, the focus up to 2001 was on early childhood education and care (0 to 6 years), but since then has been part of a unified approach to teacher education across the pre-school and school system, and early childhood professionals (*lärare för yngre åldrar*) may now also work in pre-school classes and the first grades in school. In Finland, the "kindergarten teacher" is an early childhood professional working both within a social welfare framework in early childhood centres and an education framework in pre-school classes for 6-year-olds.

Among the Nordic EU countries, Denmark has the highest level of graduates in the early years workforce (60 per cent), followed by Sweden (50 per cent) and Finland (around 30 per cent). Auxiliary staff in Sweden are educated/trained at upper-secondary level, whereas in Denmark no specialist qualification is specifically required for those working as assistants, although qualification routes are available once one is employed within the field. In Finland, staff working alongside the "kindergarten teachers" may have a degree-level qualification as social pedagogue, but are more likely to have a post-secondary qualification within the health/care professions. In Finland, it is a requirement for a third of the staff working in any one centre (0 to 7 years) to have a degree-level qualification.

Despite these well-ordered landscapes, a number of reconstructions are either taking place or being discussed. For example, since 2007 in Denmark – the country with the broadest professional profile in Europe – there is now for the first time a compulsory curriculum framework for the *pædagog* profession organised mainly according to areas of learning rather than individual subjects. The introduction of the compulsory curriculum has led to course content for each area becoming more specified at the central level; the demands on the work placements (15 months) have become higher; and the spectrum of arts subjects that may be studied has been reduced. While still adhering to a generalist and broad-based approach, the new curriculum puts more focus on a specific field of work. For example, if students choose to specialise in the early years, they will now spend their third work placement (6 months) in an early years setting and be expected to write a report on that particular field of specialisation (Jensen, 2009). Structural changes have also been taking place: The former 32 higher education colleges (*seminarier*) specialising in social pedagogy have been fused into eight large units and renamed University Colleges (*professionshøjskoler*).

In Sweden, a national evaluation of the unified teacher education/training scheme in operation since 2001, combined with recruitment problems across the education system and particularly for work in the early years, has fuelled debate about the present system of teacher education. Up to 3,600 new recruits will be needed by 2012 in order to combat the shortage of early childhood teachers and maintain the current levels of quality in centres. The fact that the new teacher education profile has resulted in a drop in the number of students wishing to work with young children is a cause for concern among experts in the field (Karlsson Lohmander, 2009). These issues and developments have led to a government proposal to introduce four separate teacher preparation specialisations instead of the current unified approach. Included in the proposals is a reduction in the length of professional study courses for early years teachers from 3.5 years to 3 years; also, they would no longer be able to work in the pre-school classes (in school) for 6-year-olds without an additional one year qualification. Understandably, these proposals are controversial in the field.

In Finland it is also becoming more difficult to recruit graduates with a specific specialisation in early years pedagogy ("kindergarten teachers"), and in some centres there are currently no staff with this qualification – again, a cause for concern in the field. On a more positive note, the Nordic countries have some of the highest participation rates of male workers in Europe, particularly Denmark where 6 per cent of workers in infant-toddler centres, 10 per cent in kindergartens and 12 per cent in age-integrated groups, are men. In Finland and Sweden the percentage of male workers in early childhood provision is 4 and 3 per cent respectively.

8.6 Three Central/Eastern European Countries: Hungary, Slovakia, Slovenia

Three countries have been chosen to illustrate some of the changes taking place in the qualification routes for early childhood professionals in Central and Eastern European countries: Hungary, Slovakia and Slovenia. Whereas the qualifications system in Hungary has developed along clearly divided lines, with specialised and separate qualification routes for work in kindergartens (3–6 years) and infant-toddler centres (0–3 years), the qualification profile for working in the age-integrated centres for 0- to 6-year-olds in Slovenia is that of an early childhood professional with a specialisation in pedagogy across the early years, including work with 7-year-olds in school alongside the first grade teacher. Again, these qualification routes mirror the country-specific system of early years administration: in Hungary it is split between Education (kindergartens) and Health (infant-toddler centres), whereas in Slovenia it is integrated under the auspices of the Ministry of Education. In the Slovak Republic the picture is again different, with kindergartens coming under the responsibility of the Education authorities, but no designated ministry is responsible for the regulation of centre-based provision for under-threes; radical cuts in the early 1990s led to the near extinction of the latter.

The required formal qualification levels also vary. In Slovenia, centre and group leaders are all educated/trained at university for 3 years (ISCED 5A), and kindergarten pedagogues in Hungary at teacher education colleges affiliated with universities (ISCED 5B). However, the requirements are lower for the childcare workers in Hungary (a 3-year post-secondary course, ISCED 4A) and for the kindergarten educators in Slovakia (4-year upper-secondary vocational, ISCED 3A). In Slovakia there are policy proposals to raise the requirement to Bachelor-level, but the target date is not until 2020. At the same time, higher education courses specialising in early childhood education at Magister-level (now MA) have long been established, but these have not been a requirement, and only an estimated 12 per cent of the workforce has this qualification. In higher education circles, both in Hungary and Slovakia, there is some resistance to the Bologna Process largely because of the fear that in introducing higher-level requirements for early years teacher education, the requirements for teacher education in general will be lowered to BA-level instead of remaining at the traditional Magister-level. In terms of work with the under-threes in Hungary, the very low pay levels, and the fact that the training route leads exclusively to work in a highly specialised field, tend to result in low motivation to undertake a higher-level training for this profession; nevertheless, there are discussions about raising the level to ISCED 5 and introducing a BA-level qualification for infant-care workers.

The overall storyline is therefore one of steadily increasing professionalisation of the workforce in these countries. However, it is only Slovenia which has a highly structured career advancement system that enables qualified early childhood pedagogues to progress to different levels of expertise (e.g. as mentor or advisory teacher). Such awards are permanent and do not have to be renewed, and they are accompanied by an increase in pay. Again, this is another region of Europe where there are considerable variations between neighbouring countries in the professional profiles followed and in requirements for work with young children. In all three countries the percentage of male workers in centre-based early childhood provision is below 1 per cent (Oberhuemer, Schreyer, & Neuman, 2010).

8.7 French-Speaking or Partly French-Speaking Countries: Belgium, France, Luxembourg

In France and Belgium there exists a very long tradition of a professionalised workforce for those working in pre-primary education institutions for 2.5-/3- to 6-year-olds (*écoles maternelles*) within the education system prior to compulsory schooling. In both countries, these developments started around 1880, with France still having the highest formal level of qualification requirement for work in pre-primary institutions in Europe (a three year university course, followed by 2 years of postgraduate professional preparation). However, in all three countries, a split system of administrative responsibility for different age groups has led to fractured qualification systems. In France, for those working in the infant-toddler centres outside the education system, qualifications are generally of a high formal level, but traditionally with a focus on healthcare rather than pedagogy. A relatively "new" profession in France, created in 1973, is that of the early childhood educator (*éducatrice/éducateur de jeunes enfants*), a professional qualified to work with children from birth to 7-year-old in diverse settings *outside* the education system. However, compared with the number of teachers in the *écoles maternelles*, this professional group is relatively small, and often with a less well-defined job profile. Nevertheless, the formal requirements are high: professional training takes place at a specialist vocational college and the award is at ISCED 5B-level.

In Luxembourg there has been a steady increase in the formal requirements for working in what is now called the "first cycle of learning" (work with 4- to 6-year-olds in pre-primary education and with 3-year-olds in early education groups) of the restructured *école fondamental* under the 2009 Education Act. However, there is now no specialisation in early childhood education, and preparation for work with these two age-groups is integrated into the 4-year general teacher education courses at BA-level; these include one mandatory semester of studies in another country. Core practitioners working with children outside the education system in childcare

provision under the auspices of the Ministry of Family Affairs are generally qualified at a higher education level in social pedagogy and special needs education.
In Belgium, practitioners working with children in services for the under-threes
are mostly infant-care workers with secondary vocational level education, whereas
the management staff are educators, medical nurses or social workers trained at
Bachelor-level.

The overall picture for these countries is therefore one of high formal requirements across the early childhood period (with the exception of Belgium for work
with under-threes), but with differing professional profiles and specialisations for
work with young children before they reach compulsory schooling age. As in most
other regions of Europe, the percentage of male workers in early childhood provision across these countries is low: 2 per cent in Belgium, and under 1 per cent
in France. In Luxembourg there are also few male teachers in the early education system (1.7 per cent), whereas the proportion of those with a social pedagogy
qualification working with young children outside the education system is higher
(8.6 per cent).

8.8 Radical Reconstructions?

This chapter has attempted to outline some of the current changes taking place
across Europe in the professionalisation strategies for work in early childhood provision and to briefly pinpoint the required qualification profiles across and within
countries. In reviewing these selected features of the ECEC workforce, a mosaic of
very differently shaped component parts has come to light.

The considerable variance in the levels of formal requirements and in the pre-
ferred qualification profiles for work with young children raises questions about the
future directions for workforce development across Europe. What kind of balance
between pedagogy and other disciplines will emerge? What kind of balance will be
pursued between age-focused, specialist and generalist concepts? Will traditional
professional demarcation lines be upheld, despite attempts to create more transparent and flexible qualifications systems? How will new qualifications sit alongside the
more traditional ones? Will new divisions emerge or will there be a move towards
more coherence and consistently high-level requirements? Could the normalising
effects of the Bologna Process also have an emancipatory effect on professional
study routes for work in early years settings? Will parity be reached with primary
school teachers who are mostly trained at Master's level? Will early years pedagogues continue to play the traditionally less prestigious role or be engulfed in a
primary school professionalisation route? Is the gender imbalance in the workforce
here to stay?

The changes taking place in rapidly transforming systems of early education and
care are not radical reconstructions with a clear vision of a desired professional
and workforce profile. The current variations suggest that there is no agreement
across Europe on the competence requirements for working with young children
up to the age of school entry. Furthermore, they imply that there is a need for

continuing research across countries such as that reported in this book, which views diverse country-specific traditions as a starting point for seeking out a "red thread" of common understandings of professionalism in the early years.

References

Barnett, W. S. (2004). Better teachers, better preschools: Student achievement linked to teacher qualifications. *Preschool Policy Matters, 2*. Retrieved July 9, 2009, from http://nieer.org/resources/policybriefs/2.pdf

CWDC (Children's Workforce Development Council). (2008). *Early years professionals: Creating brighter futures*. London: CWDC.

Donnelly, P. (2007). The Republic of Ireland. In M. M. Clark & T. Waller (Eds.), *Early childhood education and care. Policy and practice* (pp. 83–108). London: Sage.

Education, Audiovisual and Culture Executive Agency. (2009). *Tackling social and cultural inequalities through early childhood education and care in Europe*. Brussels: Author. DOI 10.2797/18055.

Hechler, D., & Pasternack, P. (2009). Bologna: Zentral- und Sonderaspekte. Zur anstehenden Reparaturphase der Studienstrukturreform. *Die Hochschule, 18*(2), 6–16.

Jensen, J. J. (2009). *Commissioned excerpts for the State Institute of Early Childhood Research* (SEEPRO project). Aarhus, Unpublished manuscript.

Karlsson Lohmander, M. (2009). *Commissioned excerpts for the State Institute of Early Childhood Research* (SEEPRO project). Gothenburg, Unpublished manuscript.

Kelley, P., & Camilli, G. (2007). *The impact of teacher education on outcomes in center-based early childhood education programs: A meta-analysis*. Retrieved April 4, 2009, from http://nieer.org/resources/research/TeacherEd.pdf

Oberhuemer, P. (2009). Frühpädagogische Ausbildungskonzepte in drei nordischen Ländern. Orientierung für die Weiterentwicklung des Professionsprofils in Deutschland? *Zeitschrift für Erziehungswissenschaft, 12*(4), 651–665. DOI 10.1007/s11618-009-0096-9

Oberhuemer, P., Schreyer, I., & Neuman, M. J. (2010). *Professionals in early childhood education and care systems: European profiles and perspectives*. Opladen & Farmington Hills, MI: Barbara Budrich.

OECD. (2006). *Starting Strong II: Early childhood education and care*. Paris: Author.

OMCYA (Office of the Minister for Children and Youth Affairs). (2009). *Towards a workforce development plan for the early childhood care and education workforce in Ireland*. Retrieved 15 October 2011, from http://www.dcya.gov.ie/viewdoc.asp?fn=/documents/earlyyears/workforce_dev_plan.pdf

Onnismaa, E.-L. (2009). *Commissioned excerpts for the State Institute of Early Childhood Research* (SEEPRO project). Helsinki, Unpublished manuscript.

Siraj-Blatchford, I. (2004). Quality teaching in the early years. In A. Anning, J. Cullen, & M. Fleer (Eds.), *Early childhood education, society and culture* (pp. 137–148). London: Sage.

Chapter 9
Childcare Professionalism in Flanders: An Inside–Outside Perspective

Jan Peeters

9.1 Introduction

Since the 1980s Flemish daycare has been expanding at a great pace. Low-schooled workers, the majority of whom are without any type of preliminary training, are being given the responsibility for very young children for many hours each day. This has led to a policy paradox. Although the quality requirements within the Flemish childcare sector (0–3 years of age), set by central government and parents, have increased sharply over the past 30 years, this has not led to higher qualification requirements; indeed, the reverse is true. Diploma requirements have been abandoned for 80% of the jobs in services for the youngest children, whereas 30 years ago a diploma was required for every job in childcare.

To discover the reasons for the 'de-professionalisation' of childcare within the Flemish community of Belgium, as a member of the Research and Resource Centre for early childhood education and care (ECEC) based at Ghent University, I questioned whether or not this policy paradox was also apparent in other countries and if there were countries that had found a solution. A European Social Fund project was set up with partners inside Belgium and other European countries entitled *Improving Childcare* (Peeters, 2008a). In the context of this European project the Research and Resource Centre sponsored a PhD study *An International Perspective on Professionalism in Childcare in Flanders* (Peeters, 2008b) in which I analysed the policy of the European Union (EU) for professionalism in the early years and conducted a comparative overview study of professionalism in different European countries (France, Germany, Denmark, Luxemburg, Italy, England, the Netherlands, the French Community of Belgium) and in New Zealand. I interviewed 14 academics and trainers from these countries about their policy on professionalism in ECEC. From the analysis of these

J. Peeters (✉)
Department of Social Welfare Studies, Research and Resource Centre for ECE,
B9000 Ghent, Belgium
e-mail: jan.peeters@Ugent.be

L. Miller et al. (eds.), *Early Childhood Grows Up*, International Perspectives on Early Childhood Education and Development 6, DOI 10.1007/978-94-007-2718-2_9, © Springer Science+Business Media B.V. 2012

interviews and an extensive review of relevant literature, four countries – England, France, New Zealand and Denmark – were selected as exemplars of contexts where the government had instigated a coherent policy to upgrade the qualifications and invest in increased professionalism. While the interpretation of the type of professionalism differs in each of these countries, the four different interpretations are especially inspiring for other countries that are in the process of professionalisation.

9.2 The De-professionalisation of Childcare in Flanders (Belgium)

9.2.1 Early Childhood Education and Care in Flanders

In this chapter I focus only on professionalism in the Flemish Community of Belgium rather than the French or German Communities. Since the 1980s, when Belgium decentralised many aspects of governance, the Communities have been responsible for all matters regarding, among others, education, welfare and culture. This means that policy developments in these autonomous Communities may be divergent. Traditionally, these three communities of Belgium have had a split system, with early childhood education for children from 2.5 to 6 years of age (kleuterschool) and childcare for children from 0 to 3 years (kinderopvang). In Flanders, early childhood education is under the responsibility of the Ministry of Education, while childcare is under the responsibility of the Ministry of Family and Welfare. Ninety-eight percent of all children aged 2.5–6 years participate in the early years schools (kleuterschool). These schools are free of charge for parents, whether the schools are private (mainly organised by Catholic organisations) or public (either municipal or state schools), and every child has the right to a place. The young children can stay from 8.30 am until 3.30 pm and there are special out-of-school provisions before and after school hours. All early years teachers have a bachelor's degree granted by University Colleges, which together form part of the University Association. Since the end of the 1990s, an early years teacher has had the same salary as a primary and a secondary teacher; this makes Flanders one of the few jurisdictions in Europe where early childhood teachers earn the same salary as their colleagues who teach adolescents.

There are childcare places (0–3 years) available in the Flemish community for 34.5% of the children. However, since one place may be occupied by more than one child (e.g., part-time attendance), the percentage figure of all children who regularly attend childcare is much higher than available places: 52.2% of children in Flanders regularly use childcare. Since children can go to kleuterschool from 2.5 years, the percentage of children attending ECEC from 0 to 3 years is slightly higher still, namely 61% (Kind en Gezin, 2008). For approximately 80% of all childcare places, the cost to parents is income related (from 2 to 20 Euros).

9.2.2 Childcare: Low Level of Training

The level of training required for working in subsidised daycare centres is lower than the vocational level training available in secondary schools for those aged 16–19 years. The family daycarers (56% of all childcare places) receive a short training course of 5 days, the out-of-school workers follow a course of 225 hours, and in the growing private sector there are no training requirements. Flanders has been criticised by the OECD (2001, 2006) and by UNICEF (2008) for this low level of training for childcare workers. Diploma requirements are being abandoned, and an increasing number of unqualified workers who did not finish secondary school (18 years of age) are finding employment in the sector. The professionalism of child-care in Flanders is characterised by a policy paradox by which the expectations that parents and government have for the profession have increased sharply while the access to the profession is, to an increasing degree, less regulated by diplomas or certificates.

In my doctoral study I showed that this de-professionalisation of the childcare professions in Flanders originated in the 1980s (Peeters, 2008b) when cool, distant and *technical professionalism* based on a *medical-hygienic meta-narrative* entered childcare training courses. This was criticised from within the academic world as well as by parents who were concerned about the distant approach taken with their young children.

9.2.3 Lack of Added Value of Initial Training Course

At the University of Ghent, a counter-movement to the trend towards technical professionalism was instigated in 1979 with the aim of constructing a new inter-pretation of professionalism. It resulted in new regulations in 1983, which included an increase in the requirements with respect to parent participation. The pedagogic aspect also gained importance in new quality requirements included in the new regulations. However, the initial training course – Childcare – at the vocational sec-ondary level, organised by the Department of Education, was not fundamentally adapted, and the medical-hygienic aspect continued to dominate the initial train-ing course and the sector. A study among parents, carried out in the early 1980s (Baeyens, 1984), confirmed that parents were dissatisfied with the *detached care* that went along with this medical-hygienic model within childcare facilities and concluded that they would rather have their children cared for by family daycarers than at childcare centres. The government used this study to permit cheap care by family daycarers – which thus far had been viewed with suspicion because of the lack of training requirements – to grow exponentially. By the late 1980s, the sector was dominated by a 'refresher course' optimism: there was a prevailing conviction within government, among researchers, and among management of childcare facil-ities that the problems of lack of professionalism could be eradicated through short refresher courses. The government promoted refresher courses, on the one hand, for the childcare workers to moderate or adjust their initial medical-hygienic training and, on the other hand, for the family daycarers to provide them with a certain degree of *professionalism.*

In the early 1990s, the government introduced the Scales for the Pedagogic Functioning of the Childcare Centres (Schalen voor het Pedagogisch Functioneren van de Kinderdagverblijven) based on the ITERS scale (Harms, Cryer, & Clifford, 1990) as an auditing tool; this sharply upgraded the quality requirements. It was not until 1997 that the vocational training course Childcare – focusing on the hygienic aspects of care – was reformed and extended by 12 months to make it a course available to 16- to 19-year-olds. As I have documented elsewhere (Peeters, 2008b), this was, however, not sufficient to satisfy the expectations of parents, and of governmental organisations like *Kind en Gezin.* The reform of the training courses was not successful in forming *reflective professionals* who would fulfil the new construction of professionalism as described in the literature. The initial training course – Childcare – was not successful in convincing the parents and the policy makers of its added value and, therefore the importance of an initial training course for a profession with young children was called into question. In consequence, the Flemish childcare sector became stuck in a spiral of de-professionalisation.

9.2.4 No Diploma Requirements for Private Centres

The beginning of the new millennium was characterised by the growth of private commercial daycare centres. In 2001, the Minister of Welfare promoted, via a media campaign, the instigation of private mini-crèches, with the argument that they could be set up without the need to meet training requirements. This campaign from the Welfare Ministry reinforced, in the public opinion, the image that only 'maternal' skills and competencies are important for a job in childcare.

During the following years, the process of de-professionalisation again gained momentum, on the one hand because of the exponential growth of the private for-profit centres, which did not meet diploma-level training requirements, and, on the other hand, by employment projects for low-schooled workers to work in childcare instigated by the Department of Employment and Social Economy.

9.2.5 Poor Working Conditions

Moreover, in the professions working with young children in Flanders, another aspect has been a cause for concern: the working conditions of employees. The two sectors showing little growth, the subsidised childcare centres and family daycare services, have managed to improve working conditions through a salary rise for the educators and better working conditions for the family daycarers. However, the fastest-growing private for-profit sector is a different story. In this sector fragmented, low-quality, poorly paid jobs are being created at a high tempo with many employees being 'illegal-independent workers and personnel without an employee's contract' (Misplon, Hedebouw, & Pacolet, 2004, p. 103) and thus working under conditions that do not comply with their basic social rights. Additionally, there are no training or qualification requirements for this sector and there is little willingness for lifelong learning. The recent OECD (2006) report warned of the negative effect of poor working conditions on the quality of the services: 'Because of poor wages, lack of professional development and long hours, staff turnover can be high and the quality offered to young children clearly inadequate' (p. 216).

9.2.6 The Policy Paradox: High Quality Requirements and De-professionalisation

In the subsidised sector some important progress has been made. The 'quality hand-book' (Vandenbroeck et al., 2009) and the scales for Well-being and Involvement (ECEGO, 2007) offer opportunities to stimulate discussion among parents and childcare workers about what is good quality, and how to implement this joint def-inition of quality in practice. Respect for diversity is also an essential part of the quality system and social inclusion is on the policy agenda of the *Kind en Gezin* (Vandenbroeck et al., 2009).

Over the past 30 years there has been a positive development in Flemish childcare in relation to discourses of quality and social inclusion and related auditing mea-sures among researchers and advocates, but a negative development in the policies that impact the professionalisation of the workforce. This has led to a policy paradox within the sector. Although the quality requirements for childcare facilities set by central government have increased sharply, this has not led to the establishment of higher diploma requirements. On the contrary, the qualification requirements for work in childcare, which provides 80% of all childcare places, have decreased dramatically in the last 30 years (Peeters, 2008b).

9.3 Outcomes of the Comparative Overview

9.3.1 Higher Professionalism in Childcare in Integrated Systems

Authors who have mapped out professionalism within the ECEC systems in Europe and in the OECD countries differentiate between the so-called *split systems* and *integrated systems* (Bennett, 2003; Moss, 2003; Oberhuemer, 2005; Oberhuemer, Schreyer, & Neuman, 2010; OECD, 2006). The split system model, in which child-care for the youngest children (under 3- or 4-year old) and the kindergarten are separate, is a common system in Europe. It exists in Belgium, Bulgaria, Czech Republic, France, Greece, Hungary, Ireland, Italy, Luxemburg, The Netherlands, Poland, Portugal and Romania. By contrast, in Austria, Denmark, England, Finland, Germany, Latvia, Lithuania, Scotland, Slovenia, Spain, and Sweden, as well as in New Zealand, policy makers have developed a system with provision for the youngest children integrated into either the educational system – as in New Zealand, Spain, England, Scotland and Sweden – or a broader 'socio-pedagogic' system, such as in Finland, Germany and Denmark. The integration of childcare into a broader entity assumes an integrated structure and a common approach with respect to access, subsidies, curriculum and personnel (Moss, 2005). Various authors have indicated that this differentiation between a split system and an integrated system has important consequences for the professionalism of the staff members who work with the youngest children (0 to 3–4-year old) (Bennett, 2005; Moss, 2005; Oberhuemer et al., 2010). According to the OECD (2006) report, it is typical in the *split regimes* that highly qualified and well-paid teachers work in the kindergartens, while childcare for 0- to 3-year-olds is undertaken by low-schooled or non-qualified personnel who are paid a great deal less. 'Early childhood educators working closest to the school gate are better trained and rewarded' (OECD, 2006, p. 158), while:

> In services for the younger children, it is difficult to identify across the different countries (with a split system) a core professional who works directly with infants and toddlers. In many countries, childcare services tend to remain hierarchical with a few professionals (often trained nurses) managing the majority auxiliary staff who care for and interact with children. (OECD, 2006, p. 161)

The OECD has identified a tendency to require a bachelor's diploma for those who work with children over the age of three. In some countries such as France, The Netherlands and Ireland, this is the same training as for elementary school teachers. In Belgium, Luxemburg and Greece, the training course for preschool teachers is a specialised one for work with 2.5- to 6-year-old children. The explanation for these low qualifications in childcare is, according to the OECD, the perception that working with the youngest children is limited to physical care; a task that can be carried out by any person without training. According to an OECD calculation, the salaries in the childcare sector (in a split system) are only 50–75% of a teacher's salary.

My analysis carried out as part of my doctoral study (Peeters, 2008b) of the practices and policies in countries belonging to the EU and to the OECD demonstrated that the integration of childcare (0- to 3- and 4-year olds) into the education system (New Zealand), or in a system of social pedagogy (Denmark), has given rise to a process of professionalisation, the demand for higher education and higher salaries. The professionalisation of family daycarers, however, remains a problem, even within integrated systems. The educational level and working conditions of family daycarers are lower in comparison to staff who work in group care.

An exception to the low level of professionalism within group care for the youngest children (0- to 3- and 4-year olds), inherent in the so-called split system countries, is France. The French example of the *éducateur jeunes enfants* (graduate level) demonstrates that it is possible to develop a high degree of professionalism within a split system. Most problems concerning professionalism within this model can be found in the private commercial childcare sector (Moss, 2009). Belgium is a striking example of the negative impact on professionalism of the split system which produces highly qualified workers in kindergarten and a low-schooled workforce in childcare. However, as we have seen in the first part of this chapter, the situation in the Flemish speaking part of Belgium (Flanders) is even worse, with no qualifications requirement at all in the private for-profit sector.

9.3.2 Professionalism Thrives in Communicative Spaces

Dahlberg and Moss (2005) have argued that the professionalisation of organisations thrives in the so-called communicative space where researchers, policy makers and staff work together to develop new knowledge. In all countries where a coherent policy has been developed, there is a clear tradition of the sector, the research world and the policy makers collaborating over long periods of time and in a democratic manner to develop a new type of professionalism. The most inspiring example is New Zealand (May, 2002) where there is a history of the early childhood education sector being in continuous dialogue with policy makers and dedicated researchers, who have made it their objective to collect new knowledge on the interpretation of professionalism. Developments have included an integrated training programme for those working in childcare and kindergarten since 1988, the bicultural curriculum *Te Whāriki*, and the collaborative development of a Code of Ethics in the 1990s (May, Carr, & Podmore, 2004). This successful collaboration reached its pinnacle in 2002 when the government commissioned representatives of the sector – chaired by Dr. Anne Meade – to develop *Pathways to the Future, a ten year strategic plan for early childhood education*. One of the objectives of this strategic plan was to have all staff members in the sector trained to the bachelor's level by the year 2012 (Boyd, 2005; Dalli & Te One, 2003 – see Chapter 7).

The creation of communicative spaces can also take place on a micro level inside ECEC centres, by introducing Utopian thinking, or what Dalli (2008) calls 'discovering what is possible' (p. 17) to increase professionalism. 'Utopian thought is most likely to thrive in spaces which enable thought to take place both beside each other and beside ourselves, listening and keeping open the question of meaning as a subject of debate' (Dahlberg & Moss, 2005, p. 17). Pedagogical mentors or *pedagogistas* can play an important role in the above process and in increasing the professionalism of childcare workers. Galardina (2008) and Peeters (2008b) have separately documented, within the municipal centres of Pistoia (Toscana) and Ghent, that it is possible to bring early childhood workers with a secondary level education towards reflectiveness, when they are supported by *pedagogistas* and pedagogical mentors in an atmosphere of co-operation and open dialogue.

9.3.3 A Reflective Practitioner for Children Under Three

The 1997 OECD report documented a tendency to set up bachelor-level training courses in ECEC. In all of the countries studied at the beginning of 2008 (Peeters,

2008b), with the exception of Belgium and The Netherlands, staff members with a bachelor's diploma worked with the youngest children (0–4 years), or initiatives were being taken to realise this. These graduates are assisted by lower-schooled personnel who generally have a secondary education. A process of professionalisation had begun or was being initiated and the countries were investing in upgrading qualifications and improving working conditions. Countries wishing to introduce professionals with a bachelor's degree must make a choice between a generic and a specialist interpretation of professionalism. In countries with a generic model, such as Denmark, the assistants carry out the same tasks as the graduates; in countries with a specialist vision of professionalism, it is mainly the lower-schooled personnel who take on the care tasks.

In many European and OECD countries the workforce in services for children aged 0–3 consists of approximately one-third staff members with a graduate bachelor's degree, one-third employees with a secondary level education, and one-third untrained personnel. The *Care Work in Europe* research project (Cameron & Moss, 2007) identified a tendency to give non-qualified employees the opportunity for abridged training courses in adult education in order to obtain a qualification through recognising various forms of work-study and earlier-acquired competencies. In this way, those with no qualifications are put on a training path in a three-tier system in which the third-lowest tier (with little or no education) is eventually phased out:

> This effectively rules out the possible use of care work as a means of bringing unqualified workers into employment (i.e., care work as a short-term measure to reduce unemployment) unless some way is found of linking education to the requisite level of qualification to the process. (Cameron & Moss, 2007, p. 145)

The graduate training courses in France, Denmark and New Zealand (Peeters, 2008a) and a number of Early Years Foundation Degrees in England (Miller, 2008) prepare students to be reflective practitioners who must be capable of constructing practical new knowledge. Within the training course *éducateur jeunes enfants*, the method of the *analyse des pratiques* is inspiring because it utilises practical experience to develop new theoretical pedagogical insights (Favre, 2004). The training course in these countries that we studied (Peeters, 2008a) is always based on the vision of the competent child. The vision in the *pedagog* training course in Denmark, teacher training in New Zealand, and the course that trains the *éducateur jeunes enfants* leans heavily on an image of the child providing his/her own interpretation of the world around them and in which the child is able to steer their own learning process. In these countries, we see methods develop in which reflection on practice steers the learning process (reflective practice cycle, *analyse de pratiques*). In the training courses in France and Denmark, this is taken a step further by also including the mentoring of low-schooled employees in the curriculum of the bachelor's training course. The interpretation of professionalism of the *pedagog* – or the *éducateur jeunes enfants* – encompasses the support of low-schooled assistants in the work-study programme.

9.3.4 More Vertical and Horizontal Mobility

The countries with a coherently developed system of professionalism have invested a great deal in expanding the possibilities for vertical and horizontal mobility, within all the professions dealing with young children. The most extensively developed model in this area is the Integrated Qualifications Framework in England, which in theory offers the possibility to move upward from the lowest level of unschooled jobs to the most highly qualified jobs in ECEC. However, horizontal mobility is also of essential importance in making jobs attractive and in avoiding shortages in the labour market in the future. The English model of professionalism, which encompasses a *common core* for all professions dealing with children, is one way to make the profession more attractive in the future by offering more opportunities for horizontal mobility (CWDC, 2006).

France has succeeded in developing a qualification structure that is simple and transparent. Non-qualified target group staff members can enter the childcare sector and follow a *contract de qualification* that can lead to a diploma of *auxiliaire de puériculture* or to a graduate degree *éducateur jeunes enfants*. The *éducateur jeunes enfants* training course is also an inspiring example because the mentoring of non-qualified staff members, via the method of the *analyse de pratique*, has been included in the competency profile (Ministère de l'Emploi, 2005).

9.3.5 A 'Reflective Practitioner' Presumes a High Degree of Autonomy

Being a reflective practitioner presumes a high degree of autonomy. There are some notable differences in the leeway for autonomy allowed by the early childhood education curriculum of various countries. The English framework provides limited autonomy and remains strongly controlled by national regulations. The French professional profile for *éducateur jeunes enfants* uses, in the description of the functions, the verbs: *établir, élaborer, mettre en oeuvre, concevoir et conduire* (develop, explore, conceptualise, create, guide), which indicate that the *éducateur jeunes enfants* graduate is not a technical executor of a curriculum or a quality handbook, but someone who interprets his/her task in an autonomous and creative manner (Ministère de l'Emploi, 2005).

Denmark provides its *pedagog* with the largest amount of autonomy. The work of the *pedagog* must be guided by a number of crucial pedagogic principles, but it is the individual *pedagog* who must contextualise these general principles (BUPL, 2006). Their professional expertise is based on personal competencies and on an awareness of the individual's own norms and values. The expertise of the *pedagog* encompasses both theoretical and practical knowledge of the development of children including play, friendships and conflicts between children (Jensen & Langsted, 2004). The New Zealand system is inspiring because the *Te Whāriki* curriculum creates a general framework within which each teacher can provide his/her own interpretation. *Te Whāriki* formulates general principles in relation to diversity between the children, the parents, and the practitioner which can be individually interpreted (Carr & Rameka, 2005; see also Chapter 7).

9.4 Conclusion: Breaking the Cycle; The Construction of a New Profession in Flanders

By collaborating together with different actors in the European *Improving Childcare* project (Peeters, 2008a), a broad consensus was developed about the need for increasing the qualifications of the workers in the Flemish childcare sector. Several actions were undertaken to persuade policy makers in Flanders of the need for higher qualifications in this field: three conferences on professionalism were organised; two books and several articles were published; a media campaign was set up; and, in personal contacts with policy makers, the need was stressed for a comprehensive approach to increase the qualifications of the childcare workforce. In those actions the results of the international comparison were taken into account. Yet, at present, there is significant lack of political will to integrate Flemish childcare in the socio-pedagogical sector or in the education system. Instead, different policy makers have opted for more professionalisation within a split system (French model), with a bachelor's degree specialisation for the youngest children and more vertical mobility for the low-qualified workers.

9.4.1 A New Bachelor Degree and a Focus on Pedagogical Mentoring

In 2008, the governmental organisation *Kind en Gezin*, which was a partner of the European project *Improving Childcare*, took the initiative to create a communicative space in the form of a working group of researchers, policy makers and representatives of the sector to develop a new licence system with the same quality criteria and qualification requirements for all forms of childcare, be they private or subsidised (Vandenbroeck et al., 2009). The new Flemish Government, which was installed in September 2009, was also convinced that the sector had to be restructured and started preparing a new decree on childcare. In this legislative work much attention was given to the professionalisation of the workforce. One of the measures proposed is the introduction of a pedagogical mentor for independent family daycarers and small private daycare centres. These pedagogical mentors can play an important role in helping ECEC workers to construct new pedagogical knowledge in an atmosphere of co-operation and open dialogue.

The group that was involved in the European *Improving Childcare* project took several initiatives in collaboration with the governmental organisation *Kind en Gezin* that can play an important role within the new legislation. A blended learning training programme (e-learning in combination with group trainings) for family daycarers was set up in collaboration with the schools for adult education. The same group also developed a recruitment selection instrument for family daycarers. This instrument helps the family daycare services to gather relevant information about candidates to aid the selection procedure.

In addition, the governmental organisation *Kind en Gezin* has developed a competence profile for a bachelor degree *Pedagogy of the young child* in Flanders, inspired by recent studies documenting the need for such a qualification (Peeters, 2008a, 2008b) and explicitly referring to the growing stream of scholarly literature documenting the link between staff qualifications and quality of care and education (e.g., Fukkink & Lont, 2007; OECD, 2006; UNICEF, 2008). The aim of the bachelor degree level training is to construct a professionalism based on abilities, competencies and qualities to meet complex demands in particular contexts.

Two options have been under discussion: the first is to embed such a bachelor degree in the training of students in social work. The French example of *éducateur jeunes enfants* is a good example of how this may lead to reflexive practitioners, valuing the social functions of childcare, without jeopardising its educational mission (Peeters, 2008a). The other option is to embed the bachelor training within the existing bachelor programme in early childhood education, focusing on the *kleuterschool* or *école maternelle*. In May 2010, two schools for higher education (one in Ghent and one in Brussels) obtained permission to start offering this bachelor degree qualification in 2012. One of the schools for higher education is part of a teacher training college (offering training to preschool teachers), the other is linked to the Department of Social Work and Health. Yet both institutions are attempting to develop a broad integrated model of professionalism linked to other social and child professions. One of the institutions has set up a project with schools of *éducateur jeunes enfants* in France about the method of *analyse de pratique*. In so doing, the tertiary institution aims at educating reflexive practitioners with a high degree of autonomy, able to construct new pedagogical knowledge.

Another goal of the new bachelor degree will be to support low-qualified workers from disadvantaged groups into learning pathways that enable them to obtain qualifications in adult education.

In 2010, the *Kind en Gezin* took the initiative to evaluate the *Childcare* course offered at secondary level. Two communicative spaces were set up: one with representatives of the schools organising the initial training courses; and one with representatives of the childcare sector. The problem of the lack of added value of this course was openly discussed and it is hoped that this may lead to a reform of this initial training course.

9.4.2 A New Decree on Childcare

In conclusion, the European project *Improving Childcare* has played an important role in breaking the cycle of de-professionalisation in the childcare sector in the Flemish Community of Belgium. Over a period of 5 years, different actors were brought together – policymakers, researchers and practitioners – to collaborate on the issues of professionalisation of the childcare workforce. They succeeded in setting up different initiatives that might lead to the construction of a new profession. It needs to be noted that the work of this group was to a large extent included in the new decree on childcare (Decreet Kinderopvang). Nevertheless, there may also be a downside to this story. Like in many countries, the financial global crisis has had a major impact on the policy of the Flemish Government. In the recent budgetary discussion, childcare is one of the few sectors that received additional funds, and is not subject to budget cuts. Yet these additional funds are in essence limited to increasing the number of available places, rather than improving the quality of existing places. Hopefully there will be enough political will to finance the necessary measures to break the cycle of de-professionalisation, so that the work on the construction of a new profession can continue.

References

Baeyens, A. (1984). *Uitbouw van de kinderopvang in de Vlaamse Gemeenschap.* Brussel: Ministerie van de Vlaamse Gemeenschap, Administratie voor Gezin en Maatschappelijk Welzijn.

Bennett, J. (2003). Starting Strong, the persistent division between care and education. *Journal of Early Childhood Research, 1*(1), 21–48.

Bennett, J. (2005). Democracy and autonomy get an early start. *Children in Europe, 5*(9), 2–3.

Boyd, R. (2005). Creating change: New Zealand's early childhood strategy. In D. Reale (Ed.), *Learning with other countries: International models of early education and care* (pp. 22–25). London: Day Care Trust.

BUPL. (2006). *The work of the pedagogue: Roles and tasks.* Copenhagen: BUPL.

Cameron, C., & Moss, P. (2007). *Care work in Europe: Current understandings and future directions.* London: Routledge.

Carr, M., & Rameka, L. (2005). Weaving an early childhood curriculum. *Children in Europe, 5*(2), 8–9.

CWDC. (2006). *Clear progression. Towards an integrated qualifications framework.* Leeds: CWDC.

Dahlberg, G., & Moss, P. (2005). *Ethics and politics in early childhood education.* London: Routledge.

Dalli, C. (2008). Early childhood teachers in New Zealand. *Children in Europe, 15*(2), 16–17.

Dalli, C., & Te One, S. (2003). Early childhood education in 2002: Pathways to the future. *New Zealand Annual Review of Education, 12*, 177–202.

ECEGO-Expertisecentrum Ervaringsgericht Onderwijs KU Leuven. (2007). *Werken aan kwaliteit vanuit het kinderperspectief: welbevinden en betrokkenheid als richtsnoeren. Eindverslag.* Leuven: ECEGO-KU Leuven.

Favre, D. (2004). Quelques réflexions de formateur sur l'analyse des pratiques professionnelles en secteur petite enfance. In D. Fablet (Ed.), *Professionnel(le)s de la petite enfance et analyse de pratiques* (pp. 17–38). Paris: L'Harmattan.

Fukkink, R. G., & Lont, A. (2007). Does training matter? A meta-analysis and review of caregiver training studies. *Early Childhood Research Quarterly, 22*, 294–311.

Galardina, A. (2008). Pedagogistas in Italy. *Children in Europe, 15*(2), 16–21.

Harms, T., Cryer, D., & Clifford, R. M. (1990). *Infant/toddler environment rating scale.* New York: Teachers College, Columbia University.

Jensen, J., & Langsted, O. (2004). Dänemark: Pädagogische Qualität ohne nationales Curriculum. In W. Fthenakis & P. Oberhuemer (Eds.), *Frühpädagogik internatonal, Bildungsqualität im Blickpunkt* (pp. 119–208). Wiesbaden: Verlag für Sozialwissenschaften.

Kind en Gezin. (2008). *The child in Flanders*. Brussels: Kind en Gezin.

May, H. (2002). Early childhood care and education in Aotearoa, New Zealand: An overview of history, policy and curriculum. *McGill Journal of Education*. http://findarticles.com/p/articles/mi_qa3965/is_200201/ai_9046141 14 januari 2008

May, H., Carr, M., & Podmore, V. (2004). Te Whäriki: Neuseelands frühpädagogisches Curriculum 1991–2001. In W. Fthenakis & P. Oberhuemer (Eds.), *Frühpädagogik International* (pp. 175–189). Wiesbaden: Verlag für Sozialwissenschaften.

Miller, L. (2008). Developing new professional roles in the early years. In L. Miller & C. Cable (Eds.), *Professionalism in the early years* (pp. 20–30). Abingdon. Hodder: Arnold.

Ministère de l'Emploi, de la Cohésion Sociale et du Logement. (2005). *Diplôme d'Etat d'Educateur de jeunes enfants: Les textes, le métier, la formation, les épreuves de certification*. Paris: Berger-Levrault.

Misplon, S., Hedebouw, G., & Pacolet, J. (2004). *Financiële leefbaarheid van de minicrèches*. Leuven: Hoger Instituut voor de Arbeid.

Moss, P. (2003). Getting beyond childcare: Reflections on recent policy and future possibilities. In J. Brannen & P. Moss (Eds.), *Rethinking children's care* (pp. 25–43). Buckingham: Open University Press.

Moss, P. (2005). *Learning from other countries*. Policy Papers. No 4. London: Day Care Trust.

Moss, P. (2009). *There are alternatives! Markets and democratic experimentalism in early childhood education and care*. The Hague: Bernard van Leer Foundation.

Oberhuemer, P. (2005). Conceptualising the early pedagogue: Policy approaches and issue of professionalism. *European Early Childhood Education Research Journal, 13*(1), 5–16.

Oberhuemer, P., Schreyer, I., & Neuman, M. (2010). *Professionals in early childhood education and care systems*. Opladen & Farminghton Hills: Barbara Budrich.

OECD. (1997). *The future of female dominated professions*. Paris: OECD.

OECD. (2001). *Starting Strong, early childhood education and care*. Paris: OECD.

OECD. (2006). *Starting Strong II, early childhood education and care*. Paris: OECD.

Peeters, J. (2008a). *The construction of a new profession: A European perspective on professionalism in early childhood education and care*. Amsterdam: SWP.

Peeters, J. (2008b). *De Warme Professional, begeleid(st)ers kinderopvang construeren professionaliteit*. Gent: Academia Press.

UNICEF Innocenti Research Centre. (2008). *Report Card 8. The child care transition*. Florence: UNICEF.

Vandenbroeck, M., Pirard, F., & Peeters, J. (2009). New developments in Belgian childcare policy and practice. *European Early Childhood Education Research Journal, 17*(3), 408–416.

Chapter 10
A Need, a Desire, a Shared Responsibility: Professional Development for a New Public Education

Irene Balaguer Felip
Introduction by Mathias Urban

10.1 Introduction

> I am completely persuaded of the importance, the urgency, of the democratization of the public school, and of the ongoing training of its educators, among whom I include security people, cafeteria personnel, and custodians, and so on. Their formation must be ongoing and scientific. Nor should it fail to instil a taste for democratic practices, among which should be an ever more active intervention on the part of educants and their families as to which direction the school is going. (Paolo Freire, 2004, p. 14)

It is unlikely that Paolo Freire knew about the seven Catalonian teachers, working in a parent–teachers' collective, who, in 1965, founded a professional association to realise their vision of a reformed and truly democratic public school in a country that was suffering badly from decades of fascist dictatorship and religious oppression. But it is not hard to imagine that the Barcelona-based *Associacío de Mestres Rosa Sensat* is exactly the kind of project that Freire had in mind when he wrote *Pedagogy of Hope*. *Rosa Sensat* describes itself as a 'movement for pedagogical renovation that works for the common interest of improving education', aiming at:

- the dissemination of pedagogical theories and practices which aim at the global development of children and are deeply rooted in respect for the child's personality and his freedom, and the promotion of the child's active participation in his own learning process
- the ongoing training of teachers, grounded both on experimentation and in theory, and developed through individual and collective reflection
- the pursuit of a public and democratic school, deeply inbred in the country's reality, with all its members, teachers, families and students actively engaged in its daily management and on the definition of its pedagogical line. (Associacío de Mestres Rosa Sensat, 2010b)

I. Balaguer Felip (✉)
Associació de Mestres Rosa Sensat, 08001 Barcelona, Spain
e-mail: irenebalaguer@rosasensat.org

L. Miller et al. (eds.), *Early Childhood Grows Up*, International Perspectives on Early Childhood Education and Development 6, DOI 10.1007/978-94-007-2718-2_10, © Springer Science+Business Media B.V. 2012

Rosa Sensat hosted the first summer school (Escola d'Estiu) after the Spanish Civil War in 1966, founding a tradition that continues until today. In 1968 the first pre-school (Escola Bressol) for children of age 0–3 was founded in Barcelona and, in the same year, *Rosa Sensat* began to organise training for early childhood educators.

All of *Rosa Sensat's* activities have been, and are, guided by a strong commitment to democratic education, to promoting freedom and to valuing the Catalan culture.

Throughout this book we have discussed professional early childhood practices as deeply embedded in the social, cultural and political realities of society. We have conceptualised professionalism as 'systemic' (Urban, 2007) and discussed the need for what we have called a 'critical ecology of the profession'. Our proposed conceptualisation of professional practice in early childhood rejects notions of education as technology, delivering predetermined outcomes regardless of context and without consideration of the lived experiences of children, families, communities and practitioners. Instead, we argue in a tradition of critical theorists and educators (e.g., Deleuze, 2001; Freire, 1970, 1998, 2004; Freire & Freire, 2007; Habermas, 1990) that there is no default option in professional early childhood practice. On the contrary, our practices – and understandings of practices – are the result of choices we make and stances we take as citizens, educators and researchers alike. Early childhood education takes place in the public sphere and, inevitably, is a fundamentally ethical and political practice (Dahlberg & Moss, 2005).

We are delighted that Irene Balaguer from *Rosa Sensat's* executive committee has contributed to our discussion because the association and its people clearly demonstrate what it means to realise systemic, ethical and political professional practice under most difficult circumstances. The history, value base and actual practice of this initiative *for practitioners by practitioners* show that there is no such a thing as apolitical education. As early as 1975, still under fascist dictatorship but with a future democratic society in mind, *Rosa Sensat* developed a document entitled *For a new public school system*. The plea for democratic reform and public responsibility was renewed in 2005, in a revised declaration *For a new public education* (Per una nova educació pública) (Associacío de Mestres Rosa Sensat, 2010a). This document argues for education in a democratic society as a shared experience, a 'process in the co-construction of identity, knowledge and values between democratic subjects who think for themselves' (Associacío de Mestres Rosa Sensat, 2006, p. 2).

Professionals, who *think for themselves* – with a critically ecological professionalism that is aware of the political and social realities that shape knowledge and practices, aiming at transforming education towards more equitable and just experiences for all – this is very much what this book is about. The ways we *talk* about our practices are active agents, argues Michel Foucault (1972). Discourses, he writes, are practices that systematically form what they are speaking about. Paolo Freire (1970) explains the importance and emancipatory force of developing one's own language in order to overcome both external and *internalised* oppression. It is more than symbolic, from this point of view, that we, as editors of this book, present *Rosa Sensat's* account below in the format chosen by the author, even though it deviates from the conventional format of academic writing.

10.2 A Need, a Desire, a Shared Responsibility: Professional Development for a New Public Education

Education is, in my view, a complex issue and hence it is difficult to set up or design a single model, a way of addressing it in its entirety. I should, therefore, mention that this contribution has a double bias, one due to the sector and the other, personal. It is well known that in Spain, as well as in many other countries, the most concerned teachers, the ones who are most interested in updating their training, are nursery school teachers, although I can't say to what this eagerness to learn that characterises professionals of this first stage of education might be attributed. As for the bias in the personal sphere, this is due to the fact that this chapter is based on the action-reflection on the education that I have had the opportunity to develop over the course of the years.

Over the last 20 years, governments in Spain have invested more than ever in teacher training. Training opportunities that can be taken up can possibly be counted in their thousands while teachers who have had the chance to undertake some kind of training are perhaps in their millions.

It should be asked if the educational reality of the country has improved in the same proportion as the investment made – and in what way it has improved. It would also be interesting to know if the investment has led to teachers becoming more interested in their daily tasks and what kind of innovations have been introduced in schools.

In this regard, certain points arise that may perhaps be of interest or use when considering training in general.

10.2.1 A First Point: Continuous Training

Nowadays nobody in any profession or trade would cast doubts on the need for continuing education in any field of knowledge. In the twenty-first century the concept of life-long learning highlights the extent to which in our times we share the idea that keeping up-to-date is necessary in all professions. It would seem, then, to be quite a widely acknowledged idea.

> But to what degree are professionals in education – at nursery, primary, secondary or university level – convinced that they need ongoing training?
>
> If no one in our profession casts any doubt on the idea of life-long learning, why do so many of them *not* feel this need?
>
> To what degree does feeling this need or not relate to the initial training received and to the ongoing training received?
>
> Is guaranteeing the opportunity of ongoing training enough?
>
> Or is the real crux of this training that it contributes to feeling the need to keep on training, to keep on questioning yourself, to keep on learning?
>
> How does one go about offering a training that generates a greater need to undergo more training?

10.2.2 A Second Point: Participation

The idea underlying any training is to give a central role to the teacher. Participation could possibly be a key element in generating new dynamics in training.

It could perhaps also be said in this regard that a consensus, indeed even unanimity, exists. Nowadays, nobody would deny that training should be co-ordinated with the participation of the teachers themselves. International bodies recommend it, governmental organisations have turned it into a basic principle and teachers continue to demand it.

But it is also possible to pose some questions from this perspective:

Who decides what training to develop and how?

How many ways can be imagined to make participation something real?

How can participation be organised, set up and directed?

Who listens to and who represents the professionals?

Should this training be individual, or in a team, or indeed in teams?

If there are limits to the number of participants in the teams, what should they be?

Could participation have any relation to proposals for change, doubts and concerns in education?

10.2.3 A Third Point: Theory and Practice

Another key element in teacher training is the coherence between theory and practice. In other words, a theory that inspires a practice and a practice that builds new theories and that, in this very simple yet simultaneously very complex way, can transform the reality, the profession of those involved in creating new education.

How can this dialogue be co-ordinated?

How can the so-called theoretical world be brought closer to the practical world?

How can the practical world inspire the theoretical world?

Who is paying attention to both these possible worlds of pedagogical construction in order to be able to relate them to each other?

How can this encounter be made visible?

How far can communication technologies today facilitate this encounter?

How could a network of permanent exchange between these two worlds be co-ordinated?

What policies would be needed so that practices and theories construct new realities and new paradigms?

10.2.4 A Fourth Point: Format and Content of Training Programmes

Generally speaking, the design of training programmes conforms to the traditional – the classical – both in planning and in theme. The generalised format is that of courses in which a traditional outline is reproduced – in which one person knows and talks and the others listen and take notes. This description is no doubt a caricature but it does also correspond to the majority of training programmes offered to teachers, at least in Spain. Why? Because most of us tend to reproduce that with which we are most familiar.

The training contents are largely defined by the priorities of the education authorities or, in some instances, by the gaps detected in the sector. With this method of proceeding, a few recurrent and, in my view, unifying, themes stand out in the analysis of the training contents of the last few years: the curriculum, the programming, the reading/writing and, more recently, the management and direction of centres, conflicts and resolutions, ethical values, immigration and integration and emotions. From our point of view, these topics are all tackled with a complete ignorance of education, nursery school and childhood development at these ages, or with an out-moded vision of them.

So at this juncture, new questions arise:

How can new ideas of childhood, education and nursery school education be realised if they are not reflected in the offerings of ongoing training?

To what extent is this dynamic of training contributing to reinforcing the traditional idea of pre-school for the education of 3–6-year-olds with the consequent prioritising of this stage?

What significance might the inexistence of the offering of ongoing training, comparable to that provided for other teachers, have for nursery school teachers?

10.2.5 A Fifth Point: The Connection Between Education and Promotion

The extensive experience of these years leads me to a troubling analysis of the connection between training and promotion. Although I understand the positive intention on which this association is based, I disagree with it.

In practice, in order to be able to evaluate whether the association between training and promotion has contributed positively to education, it is imperative that we go into its results, effects and defects in depth, so that we can redirect this association should it prove not to have made these contributions.

To carry out such an evaluation, and purely by way of suggestion, I would propose a few ideas or questions:

What is the average profile of those gaining access to the opportunities of ongoing training: classroom teachers, directors, advisors? In particular, how many male teachers are there, and how many female?

What kind of changes have they introduced, after their training, to their daily practice at school?

In what ways have their relationships to the children, families and their colleagues changed after the training?

What has brought more satisfaction to the teachers: the training or the promotion?

There is another concern that I share with teachers in other countries, who, like me, struggle with the implications of the connection between training and promotion: that it blurs the boundaries between the aims to improve educational practice on the one hand, and the evaluation of professionals on the other.

Their experience also proves that these incentives do not bring the effects desired, either from a pedagogical perspective or from the perspective of professional satisfaction or self-confidence. This evaluation has led to a rethinking of the topic in many countries, which I would like to see here.

10.2.6 A Final Point

On what realistic foundation is the training of teachers based?

In our profession, lived experience within and beyond educational institutions has as much, if not more, importance than specific professional training in shaping who we become as educators. In contrast to other professions, in the teaching profession each of us has some previous knowledge of education that is very firmly rooted, consciously or unconsciously. This is the knowledge of the school we went to. We should all be aware of this reality in order to be able to think about what training proposals could allow us in a calm, considered and unstrident way, to advance towards the changes that education in the present century requires.

10.3 An Experience: the *Rosa Sensat* Teachers' Association

In this second section, I propose to provide an initial analysis of our experience at the *Rosa Sensat* Teachers' Association as an example of a structure of long-term ongoing training carried out in a constant and persistent way for more than 40 years.

The *Rosa Sensat* Teachers' Association was born of a desire, a hope, a shared responsibility. It initially emerged from the experience of a group of several teachers keen to recover an active, secular, democratic school and to experience a school different to that imposed by 40 years of dictatorship; a group of professionals that always focused on the importance of education as a motor of change in society. The experience began in 1965 with a few teachers around the kitchen table of a private home and over the years it has had a transcendental influence on the development of schools, education and the Spanish teaching profession.

The task of these teachers was always shared by many other people: parents, artists, intellectuals, men and women of letters, relevant personalities in the worlds of culture and the sciences brought their contributions to the training of the teachers that came to *Rosa Sensat* for a theoretical and practical training that now celebrates 45 years of existence.

Forty-five years of work training teachers, however, could be an important figure or not. For me, as for many others who have had the fortune to be involved in this institution, the main point is not the years of work, but the way of working with and for teachers.

So, the experience of *Rosa Sensat* in teacher training is a story of a permanent challenge: that of a private institution with ongoing dedication to serving the public. *Rosa Sensat* has always had the desire to create or invent a training scheme that could spread the will to gather and unite teachers, starting from an institution open to the public, but, far from centralising the training, this scheme could manage to generate independence. It is a way of working that has generated and still generates interest among experts from many countries: what is routine in *Rosa Sensat* is enviable for many colleagues in many countries.

Today, after 45 years, *Rosa Sensat* is basically a movement of teachers that have faith in childhood, in education and in school, and who know that together they can improve education. A Utopia? A reality.

10.4 Summer Schools

The *Rosa Sensat* Summer School is perhaps its best internationally known activity. Of what does it consist? For 2 weeks in July, teachers from all over the place congregate at the Summer School for training, to share experiences and to learn, and they do so voluntarily and during their holidays.

The big question is, of course, what does the Summer School have that enables it to remain attractive and able to unite so many teachers, even within a context which is saturated with free courses and training possibilities funded by the education authorities both during the working day and in many cases, in the centre itself . . . Wonderful! But teachers continue to go to the Summer School during holidays, in their own time, and they continue to pay for it.

I will highlight just four of the elements that perhaps make the *Rosa Sensat* Summer School somewhat different and interesting for teachers:

1. Its organisation – the Summer School is designed for teachers who are at school every day. It is a horizontal organisation, closely tied into reality, in which reflection and pedagogic activity are combined with culture and educational policy.

2. Its contents – they vary from the grand challenges that real life imposes on education and the small questions of daily life at school. The macro and the micro are equally valued and considered, the practice and the theory meld in a co-ordinated tandem of interdisciplinary knowledge. Thus, teachers and neurologists, paediatricians, architects, gardeners, musicians and mathematicians, to cite a few examples, contribute their perspectives to transform reality.

3. In nursery school education, a third element characterises the contents of the *Rosa Sensat* Summer School: the openness, the observing and listening to everything relevant that takes place outside the country. This stance has allowed thousands of teachers to meet big international figures and converse with them: Judit Falk and Anna Tardos from Hungary; Constance Kamii from the United States; Elinor Goldschmied and Peter Moss from the United Kingdom; Claus Jensen, Ole Largs and Jytta Juul Jensen from Denmark; as well as the ongoing and tight collaboration with Italy, with Loris Malaguzzi and the Reggio Emilia team, with Anna Lia Galardini, Sonia Iozzelli, Penny Richster, Aldo Fortunatti, Francesco Tonnucci and many, many others . . . .

4. Its style – one of freedom, of dedication, enthusiasm, complicity, sharing, of continuing to work to go into more depth throughout the year, to know one is being listened to and appreciated, to be able to generate new ideas and new initiatives.

An exceptional activity takes place during the Summer School. As well as the theoretical and practical courses, the workshops and work groups, debates, seminars and pedagogical lectures, the Summer School includes what is called the *General Topic*. This is a series of debate–conferences headed by experts in different fields which centre each year around a topic of interest for education, school and professionals. The General Topic is faithful to the objectives of the Summer School; as a movement of pedagogical renewal, it aims to insert education, teachers and school into the society to which they belong and thereby jointly advance the changes through which society also moves. The General Topic is another contribution to the ongoing training of teachers in continual dialogue with professionals from other disciplines who share the common desire to improve education and school.

The influence of the General Topic is undeniable. Various declarations of great significance to education in Spain have arisen from it as fruit of the pedagogical debate. A clear example is the declaration *For a new public education*, a compendium resulting from the General Topic of 1995 – in commemoration of the Summer School's 40-year anniversary – which renewed the Association's commitment to school and teachers and summarised a way of understanding education, school and society.

Finally, it should be added that *Rosa Sensat* is not just a Summer School. The Association edits various magazines and collections of books, organises trips and studio visits and offers other courses during the year. Groups of teachers and various associations meet in the Association and work groups and regular seminars develop their work there. The Association also has a library specialising in peda-gogy with more than 50,000 volumes and an important historical collection of books and magazines.

10.5 Some Ideas or Directions in Which to Be Able to Continue Working and Exploring

The experience of *Rosa Sensat* and the points raised in the first part of this chapter come together in a final challenge: that of looking at and listening in some way to real life and questioning ourselves about it in order to rethink training.

Additionally, the marvellous constellation of events that occur every day in a nursery school allows us to become familiar with two basic elements of educational practice: the real complexity of lived experience and the diversity of responses or actions in the face of this complexity, each of them valid and coherent.

There are also numerous proposals for initial and ongoing training, but they all present us with a challenge, a change of procedure; they demand flexibility from us, as well as creativity, imagination, dynamism and adaptability. They require our commitment; they tell us that change is necessary.

10.5.1 Pedagogy and policy ought to act in a co-ordinated way

There are experiences of great pedagogical significance throughout Spain and Europe that could contribute to transforming nursery school education. To meet the challenge of new ongoing training schemes, actions must be directed towards those experiences that give rise to real pedagogical renewal; experiences which, in Spain at least, too often encounter difficulties in being able to develop their projects. It is from this perspective that the policy of all education authorities should incorpo-rate changes in their administrative activity in order to sustain and favour these new realities with measures such as:

- Designing and establishing new ways to access schools that favour and nur-ture the creation of teams. The challenge that ongoing training poses cannot be developed by individual action, it requires cohesion and the stability of teams of teachers. So from this perspective of complexity and multiple actions, the neces-sary measures have to be taken by the administration to make a school in which the ability to debate and share projects and experiences is viable.
- Facilitating and fostering the autonomy of each nursery school with the aim of guaranteeing that each acquires its own identity and personality.
- Keeping an eye on and controlling the increase of teachers or, to put it in another way, the lowering of ratios to the benefit of a more personalised treatment of boys and girls within the possibility of developing a new pedagogy.

- Guaranteeing all nursery school staff time for training within their working schedule. In order to be able to undergo ongoing training, time is needed for working in groups, time for research activity and time to explore further in order to benefit a common project.

10.5.2 A flexible and dynamic structure

It is increasingly evident that consolidated structures, rather than facilitating new dynamics, tend to become bureaucratic and inflexible and impede the agility necessary to respond to the changes that the rapid transformation of reality throughout the world imposes.

With this in mind, it is increasingly evident that network structures guarantee the flexibility and dynamism needed to co-ordinate the existing multiple realities: A network structure to escape from routine, from the traditional, the habitual, from the known, from what the safety of ignorance brings with it. Within this network structure, challenges and questions should be posed, and uncertainty, curiosity, the desire to discover, share, compare, debate, redefine, and investigate should be generated.

Such a training activity requires the group, in order to understand that which is different, to have the possibility of contrasting or comparing distinct realities, different stories, different cultures, diverse theories and practices, their coherence or incoherence, their familiarity or strangeness, and their conditioning factors. A network structure would also contribute to opening a world of possibilities about what choices can be made and would restructure its own practice and theory.

A network structure would also be able to drive the co-ordination between experiences in an effective and agile way and facilitate its work; a network of pedagogical co-ordination in which the teacher, chosen by his or her colleagues for a period of time, co-ordinates a few schools that share a project or that belong to the same area and wish to form part of the network.

The educational authorities would need to facilitate the necessary ongoing training to teachers who, for a period of time, develop this task of co-ordination, a task that has to guarantee a double condition: a period of time sufficient to be able to go forward with the task, and their return to school.

10.5.3 Rethinking promotion

To make ongoing training desirable, two parameters could be considered to promote it: first, that in the initial training the interest in continuing to learn is awakened in teachers. The initial training should therefore combine self-discipline and self-confidence. Secondly, that teachers need to have the opportunity to get to know what teachers throughout Europe do, throughout the world if possible, wherever interesting pedagogical activities are developed. Clearly, this way of doing things will open up endless possibilities, stimuli and new interests for them.

I am aware that this second parameter may seem idealistic, without a practical, realistic basis, but my experience of decades as a nursery school teacher allows me to propose it, as I have been able to see that enthusiasm is more contagious than obligation or credits to achieve work promotions, particularly if the aim of the ongoing training is that it introduce changes in everyday reality.

So, the teaching profession cannot base itself on *received credits* but on practical innovatory practices. Nursery school teachers who are in tune with this other way of understanding the profession are cheerful, happy and spread their eagerness to improve to those around them. These teachers should be recognised as the key figures of the change that nursery school education needs.

Promotion, if it must exist, has to be connected to educational practice, to the capacity to transform pedagogy in a group commitment.

10.5.4 Investigation and diffusion

Nursery school education can and must be equipped with various forms of research that contribute knowledge of real life in general, that allow us to explore more deeply what society as a whole, families and professionals, think of education; research that allows debates to be opened about education in these first years in order to contribute to diffusing ideas, beliefs and educational notions.

From this perspective, it would be interesting to know for instance, what has made a teacher change his or her way of exercising the profession or to know what it is that families value in a nursery school and to be able to relate this opinion to the reality that they have had the opportunity to know. The possibilities of investigation in this field are many, but in each case it would be necessary to make the intention explicit: what it was trying to show, in deference to what idea, what it will contribute to the community, who will participate in its design and how its results are to be interpreted.

The grand laboratory for the creation of a new kind of ongoing training is the nursery school and school itself. It is there that research should take place, that things are recorded, questions asked, discoveries made, and where educational activity contributes great information to the world of pedagogical knowledge, allowing new theories to be generated.

This way of investigating opens up a world of possibilities of interchange between schools and universities. This way of investigating allows ongoing training to be a key element of transformation, of change in both childhood education and university. In this new form of investigation, practice and theory advance together, building common ground.

It is essential also that these new possible co-ordinates of ongoing training be publicly open to investigation, that they are in the service of the community, and that their fundamental proposal is that of contributing to pedagogical renewal in nursery school education.

A good initial and ongoing training is the best augur for the change that childhood education needs. Such a renewed training proposes a new commitment from us all and a great responsibility; it is now up to teachers to measure up to the demands upon us.

References

Associacío de Mestres Rosa Sensat. (2006). *Education and democracy*. Retrieved July 10, 2010, from http://www.decet.org/barcelona06/03_education_and_democracy_martha_mata.angl.pdf

Associacío de Mestres Rosa Sensat. (2010a). *Per una nova educació pública*. Retrieved July 10, 2010, from http://www.rosasensat.org/documents/2/?tmplng=ca

Associacío de Mestres Rosa Sensat. (2010b). *Who we are?* Retrieved July 10, 2010, from http://www.rosasensat.org/quisom/en/1/

Dahlberg, G., & Moss, P. (2005). *Ethics and politics in early childhood education*. London: Routledge Farmer.

Deleuze, G. (2001). *Pure immanence: Essays on a life* (A. Boyman, Trans.). New York: Zone Books.

Foucault, M. (1972). *The archeology of knowledge*. New York: Pantheon.

Freire, P. (1970). *Pedagogy of the oppressed*. New York: Herder & Herder.

Freire, P. (1998). *Pedagogy of freedom: Ethics, democracy and civic courage*. Lanham, MD: Rowman & Littlefield.

Freire, P. (2004). *Pedagogy of hope: Reliving pedagogy of the oppressed*. London: Continuum.

Freire, P., & Freire, A. M. A. (2007). *Daring to dream: Toward a pedagogy of the unfinished*. Boulder, CO: Paradigm.

Habermas, J. (1990). *Moral consciousness and communicative action*. Cambridge: Polity Press.

Urban, M. (2007). *Towards a critical ecology of the profession: Systematic approaches to policies, practices and understandings of professionalism and professionalisation in early childhood*. Paper presented at the European Early Childhood Education Research Conference, Prague, Czech Republic.

Chapter 11
A Profession Speaking and Thinking for Itself

Mathias Urban and Carmen Dalli

11.1 This Book in Context: What Have We Learned?

Beginning this concluding chapter, it is well worth reminding ourselves how, and where, the process of writing this book began. Unlike research projects that develop in response to a call of a funding body, the *Day in the Life of an Early Years Practitioner* project is entirely the brainchild of a group of early childhood researchers who, since their initial meeting in 2004 (see Chapter 1), have pursued an apparently simple question: What does it mean to be professional as an early childhood practitioner (Urban & Dalli, 2008)? One of us recalls an early conversation with a colleague who had not been able to attend the initial meeting: 'Is this about improving teacher education, then?' she asked. Well, it is and it is not. Most assuredly there are implications for teacher education from the work of the special interest group (SIG) on early years professionalism. However, as members of the SIG we were also quite clear from the beginning that the purpose of the SIG was not merely to apply our collective expertise in order to come up with *solutions* for specific problems in teaching or in teacher education programmes. Being interested in practices in our field, our questions were more wide-ranging and included:

- What does *being professional* mean in early years settings?
- How can we understand, conceptualise and theorise *profession* in early years contexts?
- What does it mean to act professionally in different and diverse cultural contexts?
- Is it possible to have a common ground of understanding about professionalism across multiple early years settings?

M. Urban (✉)
Cass School of Education and Communities, University of East London, London E15 4LZ, UK
e-mail: m.urban@uel.ac.uk

C. Dalli (✉)
Institute for Early Childhood Studies, Victoria University of Wellington, Wellington 6140, New Zealand
e-mail: carmen.dalli@vuw.ac.nz

L. Miller et al. (eds.), *Early Childhood Grows Up*, International Perspectives on Early Childhood Education and Development 6, DOI 10.1007/978-94-007-2718-2_11,
© Springer Science+Business Media B.V. 2012

The chapters in this book illustrate the detail as well as the breadth of the issues investigated by members of the SIG both within the *Day in the Life* project and outside it. Clearly, this is by no means a result of the pastime of a group of like-minded theorists, with no particular implication for practice. Quite the contrary; the *Day in the Life* project is a concrete example of questions turned into practices (of research) and, reciprocally, practices (of the participating practitioners) turned into contributions to the professional and disciplinary body of knowledge. Similarly, the chapters in Part II open up another way of considering the topic of professionalism, and reveal the socio-political dimensions that impact this topic.

It is also worth reiterating that the *Day in the Life* project was not intended to be a comparative study (see Chapter 1). However, as a group of researchers interested in professional identities, we do share common perspectives and a desire to create understandings beyond the individual cases. As we have already noted (see Chapter 1) there is a relation among the cases. From a methodological point of view, by asking similar questions in otherwise different contexts we created a *structural equivalence* (Burt, 1982) that facilitated the creation of spaces for shared thinking and shared learning. At the same time, we sought to make space for critical reflection and for a diverse range of analytic approaches to be brought to bear on the data in individual case studies. Keeping in mind the three foci of the *Day in the Life* project, in the rest of this section we outline our insights from the project including when the cases are considered as a collection within the broader framework of the socio-political contexts and historical issues sketched in Chapters 8, 9 and 10. The three foci were to investigate: (i) what it means to act professionally in a particular context; (ii) perceptions of what being a 'professional' in early childhood means – including practitioners' self-perceptions and external perspectives; and (iii) common features of practice in each context.

In the subsequent sections of this chapter, we consider what these insights might mean in terms of the nature of the early childhood professional epistemologies, and a necessary cautionary note on the pitfalls of trans-national comparative research. We then sum up the two key arguments of this book: that early childhood education has grown up; and the need for a critical ecology of the early childhood profession. In the final section we offer some starting points for considering the implications of our insights in this book for the future of research into the profession.

11.1.1 Acting Professionally: Acting and Knowing as Two Sides of the Same Coin

In each of the case studies in the *Day in the Life* project, the country researchers sought to understand what it meant for the practitioner to act professionally through analysing the filmed day alongside the practitioner's statements.

Considered as a group, the practitioners' experiences collected in settings in Australia, England, Finland, Germany, New Zealand and Sweden paint detailed pictures of early childhood practice that reveal both commonalities and points of difference. One commonality is that they each illustrate that the practitioners constructed their professionalism in relation to their actual role – *what* they did was central to how they defined their professionalism. Additionally, the cases illustrate that acting professionally produces its own knowledge, thus leading us to conclude that acting and knowing are two sides of the same coin.

Let us consider, for example, Josie, an experienced early years practitioner and director of her centre in the Australian case study (Chapter 2). Josie's role is described by the researcher, Christine Woodrow, as multi-faceted and Josie herself stated that her actions covered 'a range of roles'. Josie sees herself as a leader with overall responsibility for everything related to the operation of her centre: 'the children, the parents, the staff, the actual building, the policies'. She talked about her centre as 'going for *best practice* in accreditation' adding that 'the parents want a quality service for their children, so I need to make sure that what we are doing is the very best we can be doing'. She estimated that almost 90% of her working time was related to staffing issues, including encouraging the rest of her team to 'engage in critical reflection, inspire them to bring change and mentor them through that process'. Josie's commitment to critical reflection included her ongoing personal engagement in professional development, stating: 'In my opinion, professionalism is... marked by the ability to first critically reflect on your own practice but secondly to make changes based on those reflections...'. Within this picture it is clear that Josie's view of professionalism is expressed in terms of her actions; and her account of her actions speak to the multiple aspects of her role. Analysing the data in Josie's case study, Woodrow highlights Josie's commitment to ongoing learning (renewal), and an emphasis on relationality alongside the importance of critical reflection as key themes in how Josie expresses her professional role. Yet, there are also 'glimpses of contradictory discourses'. For example, Josie's own commitment to ongoing learning is, at first glance, at odds with her critique of traditional views of professionalism that see this as synonymous with qualifications. Woodrow proposes that such contradictions arise from the situated and experienced nature of Josie's understanding of professionalism; Josie commented that professionalism 'is not necessarily linked to qualifications and training; . . . it's more the workplace culture, the overall community culture and yes of course government policy does set the mood and the context for feelings of professionalism'.

These insights into professionalism as a life experience focus on the relational and affective dimension of professionalism which Josie sees as more important than the 'badge' of qualifications; she also sees the 'feelings of professionalism' as impacted by the broader context leading Woodrow to argue that it is 'the practices, and the culture that produces and shapes those practices, and changes in practices and cultures, that really matter' in Josie's view of professionalism.

This focus on practices – or actions – as the site of professionalism is present in all the cases, despite the differences in the contextual details of each practitioner and in the specifics of their role. For example, for Julie, who works as a manager of a private day nursery in England, her sense of professionalism comes from the structure of her early years management role, and the way that she gives form to it, including through her daily schedule. Miller, Cable and Goodliff (Chapter 3) illustrate this with the following statement by Julie:

> Professionalism really comes from that circle where I'm saying I'm in charge and I know what's going on. If you ask me how many children are in the building, I know. If you ask me how many are going home at lunchtime, I know. If you ask me how many staff are First Aid-trained. . . , I know where to get this training and I know where to get this funding from.

This type of professionalism, one that focuses on leadership as 'managing', organising, being a 'conduit for information', keeping everything 'ticking along' and monitoring both policies and relationships – with teachers and with parents – is what Julie claimed as her professional practice – validated also by the feedback she received from management and parents. Thus, as for Josie in the Australian case study, it is *in* her actions and practices that Julie found her sense of professionalism, and not in any outside measure like qualifications, or the newly introduced role of Early Years Professional (EYP) for which she was training.

The other cases in the *Day in the Life* project provide additional support for the argument that practice and knowledge go together: The practitioner from New Zealand, Bette, for example, talked about acting professionally as existing in the bringing together of multiple layers of understandings, knowledge and thinking to the relationships within the early childhood settings, an activity that she calls 'balancing' (Chapter 5). For Frau Müller, acting professionally is also about relational practice, this time marked by what Urban calls 'a permanent attention to what is going on', and where – in a context that is uncertain – one acts with confidence as the 'uncertain expert': open to children's individuality, to diversity, to curiosity and to joint meaning making (Chapter 5). For Anna, working within a curriculum framework based on democratic values, the most important aspect of her work was that in everything that she did, she would 'take children seriously and see them, listen to what they say and do' (Chapter 6). Even for Maija, working in the Finnish context where the introduction of multi-professionalism can sometimes result in what Karila and Kinos describe as 'territorial fights' (Chapter 7), it is her actions as a kindergarten teacher interacting with other people in a state of 'being aware' that defines her idea of professional action. We note that, in each instance, action is both physical activity as well as a manner of approach, a 'permanent attention' to the other and to what is going on, 'being fully present to the child' (Bette, Chapter 6), an awareness (Anna, Chapter 7) that opens up to relationships.

It would appear therefore that for each of these practitioners, ways of knowing about professionalism are inseparable from ways of acting, as well as ways of being. This may suggest that being professional in this field means 'Linking ways of knowing with ways of being practical' (Van Manen, 1977, p. 205). There are, as Van Manen argued, many ways of being practical, and this book identifies many implications of this 'linking': for professional preparation and development, and for research and policy. Some of these have been spelled out in the discussions within the case study chapters and in the final section of this chapter.

11.1.2 Being a 'Professional': Self-Identity and External Perceptions Within Professional Ecologies

In focusing on what we have learned about how the practitioners perceived themselves as a professional, and the related issue of how they thought that the profession was seen externally, we have found it useful to apply some of the conceptual elements of the ecological framework (Bronfenbrenner, 1979, 1986) we outlined in Chapter 1.

In the previous section we argued that the way Josie (Chapter 2), Julie (Chapter 3), Maija (Chapter 4) and Frau Müller (Chapter 5) spoke about their professional action was first and foremost informed by the actual roles they occupied in their very different settings and through the interactions they had within their immediate settings, thus bringing into focus 'relationality' as a key dimension of early years professionalism.

Considering this insight from an ecological theory perspective (Bronfenbrenner, 1979, 1986; Chapter 1) reminds us that what happens in the immediate context (the *microsystem*) in which people live their lives, including their interactions with others around them, is what has the most immediate impact on self-identity. This leads us to reflect that it is also within the immediate contexts in which the practitioners are present, and their interactions with important others – the children, parents and colleagues with whom they interact on a daily basis – that the practitioners' self-identity as a professional may be most intimately constructed.

Here, then, lies one of the common features across our cases: The nature of immediate interactions may differ for a manager (Julie in Chapter 3), an educator with sole responsibility for a group of children (Frau Müller in Chapter 5) or a member of a multi-professional team (Maija in Chapter 4); yet, for each of them, it is the immediacy of their roles, *what they do* in interaction with children and adults that underpins their image of themselves as professionals. This again puts the focus on relationality as a key aspect of being professional.

Two important conclusions arise from this picture: First – as we have already signalled in the preceding section – it emphasises the inseparable nature of practice, thinking about practice, and thinking about oneself in this practice – making the boundaries between *doing*, *knowing* and *being* blurred or non-existent. Second, while there are clear indications in each setting of what it means to *be* (*act/know* as a) professional, the idea of *one* early childhood profession appears, in this study, an elusive quest. In other words, there is no such thing as *the* early childhood profession. Rather, we see a rich diversity of individuals thinking and acting professionally in their respective contexts. This, in turn, has implications beyond the individual practitioner, not least for the self-image of the professional community, or community of practice, as a whole.

Still looking across the microsystems of the six practitioners' professional ecologies, we see another commonality: the practitioners, regardless of their role and setting, describe the 'constant juggle', the 'balancing' of multiple tasks and demands, the apparent 'fragmentation' of their day – and their ability to cope with it – as key characteristics of their professionalism. Thus, while there is always a plan, or a schedule for the day, and the professional pedagogical knowledge to make it happen (Maija, Bette, Anna, Frau Müller), from the outside this can appear as a 'buzz of activity' (Chapter 6), and a collection of 'trivial routines'. Exploration of the practitioners' perceptions of their pedagogical planning suggests that this too is an outcome of the practitioners' state of 'permanent attention', the 'awareness' that characterises their professional ecology at the microsystem level. The intimate day-to-day knowledge of the children that this produced for the practitioners (with the exception of Julie) meant that plans were flexible, more like 'open possibilities...more of a question mark ... [because] ... you have to have an open mind about where any bit of any [child's] interest might go' (Bette, Chapter 6). Frau Müller explained this as an intention to make children feel that 'they are taken seriously in what they do' and that meant that 'although the day was planned...acting professionally for me means to be aware of children's interests and wishes, and incorporate them into my planning' (Chapter 5).

Julie, we said, was the exception to this commonality in the practitioners' experiences; for her the fragmentation was one of micro-practices that came from the diverse, complex and multiple management demands and removed her from sustained interaction with children and colleagues.

Reflecting on Julie's particular role – which as a manager places her some steps removed from having direct pedagogical responsibility for the early childhood programme – raises some interesting points of reflection about the future of the early years profession in multi-professional settings.

In countries such as England and Finland, working together across professional boundaries is presented at the policy level as desirable and welcomed as a possible way of dealing with the complex problems that characterise the realities of children and families in modern societies. What arises from the inevitable encounters between practitioners with diverse 'professional' backgrounds are both opportunities, and challenges and tensions. Some of the cases show how professional encounters and collaboration enable *understandings* across differences. For example, while recognising that the professionalism of her nursery colleagues 'isn't really valued. ... people from outside ... see that being in a nursery is "playing with children" all day and just an extension of the mother's role', Julie herself saw them as 'professionals too... some of them have qualifications far above what I have and... different experiences too'.

An alternative outcome of multi-professionalism is that it can lead to clearer demarcations of expertise. This is evident within the Finnish case study (Chapter 4) where Maija clarified what it meant to be an early childhood professional by emphasising pedagogical responsibility as a key marker:

> In a multi-professional team, the kindergarten teacher is the one who runs the show...she has the pedagogical responsibility and she informs and allocates the tasks together with the nursery nurses... but the training of the kindergarten teacher makes her most skilled and aware of early childhood education and pedagogy...the overall systematic alignment is the responsibility of the kindergarten teacher.

Encounters between professions, then, together with internal stratification and hierarchy, raise a number of critical issues; already mentioned is the constant need to define and defend one's status and standing as an early childhood professional. Closely related is the temptation of giving in to external expectations and to re-construct their professional identity in ways that conflict with the key characteristics of one's practice – as seen in the case of the 'uncertain expert', Frau Müller (Chapter 5). Different professions – and professionals – in one field can also lead to struggles for recognition, resources, power and privilege, bringing with them the risk of weakening the overall position of early childhood in wider societal competition – as intimated by Karila and Kinos in Chapter 4 (see also Kinos, 2008).

These issues lead us now to turn our attention beyond the individual micro level of the practitioners' professional ecologies. They highlight that deeply interwoven with the texture of modern societies, early childhood, like any profession, regularly finds itself confronted with, and affected by, developments outside its boundaries. For example, decisions taken by anonymous traders on the international financial market can have major impacts. Small businesses as well as entire national economies are put at risk; parental unemployment fluctuates and with it inequality, child poverty and exclusion. These *exosystem-* and *macrosystem*-level events, to once again use ecological theory terminology, have immediate implications for early childhood practitioners' day-to-day practice. Early childhood 'services', whether for-profit or non-profit, are immediately susceptible to pressure on private and public finances. In the case of the collapse of the East German economy, for instance, the majority of colleagues of Frau Müller, the German participant in the *Day in the Life* project (Chapter 5), had been made redundant or forced out of full-time into part-time contracts. Under these conditions, staff shortages meant that sharing time for collaborative planning and reflection had become practically impossible. In Australia, to give an example from a different geo-political context, poor financial management led to the spectacular collapse of the largest for-profit childcare provider (ABC Learning), risking the existence of over 1,000 childcare centres, making huge government bailouts necessary and, in consequence, leading to 'significant change in the landscape of Australian early childhood policy and practice' (Christine Woodrow, Chapter 2).

The practitioners in this study are unlikely to meet any of the financial traders that can trigger global financial crises, nor the human resources managers of the companies that make the children's parents redundant. Yet, their professional experiences and relationships are inevitably impacted on by these actions in their [the practitioners'] *exosystem*. The question that arises from the influence of forces and interests external to the early childhood profession is about mutuality: How can early childhood professionals and the early childhood profession make active contributions to the texture of society? How can they not only be 'informed by the political and social realities' and by the 'challenges in the settings they act in' (see Chapter 1) but also, respond?

One answer, given by Maija in Finland, Frau Müller in Germany, and Anna in Sweden (Chapters 4, 5 and 7), is to focus on the image of the child around which – as we suggested earlier in this chapter – most practitioners construct at least part of their professional self-image. Having an image of a child as a connected child: as a member of a family, a community and a society rather than an image of a detached, decontextualised child attending the centre, opens the potential of bridging the gap between individual and the society, between the *micro-* and the *macrosystem.* It requires, however, the recognition that the *context* (from families and local communities to the wider society) is as much the subject of professional practice as the child herself.

Practitioners in this study are well aware of the interrelations between the *micro*, *exo* and *macro* layers of their professional system; they relate to policy and its changes (Australia, England, New Zealand), report how changes in society and work life create new challenges (Finland, Germany) and describe their practices as ethical (New Zealand) and based on values of democracy (Sweden).

Looking beyond the *Day in the Life* project, the chapters by Peeters (Chapter 9) and Balaguer (Chapter 10) also make the same argument to bridge the gap between the micro- and macrosystem of practitioners' professional ecology. They both provide illustrations of how, through critical reflection on their political and social realities, early childhood practitioners can engage with macro-level issues and make a difference. In other words, practitioners can be, and often are, agents of change. They are not only affected by their contexts but can act to affect the context and thus also external perceptions of them as professionals.

The question we consider next is what these insights might mean in terms of the future professional epistemology and action of the early childhood field.

11.2 Professional Epistemology and Professional Action

We turn now to considering the significance of these insights for the focus of this book: the two arguments that, firstly, the early childhood field has metaphorically 'grown up'; and secondly that the future of the early childhood field should be marked by a critical ecology.

Conceptualisations of knowledge, and ways of generating it – our professional epistemology – have huge implications for the professional practices that are portrayed in this study: open-ended, relational, uncertain, intimate and discursive.

Gert Biesta and Deborah Osberg (2007), writing about the epistemological foundations of modern schooling, identify a move away from a static and representational understanding of knowledge and towards an active and adaptive one. This brings with it the understanding that 'knowledge is caught up with the activity and situations in which it is produced' (Biesta & Osberg, p. 16). Applying this reading of epistemology to our investigations of early childhood professional practices within the *Day in the Life* project challenges some taken-for-granted assumptions in our field. To begin with, it rejects the traditionally perceived hierarchical relationship between research and practice which positions them as distinct arenas of knowledge production and application (Urban, 2008). The *Day in the Life* project thus questions the false dichotomy between theory and practice and argues for an understanding of knowledge as *situational* and '*emerging* from our engagement with the present' (Osberg & Biesta, 2007, p. 40). This is not to say that the *Day in the Life* project (and this book in general) rejects all other types of knowledge, but it does mean that the project radically challenges the idea of staticity, that is the type of technicist practice that assumes that what worked in the past will necessarily work again in the present. It also rejects any narrow understanding of evidence-based practice – the simplistic but prevalent idea that scientific evidence can tell us 'what works' and therefore be employed to guide professional practices elsewhere, and in every case. Instead, it suggests that practice is in constant interrogation with existing knowledge on which it relies as a platform from which to stretch into the present, and in so doing, creates new knowledge.

As we have discussed elsewhere in more detail, we do not deny the importance of gathering *evidence* and paying careful and detailed attention to the outcomes of our practices for children, families and communities (Dalli & Urban, 2010; Urban, 2008, 2010a). We do argue, however, that in order to capture the emerging, surprising and sometimes uncertain outcomes of the complex interactions that characterise early childhood professional practice, we must acknowledge practitioners' experiences and encourage their contributions to building and interpreting the professional body of knowledge. In the professional system practitioners are key actors, not passive recipients of actions – and so are researchers, managers, trainers, teacher educators and other participants at every layer of the system. Each creates *practice-based evidence* (Urban, 2010b). As foreshadowed in Chapter 1, in this book we are suggesting that the environment that encourages such processes of collective learning, meaning-making and knowledge creation can best be described as a *critical ecology* for a profession that sees itself as a *learning community* (Kilkpatrick, Barrett, & Jones, 2003; Wenger, 2006). The *Day in the Life* project is one example of how the early childhood profession, conceptualised as a *critical learning community, or community of practice*, can move on from questioning individual practices of individual practitioners to questioning the system as a whole – including individual and collective practices in early childhood settings, in training and professional preparation and learning, in policy, administration and research.

The chapters in Part II of this book provide another example of how such a critical learning community can function. Besides providing big picture perspectives on the issue of professionalism, these chapters also function as narratives of actions that question the status quo. Oberhuemer (Chapter 8) argues what needs to happen in contexts across Europe if a better understanding of professionalism is truly sought; Peeters (Chapter 9) recounts how childcare advocates were able to bring about legislative change in Flanders; and Balaguer (Chapter 10) makes a spirited case for activism for transformation through presenting the success of the *Associacío de Mestres Rosa Sensat* in bringing about educational renewal in Barcelona, Catalonia and the whole of Spain.

Collectively, these arguments reveal that the early childhood professional system as a whole is embedded in the wider social, historical, economic and political context of society with its local, national and increasingly global dimensions. They are part of a complex socio-ecological system. It follows that the task of transformation must be one that reaches all aspects of the socio-ecological system; the challenge is to work towards a *critical ecology of the profession* (Dalli, 2007, 2010; Urban, 2007) that is informed by the political and social realities, knowledge and practices, 'together with the use of this knowledge to *strategically transform* education in socially progressive directions' (MacNaughton, 2003, p. 3, emphasis added).

11.3 How Not to Square the Circle – A Cautionary Note on Comparative Research

Having drawn together our reflections on the insights of the *Day in the Life* project, and in light of the broader picture drawn by the preceding three chapters, we pause now to comment briefly on the researchers' experiences within a project situated across six different countries.

Although we were clear from the outset (see Chapter 1) that the *Day in the Life* project was not simply about *comparing* the practices and conceptualisations we encountered in the different examples, and that none of the participating settings and practitioners represents anything but *themselves*, we have come across the pitfalls of an approach to research that is interested in the *particular* in its various manifestations. Every so often, in our internal correspondence as well as in discussions with colleagues at conferences, we caught ourselves talking about *the* Swedish, *the* New Zealand, *the* German case and so on – a practice that, for practical purposes, we have learned to live with in writing this chapter. Throughout the project, however, we have reminded ourselves regularly that the cases brought together in this study – while situated in the general socio-cultural, historical, economical and political context of specific countries, and influenced by increasingly globalised discourses on education (Spring, 2008) – allowed insights into the subjective realities of six separate individuals at a very specific point in time. Any learning and contribution to the professional body of knowledge (as discussed above) can only be drawn from across the issues, themes and reflections of these specific accounts.

Hence, a note of caution is appropriate. Tempting as it may be to think otherwise, there is no way of comparing complex experiences without losing the essence of practices in specific contexts. Things get worse when the desire to *learn from* individual cases in contexts other than our own becomes colonised by the most obsessive policy question of our time: 'what works?' (Biesta, 2007), and how what works *there* can be made to work *here*? Critical comparative educational researchers have long argued against this kind of naïve 'cultural borrowing' (Alexander, 2000a, 2000b) and warned of the oversimplification adopted by some international comparative studies, especially in mainstream education:

> [. . .] international comparison offered policy makers the tempting prospect of both plausible explanations and viable solutions. The explanations tended to be monocausal and linear, and to jump incautiously from correlation to causality. Thus, with international league tables of both economic and educational performance now conveniently available, it was assumed

that a country's position on one was determined by its position on the other. [...] The solution was clear: adopt strategies that would raise the average test scores of British children, and Britain's economic future would be assured. (Alexander, 2000a, p. 41)

Such oversimplifications as Alexander (2000a) decried ignore the fact that different cultural traditions and socio-cultural contexts produce different paradigms, particularly in education. For example, the French concept of education, based on the ideal of *raison*, aims at leading children from a state of savageness to being reasonable members of the (lay) state: the *citoyen*. By comparison, English education is more interested in forming children into useful members of society, their usefulness being determined by the assumed future needs of the labour market (see more detailed discussion in Moss & Urban, 2010). While different in their cultural meanings, both educational paradigms are grounded in the western projects of modernity, liberalism and capitalism. They might well be at odds with other interpretations of relationships between generations, between individual and community, and between private and public in many parts of this world. In fact we know they are (Elliott & Grigorenko, 2008).

Weighing against this body of comparative studies, there is a much smaller body of research that embraces different paradigms and the complexities they bring with them. It was this smaller body of research that we consciously aimed to build on when choosing our methodological approach to the *Day in the Life* project. We were inspired by the groundbreaking studies of critical comparativists whose work is recognised well beyond early childhood studies (e.g., Tobin, Wu, & Davidson, 1989), and by the work of Gillen et al. (2007), to as Robin Alexander (2000a) put it: 'bite the methodological bullet and progress beyond structure and policy to the classroom (p. 3). We deliberately chose to get into the nitty-gritty of everyday practices, the 'grassroots human detail... [in order to] illuminate their national contexts all the more effectively' (Alexander, 2000a, p. 3).

Within the case study chapters in this book, the 'grassroots human detail' of everyday practices have amply illustrated that early childhood education and care is a messy business. It follows that any research that aims at developing an understanding of *what is actually going on, and why*, and *for whom*, needs to embrace, rather than methodologically avoid, the messiness of its subject. It has to reflect the 'spatialised' nature of knowledge in this field which, in effect, is a 'motley' (Turnbull, 2003).

Ethnographers since Clifford Geertz (1973) have seen *comparison* in stark contrast to studying the particularities of the individual case and as 'actually competing with learning about and from the particular case. Comparison is a grand epistemological strategy, a powerful conceptual mechanism, fixing attention upon one or a few attributes' (Stake, 2003, p. 148). However, as Stake concluded, this grand epistemological strategy 'obscures case knowledge that fails to facilitate comparison' (p. 148) with the result that messy, complex, unique and vital *case knowledge* is obscured through methodological decisions aimed at keeping comparison manageable. A further risk is that the focus of interest will, perhaps involuntarily, shift from the 'thick of what is going on' (Stake, p. 148) to the comparison itself.

11.4 The Two Key Arguments Revisited

Let us now take stock of our two key arguments in this book: Firstly, our claim that early childhood has, metaphorically, 'grown up', and secondly, our suggestion that the future of the early childhood profession should be marked by a critical ecology.

11.4.1 Early Childhood Grows Up

As we argued in Chapter 1, policy interest in early childhood education, and the accompanying focus on the professionalising of the early years workforce, is a relatively new phenomenon.

Literature on *professionalism* in general abounds (e.g., Abbott, 1988; Berry, Clemans, & Kostogriz, 2007; Cheetham & Chivers, 2005; Larson, 1977) and a quick and rough search for *professionalism* at the Web of Science database produces over 2000 hits. However, the combined search string *professionalism and early childhood* reduces the results to less than a hundred publications. Given this apparent imbalance, we see the collaborative effort that has led to this book as a sign of confidence of an emerging profession that is shaking off its historical status as somehow inferior to other educative endeavours, and instead is taking its place as a profession alongside other parts of the education sector. It is a profession that – metaphorically – has grown up, a profession that confidently speaks and thinks for itself.

In conducting the *Day in the Life* project with participants in six different countries, and analysing the findings as a diverse group of scholars as well as through this book, sharing our findings with the wider international early childhood community, we have come together in what might best be described as a transient *learning community* (Kilkpatrick, Barrett, & Jones, 2003) or *community of practice* engaged in 'a process of collective learning in a shared domain of human endeavour' (Wenger, 2006, p. 1). It is a transient community because of the very characteristic of the practices we are interested in. As the *Day in the Life* project has demonstrated, early childhood professionalism cannot be understood as a collection of finite, technical practices where knowledge is applied (e.g., to children) in order to solve given problems. The relational and discursive practices depicted in the six case studies emerge a very different professionalism: one that is a constant exercise of creating shared understandings, negotiating actions and maintaining connections – between children and adults, laypersons and professionals, individuals and society. This is why, as a 'domain of human endeavour' – to use Wenger's term yet again – early childhood practice has been described as a deeply ethical and political one (Dahlberg & Moss, 2005; Dalli & Cherrington, 2009). Moreover, as at least three of the case studies have shown – Finland, Germany and England – professionalism in early childhood is grounded in uncertainty (Urban, 2008) and practitioners' identities are in 'flux' (Stronach, Corbin, McNamara, Stark, & Warne, 2002). Hence all answers provided to our initial question – what does it mean to be professional in early childhood? – can only be forever preliminary and allow space for change. It is clear that professional knowledge is a site of constant reconstruction, including through this book.

The history of the *Day in the Life* project outlined in Chapter 1, and its embeddedness in contemporary political, theoretical and philosophical discourses, brings forth another aspect of the collective exercise of knowledge co-creation. While the case studies and their analysis from different-but-shared perspectives contribute to increasing our understanding and knowledge of our topic – professionalism in early childhood – they also invite us to examine critically the foundations and underlying assumptions of those understandings. The process of co-construction of the professional body of knowledge (*what* to know about professionalism) will continue to bring forth the epistemological question: *How do we know what we know* about our profession and its practices? Or, phrased differently: How do we understand and conceptualise *knowledge* in relation to our profession and its practices?

This, we argue, is also a sign of 'growing up' – an indication that early childhood is a profession that can now speak, and think, for itself. Exercising the right to do so, and simultaneously acknowledging the preliminarity of our findings, we use the final part of this section to 'speak' what we think our findings say in brief summary points.

11.4.1.1 Summary of Key Insights

 i. Professionalism in early childhood means linking ways of knowing (and co-producing professional knowledge) with ways of being practical; doing, knowing and being are inseparable.
 ii. Relationality is a key characteristic of professionalism in early childhood, defined in the case studies as 'a permanent attention to what is going on', open to individuality, to diversity, curiosity and to joint meaning making; it involves an awareness of the other.
 iii. Professional self-identity is constructed partly in the most immediate (micro) contexts in which practitioners are present. What practitioners do in the immediacy of their role underpins their self-identity as professionals. Professional self-identity is also constructed through the influence of macro structures (regulations, gender) and mesosystem dynamics (community, family) which impact on the way practitioners see themselves.
 iv. There is not *one* profession but a rich diversity of individuals acting professionally in their respective contexts. This has implications for individual practitioners as well as beyond, not least for researchers attempting to understand professional practices in early childhood.
 v. Professional practitioners continuously 'juggle' multiple demands, and the ability to cope with them is a key characteristic of being an early childhood professional.
 vi. The professional teacher plans her day but works in a state of 'permanent attention' that allows the plan to be one of 'open possibilities'.

vii. Multi-professionalism can enable understandings across different professions within the same setting. It can lead to clearer demarcations of expertise, but also to further fragmentation of the sector, to struggle and competition for recognition and scarce resources.

viii. The early childhood professional system is embedded in the wider social, historical, economic and political context of society with its local, national and increasingly global dimensions. The challenge is to work towards a *critical ecology of the profession* (Dalli, 2007, 2010; Urban, 2007) that is informed by the political and social realities, knowledge and practices.

ix. The professional practitioner maintains an attitude of critical enquiry in all aspects of her role, including attention to the socio-political context.

x. Early childhood professional epistemology rejects (i) hierarchical relationships between research and practice and sees knowledge as situational and emerging from our engagement with the present; and (ii) technicist views of professionalism and narrow understandings of evidence-based practice.

11.4.1.2 Towards a Critical Ecology of the Early Childhood Profession

> There is no such thing as a *neutral* educational process. Education either functions as an instrument that is used to facilitate the integration of the younger generation into the logic of the present system and bring about conformity to it, *or* it becomes 'the practice freedom', the means by which men and women deal critically and creatively with reality and discover how to participate in the transformation of their world. (Shaull, 1970, p. 16)

Written over 40 years ago in the foreword to the first English edition of Paolo Freire's *Pedagogy of the Oppressed* (Freire, 1970), Richard Shaull's statement is as relevant today as it was then. In the six case studies of the *Day in the life* project, we have encountered early childhood practitioners who, on a day-to-day basis, *deal critically and creatively with reality*. That all of them are women (Chapter 1) sheds a light on a particular aspect of the realities of societies engaging with young children. Each encounter between professional and children, as documented in the six cases, is an active contribution to the *transformation of the world* – a transformation that unfolds in the spaces of interactions *between* professionals and children (and between professionals and others, as we have discussed above).

In a critical ecology of the profession, we pay attention to these spaces and interactions between individuals and to the relationships between the various layers of the system. Interdependency and reciprocity are key concepts of Bronfenbrenner's original *Ecology of Human Development* (1979). There is no hierarchy between the different systems he proposes. Writing about socio-cultural risks, James Garbarino (1992) explains Bronfenbrenner's ecological concept:

> In asking and answering questions about developmental risk and opportunity, we can and should always be ready to look at the next level 'beyond' and 'within' to find the questions and the answers. If we see husbands and wives in conflict over lost income, we need to look *beyond* to the economy that puts husbands out of work and now may welcome the wives into the labor force, as well as to the culture that defines a person's personal worth in monetary terms and that blames the victims of economic dislocation for their losses. But we must also look *within* to the parent-child relationships that are affected by the changing

roles and status of the parents. In addition, we must also look *across* to see how the several systems involved (family, workplace, and economy) adjust to new conditions over time. These social forces are the keys to ecological analysis, namely interlocking social systems. (p. 24)

Seeking *questions and answers* beyond, within and across social systems that affect young children, families, and communities is at the core of professional practice when this is seen as a systemic endeavour that is affected by more than the immediate context in which people are immediately present. The necessary 'attitude of enquiry', reported by Josie (Chapter 2) is an excellent example; seeing the curriculum 'much more as a question mark' than a plan is another (Bette, Chapter 6). For a critical ecologic professionalism, however, we need to shift the focus from the individual practitioner to the *professional system* and its ability to transform practices and, ultimately, realities. We would have to systematically explore the ability of the system – at every layer – to create spaces for dialogue, for asking critical questions, and for valuing a diversity of answers as a key to creating new understandings (see Chapter 10). Critical authors in our field have long pointed out the necessity to introduce a critical perspective into our professional reflections, and Josie in the *Day in the Life* project, echoes this (Chapter 2). Glenda MacNaughton (2005) explains that connecting the 'critical' to reflection is about directing the attention away from the individual and towards 'the operation and effects of power relationships *between* people' (p. 7). Critical reflection, she writes, is 'the process of questioning how power operates in the process of teaching and learning and then using that knowledge to transform oppressive or inequitable teaching and learning processes.

A critical ecology of the profession takes the concept of critical reflection one step further, beyond the individual practitioner to the entire professional system. Another way of saying this is that in a critical ecology of the early childhood profession, there would be an environment of constant enquiry – not only into individual practice but into the context and preconditions of this practice. Additionally, a reflective, self-critical community would also be 'open to responsive growth in the local – [and global] – context' (Dalli, 2010).

11.5 Implications for Research as a Practice Speaking to Other Practices – Some Concluding Thoughts

In this book we have gathered perspectives on professionalism from various international contexts, through the *Day in the Life* project, and the contextualising chapters by Oberhuemer, Peeters and Balaguer (Chapters 8, 9 and 10). We have brought these different perspectives together in a framework which we have called a *critical ecology*, hoping to offer a possibility to improve understanding of early childhood practice.

The journey that brought us from the first afternoon meeting of what would later become the special interest group 'Professionalism in Early Childhood Education' to joint research in the *Day in the Life* project and, to date, to this book, has taught us much about the complexities of early childhood practice. Every practitioner's account has increased our respect for the women (and few men) that balance numerous contradictory demands, intimacy and expertise, pedagogy, policy and management on a daily basis in return for little recognition and inappropriate remuneration. Without their commitment and interest, this project and book would not have been possible.

The journey has also taught us a lesson or two about our own role, as researchers, in the critical ecology that we use as our frame of reference. As we bring this book to a close, we want to suggest that some of them have wider implications for the role of research in relation to both policy and creation of professional knowledge in our field.

First, we think it is necessary to keep reminding ourselves – and those responsible for commissioning, funding and designing research in early childhood – that we as researchers are *in* the picture that we are painting. There is no research from the outside, no microscope or petri dish in researching early childhood practice. 'To *know* the world' writes Max Van Manen in *Researching Lived Experience* (Van Manen, 1990), 'is profoundly to *be* in the world in a certain way. The act of researching-questioning-theorizing is the intentional act of attaching ourselves to the world' (p. 5).

Second, in a critical ecological frame of thinking, there can be no false dichotomy between theory and practice. Research is a practice in itself, as much as the cases in this study show that practice is constant enquiry – a question mark. On a positive note, this opens many possibilities, not least for addressing what Gert Biesta (2007) has called the *democratic deficit* of mainstream educational research, and the prevalent bias towards a technocratic understanding of knowledge production and *evidence-based practice*. One important step towards overcoming this bias would be for us, as researchers, to engage in more of the 'great conversations' suggested by Gilles Deleuze (2001):

> Theory is an inquiry, which is to say, a practice: a practice of the seemingly fictive world that empiricism describes; a study of the conditions of legitimacy of practices in this empirical world that is in fact our own. The result is a great conversation of theory to practice. (p. 36)

Third, such an understanding of research and practice as reciprocal and *equal* has wider policy implications. To begin with, it will be necessary to recognise that practice is *evidence*. Put differently, the professional body of knowledge that is continuously produced by *all* actors in the professional system brings into the picture a new focus on practitioners' everyday experiences in working with young children and their families. These everyday experiences, as Donald Schön (1983) argues, are gathered in situations that are complex, open and necessarily *uncertain*. Research in this book shows that early childhood practice is itself an ongoing experiment, a continuous invention which, as Jerome Bruner (1996) once argued about education generally, is 'risky' (p.14) because its outcomes are not predictable, yet they affect the future of society.

At a time when early childhood education has metaphorically 'grown up' and is taking its place on the policy agenda of many nations, it seems important to guard against an overemphasis on seeking to pin down the unpredictable and the uncertain in favour of top-down models that seek to enforce *effective* practices that are supposed to be guided by externally produced *evidence*. Top-down models based on the search of certainty are likely to lose sight of the surprising, promising and innovative effects and outcomes of early childhood practices. Rather, we are in need of alternative and secure policy frameworks that provide funding, resources to gather, document, disseminate and theorise these experiences as *practice-based evidence*.

The 'great conversation' has only begun.

References

Abbott, A. D. (1988). *The system of professions: An essay on the division of expert labor*. Chicago: University of Chicago Press.

Alexander, R. J. (2000a). *Culture and pedagogy: International comparisons in primary education*. Oxford: Blackwell.

Alexander, R. J. (2000b). *Other primary schools and ours: Hazards of international comparison*. Warwick: Centre for Research in Elementary and Primary Education, University of Warwick.

Berry, A., Clemans, A., & Kostogriz, A. (2007). *Dimensions of professional learning: Professionalism, practice and identity*. Rotterdam: Sense.

Biesta, G. (2007). Why 'what works' won't work: Evidence-based practice and the democratic deficit in educational research. *Educational Theory, 57*(1), 1–22.

Biesta, G., & Osberg, D. (2007). Beyond re/presentation: A case for updating the epistemology of schooling. *Interchange, 38*(1), 15–29.

Bronfenbrenner, U. (1979). *The ecology of human development: Experiments by nature and design*. Cambridge, MA: Harvard University Press.

Bronfenbrenner, U. (1986). Ecology of the family as a context for human development. *Developmental Psychology, 22*(6), 723–742.

Bruner, J. (1996). What we have learnt about early learning. *European Early Childhood Education Research Journal, 4*(1), 5–16.

Burt, R. S. (1982). *Toward a structural theory of action: Network models of social structure, perception, and action*. New York: Academic.

Cheetham, G., & Chivers, G. E. (2005). *Professions, competence and informal learning*. Cheltenham: Edward Elgar.

Dahlberg, G., & Moss, P. (2005). *Ethics and politics in early childhood education*. London: Routledge Farmer.

Dalli, C. (2007). *Towards a critical ecology of the profession: Systematic approaches to policies, practices and understandings of professionalism and professionalisation in early childhood*. Paper presented at the European Early Childhood Education Research conference, Prague, Czech Republic.

Dalli, C. (2010). Towards the re-emergence of a critical ecology of the early childhood profession in New Zealand. *Contemporary Issues in Early Childhood, 11*(1), 61–74.

Dalli, C., & Cherrington, S. (2009). Ethical practice as relational work: A new frontier for professional learning? In S. Edwards & J. Nuttall (Eds.), *Professional learning in early childhood settings* (pp. 61–80). Rotterdam, The Netherlands: Sense.

Dalli, C., & Urban, M. (Eds.). (2010). *Professionalism in early childhood education and care: International perspectives*. London: Routledge.

Deleuze, G. (2001). *Pure immanence: Essays on a life* (A. Boyman, Trans.). New York: Zone Books.

Elliott, J., & Grigorenko, E. (2008). *Western psychological and educational theory in diverse contexts*. London: Routledge.

Freire, P. (1970). *Pedagogy of the oppressed*. New York: Herder & Herder.

Garbarino, J. (1992). *Children and families in the social environment* (2nd ed.). New York: Aldine de Gruyter.

Geertz, C. (1973). *The interpretation of cultures: Selected essays*. London: Fontana.

Gillen, J., Cameron, C. A., Tapanya, S., Pinto, G., Hancock, R., Young S., et al. (2007). A day in the life: Advancing a methodology for the cultural study of development and learning in early childhood. *Early Child Development and Care, 177*(2), 207–218.

Kilkpatrick, S., Barrett, M., & Jones, M. (2003). *Defining learning communities*. Paper presented at the Australian Association for Research in Education. Retrieved from http://www.aare.edu. au/03pap/jon03441.pdf

Kinos, J. (2008). Professionalism: A breeding ground for struggle: The example of the Finnish day-care centre. *European Early Childhood Education Research Journal, 16*(2), 224–241.

Larson, M. S. (1977). *The rise of professionalism: A sociological analysis*. Berkeley, CA: University of California Press.

MacNaughton, G. (2003). *Shaping early childhood. learners, curriculum and contexts*. Berkshire: Open University Press.

MacNaughton, G. (2005). *Doing Foucault in early childhood studies: Applying poststructural ideas*. London: Routledge.

Moss, P., & Urban, M. (2010). *Democracy and experimentation: Two fundamental values for education*. Guetersloh: Bertelsmann Stiftung.

Osberg, D., & Biesta, G. (2007). Beyond presence: Epistemological and pedagogical implications of 'strong emergence'. *Interchange, 38*(1), 31–51.

Schön, D. A. (1983). *The reflective practitioner. How professionals think in action*. New York: Basic Books.

Shaull, R. (1970). Foreword. In P. Freire (Ed.), *Pedagogy of the oppressed* (pp. 11–16). New York: Continuum.

Spring, J. H. (2008). *Globalization of education: An introduction*. New York: Routledge.

Stake, R. E. (2003). Case studies. In N. K. Denzin & Y. S. Lincoln (Eds.), *Strategies of qualitative inquiry* (pp. 134–164). London: Sage.

Stronach, I., Corbin, B., McNamara, O., Stark, S., & Warne, T. (2002). Towards an uncertain politics of professionalism: Teacher and nurse identities in flux. *Journal of Education Policy, 17*(1), 109–138.

Tobin, J. J., Wu, D. Y. H., & Davidson, D. H. (1989). *Preschool in three cultures: Japan, China, and the United States*. New Haven, CT: Yale University Press.

Turnbull, D. (2003). *Masons, tricksters and cartographers: Comparative studies in the sociology of scientific and indigenous knowledge*. London: Routledge.

Urban, M. (2007). *Towards a critical ecology of the profession: Systematic approaches to policies, practices and understandings of professionalism and professionalisation in early childhood*. Paper presented at the European Early Childhood Education Research Conference, Prague, Czech Republic.

Urban, M. (2008). Dealing with uncertainty. Challenges and possibilities for the early childhood profession. *European Early Childhood Education Research Journal, 16*(2), 135–152.

Urban, M. (2010a). Rethinking professionalism in early childhood: Untested feasibilities and critical ecologies. Editorial. *Contemporary Issues in Early Childhood, 11*(1), 1–7.

Urban, M. (2010b). Untested feasibilities and zones of professional development: Arguments for reclaiming practice-based evidence in early childhood practice and research. In J. Hayden & A. Tuna (Eds.), *Moving forward together: Early childhood programs as the doorway to social cohesion: An east-west perspective* (pp. 177–191). Newcastle upon Tyne: Cambridge Scholars.

Urban, M., & Dalli, C. (2008). Editorial. *European Early Childhood Education Research Journal, 16*(2), 131–133.

Van Manen, M. (1977). Linking ways of knowing with ways of being practical. *Curriculum Inquiry, 6*(3), 205–228.

Van Manen, M. (1990). *Researching lived experience: Human science for an action sensitive pedagogy*. Albany, NY: State University of New York Press.
Wenger, E. (2006). *Communities of practice: A brief introduction*. Retrieved August 6, 2010, from http://www.ewenger.com/theory/index.htm

Index